CUSTER'S THORN

The Life of Frederick W. Benteen

J. C. Ladenheim

HERITAGE BOOKS
2007

HERITAGE BOOKS
AN IMPRINT OF HERITAGE BOOKS, INC.

Books, CDs, and more—Worldwide

For our listing of thousands of titles see our website at
www.HeritageBooks.com

Published 2007 by
HERITAGE BOOKS, INC.
Publishing Division
65 East Main Street
Westminster, Maryland 21157-5026

Copyright © 2007 Jules C. Ladenheim

Other books by the author:
Alien Horseman: An Italian Shavetail with Custer

All rights reserved. No part of this book may be reproduced or transmitted in any form or by any means, electronic or mechanical, including photocopying, recording or by any information storage and retrieval system without written permission from the author, except for the inclusion of brief quotations in a review.

International Standard Book Number: 978-0-7884-3646-5

To
The Puzzleheaded Girl

TESTIMONIALS

"Benteen is one of the bravest men I ever saw in a fight."
— *George Herendeen, scout*

"I think he is one of the coolest and bravest men I have ever known."
— *Lt. Francis Gibson*

"I found my model early in Captain Benteen, the idol of the Seventh Cavalry."
— *Gen. Hugh Scott*

"...just about the finest soldier and the greatest gentleman I ever knew."
— *Sgt. Charles Windolph*

"He was the only man I ever saw who did not dodge when bullets flew."
— *Lt. Charles A. Varnum*

"Too much cannot be said in favor of Captain Benteen."
— *First Sergeant John Ryan*

"I do not believe a more gallant man ever lived, and he was the coolest man under fire that I ever saw."
— *Lt. Ezra Fuller*

"Benteen was one of the bravest officers I ever met."
— *Pvt. Jacob Horner*

"Benteen saved the command, according to my opinion. He was a brave and nervy man."
— *Sgt. Stanislas Roy*

CONTENTS

List of Illustrations ix
Introduction xi
Acknowledgments xv
Early Years 1
Civil War 17
The Southern Plains 65
The Northern Plains 127
Little Bighorn 147
Nez Perce 211
Final Years 235
Notes 273
Bibliography 313
Index 321
About the Author 349

LIST OF ILLUSTRATIONS

Sheet music cover, "The Very Last Polka," 1843(?)
....*between pages 7 and 8*

The versatile Theodore Charles Benteen, Sr. ("Charley")
....*between pages 7 and 8*

Map of Benteen's Civil War battles *16*

Captain Benteen of Bowen's Battalion of Volunteers in 1862
....*between pages 25 and 26*

Major Benteen of the 10th Volunteer Missouri Cavalry in 1863 ....*between pages 25 and 26*

Map of the Southern Plains *64*

Lieutenant Colonel George A. Custer in civilian dress
....*between pages 93 and 94*

Lieutenant General Philip Sheridan....*between pages 93 and 94*

Diagram of the Washita attack ....*between pages 96 and 97*

"Cheyenne Squaws & Pappooses - captured at the battle of the 'Washita'" ....*between pages 96 and 97*

Captain Benteen ....*between pages 118 and 119*

Major Marcus Reno, 7th Cavalry ...*between pages 118 and 119*

Captain Benteen of the 7th U. S. Cavalry in Nashville, 1872. His hair is beginning to turn white.
....*between pages 134 and 135*

Catherine Norman Benteen in 1872
....*between pages 134 and 135*

Map of the Northern Plains ....*between pages 134 and 135*

Major Benteen in dress uniform in later years
....*between pages 134 and 135*

Benteen and Freddie in New York, 1882 ....*234*

Officers' Quarters, Fort Sill, Indian Territory, 1884.
Major Benteen, Cathy and Violet are standing outside.
....*between pages 244 and 245*

Theatre of Operations, 9th Cavalry
....*between pages 244 and 245*

Benteen and family at Fort Du Chesne, 1886
....*between pages 258 and 259*

Benteen (standing) at Fort Douglas, 1887, while awaiting review of his court martial...............*between pages 258 and 259*

Theodore Goldin, Benteen's confidant (of sorts).................*272*

INTRODUCTION

This book is offered as a concise biography of Frederick William Benteen. The author has focused the study primarily on the man and spared the reader a detailed description of the great events in the Civil War and the Plains Wars, so well treated elsewhere. In this connection, attention is directed to the almost encyclopedic work of Charles K. Mills,[i] which furnishes a description of anyone even distantly connected to Benteen. For an overview, the informative magazine article *Custer's Nemesis* by Steven M. Leonard[ii] is helpful. Also, my biography of Lieutenant Charles De Rudio,[iii] contains material relating to Custer and the 7th Cavalry, which has not been duplicated in this work.

A study of Benteen's life can be daunting. The many letters he left behind support divergent views of his character. Throughout her long life, Custer's resourceful widow had unremitting contempt for Benteen, which she made no effort to conceal. Even today, his detractors are many. If the Reno Hill was later renamed the Reno-Benteen Hill, the change owes more to a desire to humiliate Reno, than to an intent to honor Benteen. Few of Benteen's fellow officers mourned his departure from the army, as they watched him sink deeper into alcoholism and petulance.

Benteen's shortcomings were many. He may well be faulted for a long list of character defects–but never for want of bravery. Something about the person made men respect him, spring to his orders and unhesitatingly follow him into battle. That essence deserves to be explored, and the testimonials he accrued during his lifetime have earned him the right to a balanced inquiry.

A word about method. The author at times has shamelessly rounded out distances and numbers, in situations where exactitude can be tedious. If the reader nurtures an overwhelming desire to know the exact number of soldiers in Nathan Bedford Forrest's army or the exact distance between Fort Riley and Fort Harker, he (or she) is advised to look elsewhere. The numbers of dead (not the casualties) are given after each of Benteen's Civil War battles, to put the encounter into proper historical perspective, so that its importance will not be overstated. The author surely does not intend to demean the contributions of the wounded. Since the history of the 7th Cavalry is an oft-repeated story, I have omitted many familiar details. Thus, "Garry Owen" and "The Girl I Left Behind Me" go unmentioned. Some difficulties were encountered in identifying a few items in Benteen's army file, where the accession number was absent or obscure.

664 River Road
Teaneck, NJ 07666
201-836-6365
Julescalvin@aol.com

[i] Charles K. Mills, *Harvest of Barren Regrets*, Glendale, CA: Clark Co., 1985.
[ii] Steven M. Leonard, "Custer's Nemesis", *Wild West Magazine*, June 2001.
[iii] Jules C. Ladenheim, *Alien Horseman: An Italian Shavetail with Custer*, Bowie, MD: Heritage Books, 2003.

ACKNOWLEDGMENTS

I acknowledge with deep thanks the courtesies shown me during the preparation of this study by the librarians of the National Archives; the Hagner Collection of the New York Public Library, the Hargrett Collection of the University of Georgia, the Western Historical Manuscript Collection of the University of Missouri, the Bobst Specialty Collection of the New York University Library, the Manuscript Collection of the Military Academy of West Point, the Portland, (Maine), Public Library and the Bismarck, North Dakota, Municipal Library. I also wish to thank the reference staff of the Enoch Pratt Free Library of Baltimore, Maryland, and Lucille Bertram of the Teaneck, New Jersey, Public Library for their help with the Benteen genealogy. Dr. Richard Sommers of the Army Historical Library was most helpful. Mrs. Jean Ganley relieved me of distracting chores.

Willie Peters accompanied me to the "Crows Nest," "White Man's Crows Nest," "Benteen's March to the left" and to the putative site of the Lone Tepee. Bill Redford provided answers for several perplexing questions. I thank the Crow Nation for allowing me to wander over their reservation. To Eric Ladenheim and Alex Ladenheim who accompanied me along Custer's March and helped me revisit Ford A and retrace Reno's retreat, I express my deep gratitude. The assistance of my editor, Roxanne Carlson, was invaluable.

EARLY YEARS

The grandfather of Frederick William Benteen arrived on these shores before the Revolutionary War and settled in Baltimore. He anglicized his given names to Theodore Charles, probably from Teodor Karl. A son stated for the 1880 census that his father had been born in Germany. There is a "family tradition" that the lineage came from the Netherlands and that the young immigrant supported the English Crown during the Revolutionary War,[1] but these, and many other family stories, should be regarded with suspicion. The Benteens in those days were working people, without pretensions. The southern gentry myth came later.[2]

Baltimore was an attractive destination for an immigrant. Commerce was thriving, thanks to the city's splendid sheltered harbor. Its rivers supplied adequate power for early manufacture,[3] and soon, the National (Cumberland) Road, would provide access to trans-Appalachia.[4] Baltimore had early encouraged a rail system,[5] especially after the Potowmack and

Chesapeake and Ohio Canals threatened to divert trade to Alexandria, Virginia.

Theodore C. Benteen married a woman who had been born in Pennsylvania. One of their sons was Frederick Damish Benteen, who began his working career as a piano dealer, then became a music publisher. Music was greatly appreciated in Baltimore. German immigrants brought with them a love of music, which the slave-owning families had the leisure to enjoy. As early as 1840, William Knabe and Charles Steiff were well established in Baltimore as piano makers.

Among Frederick D. Benteen's clients was a Pittsburgh composer, Stephen Foster. Benteen had published "Oh Susanna,"[6] as well as other Foster songs, especially those composed early in Foster's career. For the period from 1849-60, Benteen remitted to Foster a total of $15,000 in royalties, based on a royalty of two cents for every twenty-five cents of sale.[7]

More to the purpose of this story was another son, Theodore Charles ("Charley") Benteen. Born in Baltimore in 1809, he became a commercial painter and paint supplier, and shared the same residence as his brother, the music publisher. Charley Benteen married Caroline D(a)vis on February 17, 1829.

There was much construction in Baltimore during the middle third of the nineteenth century. In one year, two thousand houses were built.[8] Professional painters artfully decorated many of the more expensive homes. A visiting Englishman extolled the tradespeople, shopkeepers and mechanics of Baltimore as being "better informed, more industrious and in better

Early Years 3

condition as to circumstance than the same class of people in England."[9]

A year after the birth of their daughter, Henrietta Elizabeth ("En") in 1831, Charley Benteen moved the family to Petersburg, Virginia. The reasons for the relocation are not known. Some Baltimoreans were aggrieved by the collapse of the Bank of Maryland,[10] others by the growth of the "Know Nothing" party, which quickly degenerated into a corrupt political machine;[11] but it is more likely Charley moved for better business opportunities.

Petersburg was a thriving manufacturing and transport center. It was situated twenty miles south of Richmond, and in some regards overshadowed it.[12] The city was on the tidal Appomattox River and accommodated schooners and sloops with shallow draft.[13] Although Petersburg led Virginia in the manufacture of cotton products, tobacco was its chief commodity.[14] It had twenty tobacco factories; six cotton mills; two cottonseed mills, a flour mill and a brass and cast iron foundry.[15] In 1840, there were 121 retail stores representing a capital of one million dollars.[16]

A son, Frederick William, was born to the Charley and Caroline Benteen on August 24, 1834 and another son, Theodore Charles, Jr. six years later. According to the 1840 census, Benteen owned two slaves—an adult black woman (age 30-40) and her child (age 5-10), destined for work in the home. Caroline's health was at best precarious. She contracted pulmonary consumption and died on October 31, 1841, at the age of forty-seven, leaving three children in the care of their father, who seemed on the way to commercial success. The death of his mother must have deeply touched ten-year-old Fred. Years later, on a trip from Atlanta to Washington, he visited the Blandsford Churchyard in Petersburg on Christmas Day.[17]

Charley Benteen plied his trade as painter and paint purveyor. At various times, he had two partners. Judging by the frequency of their advertisements in the *Petersburg Republican*, the partners seem to have been moderately successful. Their services included "house painting and plain lettering, glazing of marble, graining and imitation wood, picture frames, chairs, ornamental painting and gilding." Charley and his partners may have performed the painting themselves wholly or in part; or, more likely, supervised hired men. The partners were in direct competition with free black house painters. Included in Petersburg's population of fourteen thousand in 1850 were six thousand blacks, two-thirds of whom were free[18] and all well represented in the trades and crafts. In Charleston, South Carolina, for example, with a population of thirty thousand, there were sixteen white and sixteen black painters. The slave craftsmen could be hired for twenty-five to thirty dollars a month.[19]

There were "free" schools in the city, supported by public funds and private endowment, but ambitious families preferred to send their boys to private academies.[20] Fred, the older son, was sent for his schooling to the Petersburg Classical Institute. This "prestigious academy for boys,"[21] founded in 1819,[22] had 140-150 students. It was under Presbyterian sponsorship and promised to promote "the higher branch of liberal education."[23] Virginia had hundreds of these private academies, some lodged in rude log cabins, others in noble houses. The tuition for Fred's school is not known, but the Chesterfield Boarding School, twenty miles from Petersburg, charged thirty-two dollars a session.[24]

The school building of the Petersburg Classical Institute was of the "noble" variety and lasted well into the twentieth century. Judging by similar schools, it had two or three programs of instruction,[25] depending on the prospects of the student. For the student destined for higher study, the curriculum might consist of Latin, Greek, French, Italian, surveying, algebra, etc.[26] The non-academic student might be taught such subjects as practical arithmetic, natural and moral philosophy, English grammar and composition, geography, history and literature.[27] Fred Benteen was more likely in the latter group.

As a boy, Fred Benteen showed a talent for art. In 1843, he painted an elegant Baltimore street scene, which was used for the cover of one of his uncle's sheet music, "The Very Last Polka."[28] Perhaps the painting was based on a sketch made by someone else. At any rate, Fred Benteen was comfortable with art, as evidenced by his later sketches and elegant calligraphy.

Military instruction, too, was included in his studies, although the Petersburg Classical Institute was not, as Benteen later claimed,[29] a military academy. A well-bred Virginia student was expected to have some knowledge of military matters,[30] and a military education was highly prized.[31] White Virginians lived in fear of a slave uprising and long ago, refugees from San Dominigue (Haiti) had warned of the dangers of black revolts.[32] In 1831, in Jerusalem, Virginia, seventy miles east of Richmond, Nat Turner rose up with a band of forty slaves and free blacks and killed fifty-nine white Virginians. Bells clanged day and night in Petersburg,[33] and rumors spread of thousands of blacks roaming the highways.[34] Nat Turner and his band were quickly captured and hanged.

Almost every community throughout the state had a slave patrol. These night watches policed the black section of town, challenged strangers, captured runaways and dealt so-called summary justice. In addition, Petersburg lent generous support to the 39th Regular Virginia Militia, whose principle charge was to ensure "law and order" among the black population.

In 1848, the news of the discovery of gold in California stirred the east as no other event had done in recent memory. Farmers scrambled to prepare themselves for a six-month trek across the plains, clerks scraped together the four hundred dollars needed for passage around the Horn or across the Isthmus of Panama, but the canny tradesmen and craftsmen sought advantages closer at hand. Charley Benteen, too, was smitten with the fever and felt a desire to cut loose. He carefully studied the glowing reports, and could see great prospects in St. Louis.

St. Louis by 1850 was the seventh largest American city, with a population of 77,000 people. Commerce and manufacture flourished.[35] As well as being the entrepot for the westward movement, St. Louis was a world-class port, with traffic converging from the Ohio, Missouri, Mississippi and Illinois Rivers. The splendid engineering efforts of the army in 1837-39, under the direction of Lieutenant Robert E. Lee, greatly benefited the natural anchorage and, by the construction of jetties and levees, insured that the river did not meander and leave St. Louis inland. Above St. Louis, the Mississippi lost depth, requiring transshipment to shallow-draft vessels, while cargo descending the river was transferred to larger vessels at St. Louis, for purposes of efficiency and economy. Even the difficulties experienced with low water or winter ice benefited the city, since they encouraged the construction of railroads.

Before departing for St. Louis, Charley Benteen traveled to New York, where on March 3, 1849, he married Beulah Kane, a widow with three small children.[36] Nothing further is known about this marriage, nor do we hear of the new Mrs. Benteen in St. Louis. On the contrary, we learn that in St. Louis Charley Benteen courted the older daughter of the Norman family. One might suspect that the bridegroom mentioned in the newspaper article was someone else with the same name, perhaps a son of Frederick Damish Benteen, but the notice of the marriage appeared in the *Petersburg Republican*, and there was no subsequent retraction. The same confusion of names may concern a foreclosure in New York by the Fire Insurance Company in December 1850 of property owned by a Theodore Benteen.[37] Fortunately, the narrative can proceed without a resolution of these ambiguities.

Sheet music cover, "The Very Last Polka," 1843(?). Artist: Frederick William Benteen. Publisher, F. W. Benteen. [Manuscript Department, Enoch Pratt Free Library, Baltimore]

The versatile Theodore Charles Benteen, Sr. ("Charley"). [Benteen Photo Collection, Hargrett Rare Book and Manuscript Library, University of Georgia]

In any event, Charley Benteen packed the family belongings and started out for St. Louis. It is likely for reasons of economy that they traveled on the National Road, rather than by riverboat down the Ohio, from Wheeling.

The macadamized National Road began at Cumberland, Maryland and stretched over the Appalachians to Vandalia, Illinois; where it joined a crushed rock state road leading to East St. Louis. Wagon freighters could be hired to transport household effects, but Charley Benteen may have made his own wagons and done his own transport, having, as we shall see, a pair of skillful hands, as well as the help of his two sons and a daughter. Most travelers spent nights under canvas and sometimes in "wagon houses."[38] Always the threat of highwaymen required vigilance. East St. Louis was eventually reached and a steam ferry conveyed the party to St. Louis.

The year the Benteens arrived, the city was beset by a deadly cholera epidemic that killed 8,000 people, and by a great fire that destroyed much of the commercial center. St. Louis took little time to mourn. With business booming, rebuilding was prompt and energetic. Cast-iron construction replaced the wooden building fronts, providing a further spur to the local foundries.[39] The family settled in the city and Benteen started up his business. On May 18, 1850, his daughter, Henrietta, married James L. Doyle.[40]

Although Missouri was a slave state, the "peculiar institution" was less entrenched there than elsewhere in the South. Of the 54,000 Missouri farms, only 8,000 had slaves, few more than two or three. These slave farms were concentrated along both banks of the Missouri River[41] and to a lesser extent, along the fertile Mississippi bottom land north of St. Louis ("Little Dixie"). To these regions flocked slave owners from the exhausted farms of Kentucky, Tennessee, North Carolina and Virginia, determined to try their luck in virgin soil with tobacco, hemp, grain or livestock. Closely allied to these slave owners were the poor white emigrants from the south ("clay eaters" in South Carolina, "sand diggers" in Virginia) who had left "hollers and gullies" back east, only to gravitate toward the same marginal existence in Missouri.[42] These poor white families, which settled in rural Missouri, continued to support the slave squirarchy[43] as they had done previously. They were destined to play an important role in the forthcoming Missouri insurgency.

The painting business offered great opportunities in St. Louis. Factories, homes, steamboats all required the painter's services. Fred began in his father's trade but left it for sign painting, which may have better accommodated his artistic talents. He was not, however, "an artist with a military education" as he later claimed.[44] His brother, Theodore, took up paper hanging. Whether Fred pursued his talent for art, is not known. The St. Louis Museum of Art was then in the early stages of formation. There must have been considerable public interest in fine art painting, since advertisements for an art supply store appear frequently in the newspapers.

Charley plied his trade with great vigor. As in Petersburg, he had partners at various times, offering their services as painters and purveyors of paint and glass. Steamboats especially required painting, when they arrived at St. Louis with decks and bulkheads begrimed with ash. If one judges by the newspaper ads, Charley Benteen had lively competition. The names of three paint firms appear in the 1860 advertisement columns of the *St. Louis Democrat*.

The years passed, and the sixteen-year-old boy grew into manhood. He had a thin, lanky frame and was five feet, ten and one-half inches tall. It is not known if he had further schooling—probably not. Charley Benteen had given him a good start; now it was time for business. In his spare time, he played baseball. Benteen had a great love for the sport, but apparently he did not let it interfere with work. There were at least five baseball teams in St. Louis, but Benteen's name is not listed among the players in 1860. There were also local drill clubs and militia units, but it is not known whether Benteen showed an early interest in these activities. Eventually, Frederick and his brother, Theo, moved to rooms, no long residing with their father.

Around 1855, the nineteen-year-old Philadelphian, Catherine Louise Norman,[45] found her way to St. Louis on a family visit. She was forewarned by her father to "let no flattery or eloquent language of any man make any impression upon your mind especially when you are far from your home [in Philadelphia] and in absence of your admirable and estimable mother whose council

Early Years 11

consent and advice you should always take in such matters of so much importance to your self."[46]

Henry R. Norman, her father, was born in Philadelphia in 1806.[47] He married twenty-year-old Elizabeth Lowrey[48] on June 10, 1833. In addition to Catherine, the Norman children included William H., Leslie R. and an older sister, Anita.[49] A year after Catherine arrived on her visit, her father died in Philadelphia, and her mother, in some financial difficulty, moved the family to St. Louis. The Norman family was said to have had strong anti-slavery sentiments that doubtless were made known to the young sign painter, who had begun to show an interest in Kate. Charley was attracted to Kate's older sister, Anita Norman,[50] but nothing came of it. In later years, Anita would prove a great nuisance to Frederick William Benteen.

The black population in St. Louis numbered only six thousand,[51] with slaves and free blacks in equal numbers.[52] Slavery had not prospered in that city, since its economic benefits were undercut by the influx of foreign labor. A slave cost his owner more than $1,300 and required clothing, food, shelter, insurance and medical care,[53] while an immigrant laborer could be hired for two hundred dollars a year. Even so, slaves supplied the manual labor for warehouses and piers, and black painters competed with the white craftsmen, either as freemen or as slaves. Often the slave worked independently and shared his earnings with his owner. This lively competition between black and white artisans may have been the source of Charley's fierce partisanship with the southern cause.

As the decade of the 50's drew to a close, life in St. Louis was pleasant and promising, at least for the white population. The depression of 1857 had dampened spirits, but the city recovered quickly. Employment opportunities abounded, and a teenager named Samuel Clemens (Mark Twain) found work as a journeyman printer for the *St. Louis Evening News*. Baseball games were well attended. Drill companies were popular, among them the State Militia, the Washington Guards, the St. Louis Guards, the St. Louis Greys, the Emmet Guards and the Zouaves.[54] Other events engaged public interest, among them a balloon ascent, the annual Agricultural and Mechanical Fair, the Philharmonic concerts and opening of the Academy of Art, visited by the Prince of Wales. Through it all, Fred Benteen continued to court Catherine Norman. No decision had been made about marriage. Perhaps a sign painter's prospects were not as promising as Mrs. Norman would have desired for her daughter.

By 1860, Charley is no longer named in the Kennedy City Directory for St. Louis. Instead, Frederick W. Benteen is now listed as painter, instead of sign painter, while Theodore Jr. continues as a paper hanger. This suggests, perhaps, that Charley may have left the city and turned the business over to his son.

The inevitable confrontation between the slave and free interests came with the election of 1860. The fundamental issue before the voters was the introduction of slavery into the new territories. The Republican candidate, Abraham Lincoln, opposed the expansion of slavery but denied any intent to interfere with the institution within the southern states. Senator Stephen Douglas, the candidate of the Democratic Party, held that the territories themselves should decide the slave issue. Neither stand satisfied the southern members of the Democratic Party, and they put forth the incumbent Vice-President, John C. Breckinridge, who pledged to allow slavery in all the territories. A fourth group, the Constitutional Union Party, composed of old-line Whigs and Native Americans (i.e. anti-immigrant whites), nominated John Bell of Tennessee, an advocate of compromise and conciliation. An overwhelming majority of Missourians supported Douglas or Bell.

The St. Louis election campaign was especially tumultuous. For many immigrants who had arrived after the Revolution of 1848, this was their first Presidential election. Crowds of Republican "wide awakes," composed of torch waving, glossy caped, young Germans and others, carried on a noisy and vigorous campaign. They were opposed by the Democratic "minute men"—paramilitary units, smaller in number but no less vociferous. Missouri found itself divided into four camps,[55] corresponding to the number of candidates. On Election Day, only ten percent of the electorate voted for Abraham Lincoln, while seventy percent voted for Douglas or Bell; and the remainder for the pro-southern Democrat, John C. Breckinridge.

Abraham Lincoln won the national election with forty percent of the popular votes and 180 of the 303 electoral votes, but not a single vote was cast for

Lincoln in ten of the southern states; or if any were cast, they were not counted. Lincoln ran a poor last in the border states. Six weeks after the election, South Carolina voted an Ordinance of Secession, and the dissolution of the Union had begun. A last-minute attempt at compromise was proposed by extending the line of the Missouri Compromise to the Pacific Ocean, but the President-Elect, who opposed any extension of slavery into the territories, adamantly rejected this.

A month before Lincoln's inauguration, the delegates from six southern states met at Montgomery, Alabama and elected Jefferson Davis as President of the Confederate States. Events moved quickly. When Lincoln attempted to supply Fort Sumter in Charlestown Harbor, insurgents fired upon the fort, prompting another four states to join the Confederacy. The Civil War had begun. Since the 13,000-man regular army had been deliberately scattered over the frontier by the outgoing President Buchanan, Lincoln was obliged to call on 75,000 three-month volunteers, for a show of force. Lincoln steadfastly believed that a majority of white southerners were at heart Union men and that the secession was thrust upon them by the so-called secession state conventions, which had been manipulated by the slave interests. He maintained that the slave leaders dared not put the issue to statewide vote nor, in most cases, to the regular state legislatures.[56]

Little did he appreciate the unyielding grasp of the slave interests on the southern white population.

Throughout the early days of secession, Lincoln hoped that the wayward states could be cowed by a strong Federal *coup de main*. General Winfield Scott, the General-in-Chief, gave little encouragement to this belief. Scott knew the quality of the southern soldier, honed by diligent participation in night patrols and in the trained militia. In contrast, service in the northern peacetime militia was often little more than an excuse to drink and to strut. Scott foresaw the difficulty of invading Virginia, with its four rivers running to the sea, separating the countryside into long strips of land, where an invading army would have trouble in maneuvering and in bringing up timely reinforcements.

Rather than invade the South, Scott proposed to isolate it by a blockade of southern ports along the Atlantic coastline, the Gulf of Mexico and the Mississippi River. The impatient President Lincoln thoroughly rejected this grand strategy, derisively called the "Anaconda Plan," but in time, even George B. McClellan found merit in it.[57] Events would later show that the four years of bloody campaigns in Virginia resulted in little more than a stalemate, while military success came largely from western initiatives, based on control of the Mississippi.

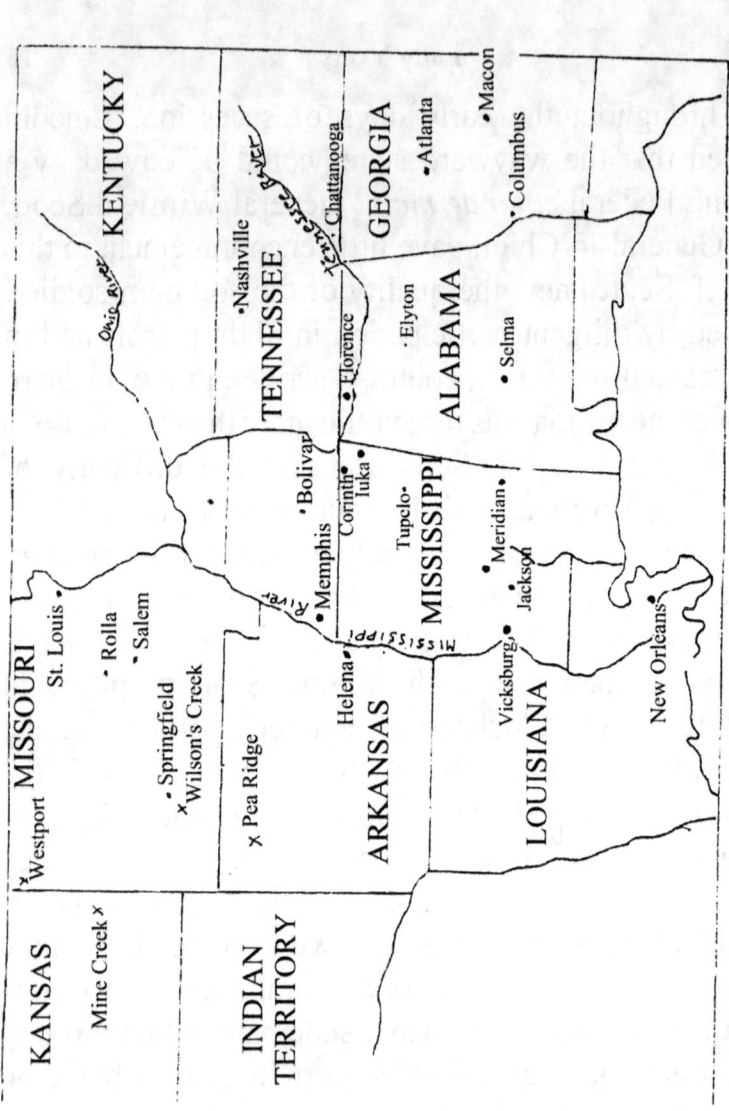

Map of Benteen's Civil War battles.

CIVIL WAR

Following the secession of the southern states, St. Louis experienced violent civil disorder, as mobs roamed the streets proclaiming their sympathies. "St. Louis trembled on the verge of madness," wrote a reporter. "Plots, counterplots, hysteria shook the streets and levees."[1] The Union Home Guard mobilized its members, determined to protect the St. Louis Arsenal, the largest in the country.[2] Fred Benteen helped drill the Union Home Guard, but was reluctant to accept a commission, he says, out of loyalty to his father, a rabid Confederate sympathizer.[3] Southern sympathizers, on the other hand, formed the state militia unit. Both units paraded the streets in St. Louis. Watching in the crowds were William T. Sherman, president of a streetcar company, and U. S. Grant, civilian mustering officer for the Governor of Illinois, on his way to visit his father-in-law living outside of St. Louis.[4]

Captain Nathaniel Lyon, a regular army officer, commanded the ten-thousand-man Home Guard and the

Federal regulars stationed at the arsenal. He led them in a preemptive dawn strike against the eight-hundred-man state militia, camped on the outskirts of the city; and forced a surrender.[5] While conveying their prisoners through the streets, the Union soldiers were attacked by pro-Confederate sympathizers, resulting in the death of one soldier; whereupon the Home Guard fired at the mob, killing twenty-eight. Southern sympathizers were arrested and detained, until they took an oath to uphold the Constitution of the United States.[6] This episode hastened the polarization of public opinion. During the ensuing hostilities, Missouri was to provide 110,000 soldiers for the Union and forty thousand men for the Confederacy, but these statistics do not reflect the hoards of irregulars that kept the state in turmoil. Outside of St. Louis, the Union never had a firm hold on Missouri.[7]

The Confederates sensed that Missouri was ripe for a quick military initiative. Confederate Brigadier General Sterling Price ("Old Pap"), a former governor, scoured the state for recruits. He found twenty thousand for his army, many without weapons, and gathered them in southern Missouri. Apprised of this threat, Lyon the Union commander, now a brigadier general, moved his hastily organized army south. His troops had half the rebel strength, but were better equipped, with weapons from the armory. With the Union troops went Fred Benteen and some of the civilians he had been drilling. Perhaps they had not had the opportunity to be mustered into the army, or, perhaps, they did not choose to enlist. At the time, soldiers usually elected their company officers. If someone wanted to become an officer, he had first to join the company; and if he was not elected, he had to serve as an enlisted man. Perhaps Benteen was not willing to take that risk and was waiting for a surer opportunity.

From his staging area in southwest Missouri, Price moved north to seize control of the state. On the night of August 9, 1861, the southern troops were bivouacked near Wilson's Creek,[8] Missouri. Under cover of darkness, Lyon executed a daring attack. He ordered a column under Colonel Franz Sigel to swing wide around the rebel camp and attack it from the rear. A Union regiment of three-month volunteers, under the command of regular army Major Samuel Sturgis, was ordered to attack the left flank of the enemy encampment, while Lyon led the main frontal attack. Sigil's attack was launched, but on an early sign of resistance, his troops faltered and fled. Sturgis's attack likewise lacked sufficient strength to roll back the enemy flank. Among Sturgis's company commanders was a former cavalry sergeant named Myles Moylan, whom we shall meet again.

Lyon led his men bravely toward the Confederate line. He was wounded three times and had his horse shot out from under him. After procuring another horse, he continued to rally his men, until he was shot in the heart and fell dead. His men fled the battlefield, abandoning the body of their brave commander. Major Sturgis helped guard the rear of the fleeing soldiers. Fortunate for the Union troops, the rebels lacked the vigor to pursue. Not until eight days later when the

Union soldiers reached Rolla, the railroad terminus, did the retreat halt. The numbers of dead shocked both sides: Union, 1,300 killed; Confederates, 1,200. More than the first major clash west of the Mississippi, Wilson's Creek had a higher percentage of casualties than any other battle in the Civil War: e.g., ten percent for Bull Run, twenty-three percent for Wilson's Creek.[9] It was the first of almost one thousand battles and skirmishes to be fought in Missouri,[10] eleven percent of those fought in the nation, exceeded only by the fighting in Virginia and Tennessee.

What had Fred Benteen been doing during the battle of Wilson Creek? It is unlikely he accompanied Sigil's "Dutch" Brigade. More probably, he remained with the men that he had helped train or with some other gaggle of volunteers in Lyon's column, not yet enrolled. In any event, Benteen retreated with the rest of the Union forces, and by the time they reached the rail terminus in Rolla, Benteen had decided to formally join the Union army. He later stated that his decision angered his kin, meaning his father, a rabid southern sympathizer, who expressed a wish that a bullet would cut short his son's military career: "I hope the first goddamned bullet gets you!"[11] Family feelings ran high, but Benteen was not above exaggerating.

At Rolla, a small town with scraggly shacks,[12] the dispirited Union soldiers were loaded onto railroad cars and sent off to St. Louis for reorganization. Benteen remained behind, as did several hundred others, who, although they had participated in the battle, they had not been formally enrolled in any specific company. An effort was made to recruit these men into a cavalry battalion. Four cavalry companies were organized and on September 1, 1861, an election was held. William D. Bowen was elected captain of C Company, and Frederick William Benteen was elected his first lieutenant, replacing another officer who had resigned. It seems likely that Bowen had persuaded the men to accept Benteen as second choice. A month later, Bowen was given command of the battalion, the First Battalion Missouri Cavalry or "Bowen's Battalion," and Benteen was elected captain of C Company. Benteen, then, received his empowerment from the soldiers of his company, unlike the West Point officer, who received his from the President of the United States.

Benteen chose the cavalry since it offered the best opportunity at the moment. Perhaps he meant to impress Kate, for the cavalry had a certain élan. If he lacked cavalry training, so did the peacetime Army, with its paltry five regiments of mounted troops.[13] Initially, Lincoln saw no need for cavalry. He envisioned a quick victory, at least within the period of the ninety day volunteer enlistment. Moreover, cavalry was thought to take two years to train and to cost $500,000 for raising and equipping a regiment. Only after the Union defeat at the first Battle of Bull Run, where the worth of Jeb Stuart became painfully evident, did the Union army reconsider the need for cavalry. Within six weeks after Bull Run, thirty-one cavalry regiments were on order.[14]

In the west, both armies from the start recognized the need for cavalry. Here, the Union horseman was the equal of the Confederates,[15] while in the east, they were clearly the inferior, at least during the first two years of the war.

Outfitting the Union cavalryman with uniform, revolver, saber, carbine, saddle and horse presented no problem, given the resources of the St. Louis Armory and the large stock of Missouri horses and mules.

There was no standardization of arms. When it came to weapons, "no army ever went to war with such a variety of firearms as the Federal volunteers."[16] The government had accepted seventeen different carbine breech-loading models, all requiring different ammunition. Early in the war, the Sharps was the most popular single-shot carbine,[17] using a linen cartridge, and having a barrel length of thirty-eight inches, compared to the fifty-six-inch rifle barrel. The Colt revolver was most commonly issued sidearm, which was eventually distributed to eighty percent of all Federal cavalry. It came in .36 caliber (1851) and .44 caliber (1860). A paper cartridge containing ball and powder was inserted into each revolver chamber and compacted with a ramming rod seated under the barrel. The percussion cap was placed on a nipple at the back of each chamber.

Union horses were purchased by the army procurement agency. Before they were delivered to the battalion, the horses had been poorly fed, carelessly watered and kept in filthy corrals, knee deep in mud and excreta. The hooves were often untrimmed and in sad condition. The first task was to shoe or re-shoe. If the company lacked a trained farrier, a knowledgeable stable hand might be substituted, who in time would perfect his skills. The McClellan saddle was issued to the Union cavalry and maintained by the company saddler, or as close to one as could be found. The saddle was light and comfortable, but split with wear. Officers often preferred an English saddle, which they bought at their own expense.[18] Since the Union cavalryman was unfamiliar with his mount, he needed time to adjust; unlike the Confederate cavalryman, who brought his own horse.

After receiving his mount and equipage, the recruit underwent intensive training. In the time-honored cavalry tradition, he first learned to care for his horse—better than for himself. He received instruction in military etiquette and camp hygiene; then in dismounted drill, mounted exercises and lastly in the march: walk four, trot six, gallop sixteen miles per hour.

Officers were furnished with copies of the *Manual of Cavalry Tactics and Regulations*, which they studied carefully, so that they could remain one step ahead of the men. Illustrations in the manual depicted basic cavalry evolutions up to platoon strength. Larger manoevers had to be learned through trial and error. The primer was an exposition of the tactics of Napoleon, now four decades old. Napoleon employed as many as twelve thousand horsemen in a single battle and, in the popular perception, overwhelmed the enemy with the saber charge. "The strength of cavalry is in the spurs and saber," wrote George B. McClellan in his introduction to the 1861 edition of the *Cavalry Manual*. In fact, Napoleon was a trained artilleryman, who more often used the field artillery to blow a hole in the enemy line, the so-called "artillery charge," before sending in the cavalry.[19]

Early in the war, much time was spent on saber drill. The saber was highly regarded by the northern cavalry, less so by the Confederates.[20] Wrote John Singleton Mosby, the celebrated Confederate cavalryman, "The only real use I ever heard of their being put to was to hold a piece of meat over the fire for frying."[21] Quickly the revolver and the carbine supplanted the saber, and for the Confederate cavalryman, even a shotgun, was preferred.

Cavalry was initially deployed to scout, to protect flanks, to tear up tracks and telegraph lines, and to harass rear columns and supply depots. Over unchallenging terrain, it could travel thirty-five miles in an eight-hour day without undue strain on horses or men. However, as an instrument for intruding into an ongoing engagement, the cavalry had limited value, since the effective range of the carbine was only two hundred yards, and the horse performed poorly amid the noise of battle. Moreover, the introduction of the rifled minieball, with double or triple the carbine range, also served to keep the cavalry away from the line.[22] The minieball had a hollow base that expanded after the firing, to grip the rifling. Its conoidal shape helped maintain a steady spiraling in flight. Soon, the acquisition of the twelve-pound howitzer cannon would give the cavalry a more meaningful role in the battle.

After a month of training, Bowen's Battalion took its first faltering step. It was sent to central Missouri, to accompany an infantry regiment. On October 13, 1861, at Dutch Hollow,²³ Missouri, they encountered a column of mounted Confederate irregulars, called "bushwhackers." Benteen's C Company was ordered to dismount and deploy to the left of the rebel line, while Bowen held the center. The battle wavered, until another brigade of Union cavalry appeared and broke the rebel position. The cavalry pursued the Confederates, killing eighty. The Union loss was one man.

For Benteen and his men, this was the beginning of four long years of campaign, which would take them to seven states. Many of their battles and most of their skirmishes are long forgotten. Through the efforts of these citizen soldiers, many without a headstone to mark their graves, the war in the west was won for the Union.

After their baptism of fire, Benteen's men saw no action for the next six weeks. The company meanwhile was formally enrolled in the army. This had not been done in September, since a mustering officer was not then available. The company had ample time to study its captain. They saw a wiry, twenty-seven-year-old with cherubic face and scraggly mustache, who seldom raised his voice and seldom needed to repeat an order. His broad shoulders, muscular arms and huge, calloused hands advised the company that their captain was no stranger to hard work, although he later insisted that his gnarled fingers were the result of baseball playing.²⁴

On December 3, 1861, while Bowen's Battalion was asleep in camp near Salem,²⁵ Missouri, twenty-five miles from Rolla, three hundred Confederate irregulars attacked them in the early hours of the morning.

Captain Benteen of Bowen's Battlion of Volunteers in 1862. [Benteen Photo Collection, Hargrett Rare Book and Manuscript Library, University of Georgia]

Major Benteen of the 10th Volunteer Missouri Cavalry in 1863. [Benteen Photo Collection, Hargrett Rare Book and Manuscript Library, University of Georgia]

Benteen quickly roused his company, and they struggled to hold off the intruders. The mounted battalion eventually drove off the enemy, who left behind eighteen bodies. The Union suffered four deaths.

Guerrilla warfare in Missouri was to cause twenty-seven thousand deaths by the end of the war. Shooting and looting quickly became endemic, with the emergence of such desperados as "Captain" William Quantrill, Cole Younger, the James brothers and "Bloody Bill" Anderson.

The battalion spent the next four days pursuing the irregulars and captured twenty prisoners. They then returned to Rolla.

Here, Benteen learned that his sister, Henrietta Doyle ("En"), residing in New York, was in dire straits. She had been cruelly mistreated by her husband and had expressed a desire to move back to St. Louis with her three daughters. Benteen's request for "emergency" leave was approved by his superiors on January 1, 1862.

Whatever the motive behind his request, Benteen used his leave as an opportunity to propose to Catherine Louisa Norman, then twenty-five years old. The two were married January 7, 1862, at St. George Episcopal Church in St. Louis, with the bride's mother and sister in attendance. Neither Charley nor Henrietta were present. It is likely that Charley had left St. Louis in 1860, perhaps to become a steamboat engineer, and that Henrietta had not yet arrived, notwithstanding Benteen's representations to his commanding officer. Benteen and Catherine moved into their own home at 281 Franklin Avenue and, after three days of honeymoon, Benteen was back in Rolla with his company.

Meanwhile, Sterling Price was again on the march. He gathered a large army that included Missouri irregulars, Arkansas militiamen and Native Americans from the Indian Territory. Price's aim, as always, was to invade Missouri and capture St. Louis. To the South, the city beckoned as a colossal supply depot; to the Union, it was a steppingstone to the capture of the Confederate river cities.

Command of the Union forces in Missouri meanwhile had passed to Brigadier General Samuel Curtis, a West Point graduate, who had earlier resigned his commission to practice law. Curtis was determined to halt the invasion by moving quickly.

He marched his four divisions to Lebanon, fifty miles southwest of Rolla. Bowen's Battalion was attached to General Curtis's headquarters. Significantly, one of the companies was issued four twelve-pound muzzle-loading howitzers. Although called a "howitzer," the field piece had a comparatively flat parabolic trajectory (arc of fire), and its barrel was capable of only a five degree elevation.[26] The Model 1857 smooth bore was usually made of bronze and had an effective range for solid shot of less than 1,500 yards. It could fire solid shot, explosive shells, grapeshot or canister (scatter load). Smooth bore had the advantage over the rifled cannon, in that it allowed for a larger caliber of solid shot and could fire the deadly canister.

A battery could now be rushed to a strategic location to pour fire onto the retreating or advancing foe. In such instances, the other cavalry companies in the battalion might be called on to defend the field pieces. When firing canister, with a range of less than four hundred yards, the twelve-pounder was more effective for defense than for offensive action.[27]

The Union Army swept through Springfield, Missouri, and continued toward the Arkansas border. At Crane Creek,[28] Missouri, on February 14, 1862, Bowen's Battalion had its first opportunity to use the howitzers, when it came upon a small Confederate force and fired ten canister shells. The Union cavalry charged but had to withdraw when confronted by heavy enemy reinforcements. Two days later the battalion exchanged cannon fire with a rebel battery, which fled after a Union cavalry charge. On February 16, at Sugar Creek,[29] Arkansas, a strong Confederate battery fired on the battalion. Bowen brought up two of his howitzers and continued to return fire, until relieved by a heavy artillery battery. Bowen's Battalion was fast mastering the use of the howitzer and learning to integrate its fire with the battalion mission. During the battle at Sugar Creek, Bowen sustained a wrist wound, which would later have significance for Benteen.

Benteen was ordered to provide an escort for one of General Curtis's quartermaster-subsistence officers, a Captain Philip Sheridan. Benteen assigned him twenty-five of his best troopers and a dependable second lieutenant. The caliber of the escort left Sheridan with kindly thoughts towards Benteen, which would later pay rich dividends.[30] Such is what Benteen would have us believe, and it may be true, but Sheridan was a hard-nosed realist, whose gratitude was notoriously short-lived.

Curtis marched his ten-thousand-man Union army into Arkansas. Word reached him from James Butler ("Wild Bill") Hickok and the other scouts that seventeen-thousand rebel soldiers under General Earl Van Dorn were coming north to meet him. Curtis positioned his four divisions on the north bank of Sugar Creek with Pea Ridge[31] Mountain behind him, to protect his rear. Curtis anticipated an enemy flanking maneuver. Instead, Van Dorn made a weak frontal attack, and sent two divisions behind Pea Ridge to come up onto the Union position from the rear. Curtis had stationed two divisions to confront what he thought would be the main attack, but, fortunately, he also deployed a weak division to the rear at the base of Pea Ridge, to oppose what appeared to be a minor rebel deployment. None of the Union officers expected that the main thrust would come from that direction.

On March 6, 1862, the rebels launched their attack. Two Confederate divisions marched around Pea Ridge and engaged the Union division near the site of Einhorn Tavern. The Union division commander desperately struggled to hold back the enemy. He urgently requested reinforcements, but Curtis could only send Benteen's company and four howitzers, all under Bowen's command. The small detachment took up a position on a road. Benteen and Bowen themselves fired two howitzers until they ran out of ammunition. After receiving a fresh supply of canister, they renewed the firing. Bowen's detachment withstood three strong enemy assaults, which allowed the Union division commander to stabilize his position and resist the enemy onslaught, until reinforcements arrived to repel the Confederate attack.³² The following day, Union forces captured the heights at Pea Ridge. This compelled the enemy to retreat across the Mississippi River and to abandon Arkansas. The Union dead was two hundred, the exact number of Confederate dead is unknown. The Battle of Pea Ridge postponed for two years another Confederate attempt to take Missouri. Many of the Missouri irregulars took leave of Price's army and slipped back home.

Rather than advance prematurely into Arkansas, General Curtis withdrew his army back to Missouri in order to shorten his supply line and to properly prepare for the invasion of Arkansas later in the spring.

On April 12, while the army rested, Major Bowen went off on a thirty-day leave to recuperate from his wrist wound, leaving the senior captain, Stanford Ing of B Company, in temporary command of the battalion. Benteen was unhappy with Ing, and trouble soon followed. Someone in Army headquarters wanted one of Benteen's corporals sent to headquarters for orderly duty. The order detailing the transfer came from the Assistant Adjutant of the Army of the Southwest, who happened to be the son of the commanding general. When shown the order by Captain Ing, Benteen uncharacteristically lost his temper.

Men previously had been transferred to headquarters for orderly duties, but never a non-commissioned officer (NCO), without Benteen first giving consent. In quick succession, Benteen rejected the written directive, refused to accede to Captain Ing's order, berated Ing and wrote on the transfer order:

"Corporal Weaver declines the polite invitation to leave the mess and feels highly insulted at his rank not being attended to."

And again:

"Corporal Weaver cannot and shall not come, nor do I recognize the right of anyone to detail the men of my company by name—they have taken of some of the best of them and if they want them all, my resignation is at their service..."

Captain Ing drew up charges, specifying disrespectful behavior towards the commanding officer and conduct prejudicial to good order and military discipline, etc. Benteen assured his commanding officer by letter that he had meant no disrespect.[33] The matter was mooted when a few weeks later Captain Ing withdrew his charges and resigned, for reasons of his own.

On April 19, 1862, Bowen's Battalion joined the 3rd Iowa Cavalry in a raid into Arkansas at Talbot's Ferry, which preceded the general advance of Curtis's army. An enemy saltpeter factory was destroyed. Thereafter, the Union army moved into Arkansas and on May 4, attacked Batesville. The regular Confederate soldiers quickly fled the field, leaving the defense to the local irregulars. Bowen's Battalion attacked, inflicting several deaths without injury to itself.

Securing Arkansas for the Union presented few problems, since the regular Confederate army had been withdrawn from the state. Curtis moved his army southeast through Arkansas to the Mississippi River, more or less paralleling the movements of U. S. Grant on the east bank, who had his sights set on Vicksburg.

A detachment of Benteen's company, led by a junior officer, helped beat off a guerrilla attack on a wagon supply train near Waddell's Farm[34] on June 10, inflicting twenty-eight deaths without loss of life to its own men. The commanding officer of an Illinois cavalry regiment was impressed with C Company and described its performance as "the finest cavalry charge I have ever witnessed." It is uncertain how many cavalry attacks the commanding officer had seen, but it was a handsome compliment. In July, Bowen was promoted to lieutenant colonel.

Anxious to attract Grant's notice, Curtis devised a plan to move his army by river from Helena, Arkansas, down the Mississippi to the vicinity of Vicksburg. The navy supplied several armored ram boats, gunboats and transports. The troops were embarked under the command of Colonel Charles Woods and included Bowen's Battalion and Benteen's C Company.

The flotilla made good progress down the Mississippi to a point thirty miles above Vicksburg where the river makes a long horseshoe turn, known as Millikin's Bend,[35] (Louisiana), with the bend of the horseshoe facing the city, and one end of the horseshoe above and the other below Vicksburg. Anchored in Millikin's Bend on August 18, 1862, was a well-appointed civilian steamboat, the *Fair Play*, which had been commandeered by the Confederates and converted into a supply ship. It carried a cargo of armaments and supplies destined for the irregular troops in Louisiana and Arkansas. A Union gunboat had little difficulty in capturing the steamboat, its crew, and the tons of ammunition.

Among the prisoners was Charley Benteen, who had been the chief engineer aboard the riverboat. How he came to that position is not known, but Charley was a man of many talents and was probably well known to the riverboat owners, who had often needed his services to paint their vessels. As mentioned, he may have left St. Louis as early as 1860 to further a career as steamboat engineer.

Bowen's cavalry pursued the fleeing Confederate soldiers that had been guarding the *Fair Play*. It managed to catch a few and to destroy the wares at a nearby Confederate depot. Since Charley Benteen had been captured at Milliken's Bend by the crew of the gunboat, he never knew how close he had been to his son.

Captain Benteen is supposed to have prevailed on the provost to jail Charley for the duration of the war, to keep him from returning to Confederate service. The information was supplied by Captain Benteen's son in an interview in 1923.[36] The son had not yet been born in 1862 and could relate only what Benteen had told him. At the time of Charley's capture, most prisoners were released on parole after swearing to abstain from again taking up arms. Until the practice was halted in 1863, 250,000 Union and 16,000 Confederates had been freed on parole. Would the Union authorities retain in custody a civilian who had been employed as a chief engineer aboard a commandeered civilian ship, even if the ship had been converted into a blockade-runner? Where would they keep him? The Union prisons had horrible mortalities, some as high as sixteen percent (Elmira, New York; Rock Island, Illinois). Is this what Benteen would have wanted for his father? There is no listing of a Benteen in the prisoner lists of Gratiot Street, Johnson Island, Alton, etc., not that the lists are especially complete, especially for civilian prisoners. The family "recollection" is that he might have been held at Fort Jefferson on the Dry Tortugas,[37] but this prison was used for Union deserters during the Civil War, although it later housed the four rebel sympathizers implicated in Lincoln's assassination. To carry the story further, Charley Benteen is supposed to have found out years later from his grandson that it was his own son, who was responsible for his incarceration.[38] Even if Charley were told that, there is no certainty that it was true. In any event, Charley's whereabouts for the rest of the war are not known. He does not appear in the business directories for St. Louis after 1860, so it is not likely that he returned there.

The Woods flotilla proceeded up the Mississippi, stopping to destroy rebel installations, cut telegraph wires and spar with the enemy. At Bolivar,[39] Tennessee, on August 18, the infantry was disembarked in an area with steep embankments, too steep for horses. Bowen managed to put his cavalry and field pieces ashore further up the river. Dismounted, C Company fought off an unexpectedly large concentration of enemy, then retired back to the boats. The battalion lost three men.

The flotilla delivered prisoners and spoils back to headquarters in Helena, Arkansas. Conveniently for Benteen, Bowen's Battalion was then sent to Benton's Barracks in the center of St. Louis for reorganization, while Captain Benteen went on leave.

The War Department ordered the consolidation of all cavalry units below regimental strength, which would include Bowen's Battalion. Accordingly, four companies of Bowen's Battalion were combined with four other cavalry companies to form the 9th Missouri Cavalry, losing two of Bowen's companies in the process. This organization lasted for only two months, following which the unit was combined with another regiment to become the 10th Missouri Cavalry, with a complement of 1,200 men.

Colonel Florence Cornyn became the new commanding officer of the 10th Missouri. The regiment was sent for refitting to Jefferson Barracks, a cavalry center ten miles from St. Louis. Cornyn was a fearless surgeon whose exemplary leadership at Wilson's Creek first earned him a field command. Second in command was Lieutenant Colonel Bowen, and on December 4, 1862, Fred Benteen was promoted to second major. Many resignations were submitted, as the officers from Cornyn and Bowen's previous commands jostled for rank.

Orders were received for the new 10th Missouri to report to Corinth, Mississippi, to join a new division commanded by Brigadier General Grenville Dodge. Corinth was a hugely important junction of the Memphis-Charleston and Corinth-Mobile railroads and a launching site for future campaigns in the south. The regiment boarded transports in December 1862 for passage down the Mississippi. After disembarking at several cities, the companies made their way by march to Corinth, arriving by February 7, 1863. General Dodge promoted Colonel Cornyn to cavalry brigade commander, and Lieutenant Colonel Bowen became acting commander of the 10th Missouri Cavalry.

Grant had been massing his army in December 1862 in preparation for the first of several efforts to capture Vicksburg. For this attempt, a two-pronged attack was planned, with Grant approaching from the south with the Army of the Mississippi; and Sherman approaching down the Mississippi from the north with the Army of the Tennessee. To Grant's chagrin, his supply lines were cut by Nathan Bedford Forrest; and Sherman was turned back by strong Confederate defenses at Chickasaw Bluffs, Mississippi. Grant returned to Memphis to devise a new strategy.

On February 18, Colonel Cornyn led his brigade on a scouting expedition into Alabama. The first day out, Bowen got into an argument with his second in command, who had strayed from his post without notifying Bowen. A heated argument led to charges against the officer for "disobedience of orders, disrespectful conduct toward his superior officer," etc. The said major underwent court martial, never to return to the regiment. Unfortunately, he took with him the records of the brigade, supposedly to prepare for his trial. Fred Benteen became second in command of the 10th Missouri Cavalry. On February 22, the brigade stormed Tuscombia,⁴⁰ Alabama, and captured an unimpressive cache of arms, which it brought back to Corinth.

Benteen interrupted the dull encampment life with a few days of temporary duty in St. Louis and Rolla, to arrest deserters. By now, Kate was in the fifth month of pregnancy.

Grant began construction of a canal across Millikin's Loop in April 1863, in order to bypass Vicksburg and bring his men south of the city. This effort would prove to be unsuccessful, but meanwhile he needed to distract as many of the Confederate cavalry as possible, especially the hated troops of Nathan Bedford Forrest. Three legendary Union cavalry deployments were sent deep into Confederate territory: Grierson's Raid into Louisiana, Streight's Raid on mounted mules into Georgia, and Dodge's Raid into Alabama, Mississippi and Tennessee. Cornyn's brigade was a part of the Dodge expedition.

The brigade set out from Corinth on April 14, 1863, in advance of Dodge's division. While pursuing a small Confederate force, Cornyn allowed his column to lengthen. This prompted a Confederate attack and the loss of two field pieces.⁴¹ The brigade pursued the rebels, but could not entice them into battle.

Four days later, while the brigade was tearing up railroad tracks, the enemy reappeared, but when Cornyn deployed his men, the rebels withdrew. This pattern was repeated several times, with the brigade pursuing and the enemy withdrawing, until Nathan Bedford Forrest appeared with 3,500 men and did not withdraw. Badly outnumbered, Cornyn immediately sent for reinforcements; but General Dodge ordered the brigade to disengage and return to Corinth.

Grant, meanwhile, had devised what was to become his final plan. Marching his troops along a circuitous route on the west side of the Mississippi to a point far below Vicksburg, he ferried them over to the east bank on Union vessels that had slipped past Vicksburg in the dead of night.

In order to further divert attention from Grant, Cornyn was instructed to proceed to Tupelo,[42] Mississippi, and join up with remnants of Grierson's Raid. When the brigade arrived on May 5, 1863, two thousand Confederate soldiers met them, eager to repay Grierson for his recent foray. Benteen was given several dismounted companies and ordered to capture a bridge. The enemy fiercely resisted, but were overwhelmed by Union field artillery and by troops equipped with the rapid-fire Colt revolving rifles. One Union soldier was killed. The brigade returned to Corinth laden with considerable booty. Thenceforth, the regiment was known as the "Fighting Tenth," and Benteen received special praise for his spirited leadership.[43]

Cornyn's brigade spent three weeks in Corinth, improving conditions in their camp. The long-awaited mail finally arrived. News of the vicious guerrilla activity in Missouri greatly disturbed the soldiers, especially those who had families living in rural areas. Many considered leaving without permission to return home. By now, the brigade had shrunk from the original 1,200 when they left St. Louis to no more than five hundred. A few companies had been transferred to other units.

Grant was fast making progress. After crossing the Mississippi River onto the east bank, he moved his army northeast, drawing on the countryside for supplies. He defeated a Confederate army at Jackson, Mississippi, then moved west to Vicksburg and lay siege to the city along a twelve-mile front.

To divert Confederate resources from the Vicksburg campaign, Cornyn's Brigade was ordered on May 26, 1863, to raid Florence,[44] Alabama. A small riverboat was on hand to ferry the brigade over the Tennessee River. Marching through the night, the brigade surprised and overcame the garrison in Florence. Large quantities of ammunition were destroyed and blacksmith shops and tanneries burned. The Union soldiers set booby traps in houses to rattle the enemy. On their way back to Corinth, the brigade burned a cotton factory, destroyed fields and liberated slaves, arriving back at camp on June 1, with the loss of one man.

In July, as victory in Gettysburg and Vicksburg was being celebrated, Benteen learned that Kate had given birth to their first child, a girl named Caroline Elizabeth, after her two grandmothers. She was to die within the year.

Problems arose within the brigade. Cornyn had arrested Bowen, the commanding officer of the 10th Missouri, in one of their incessant internecine disputes,[45] leaving Benteen in command of the regiment. Meanwhile, Cornyn had received orders to prepare for a pre-dawn march. The brigade took an extra hour and a half to prepare for departure, during which time Confederate cavalry raided the government stables near Corinth and made off with 240 horses. A furious General Dodge held Cornyn responsible, since, according to army logic, had Cornyn been on the road at the appointed time, he would have halted the rebel cavalry.

Cornyn set off in pursuit, but the narrow roads hampered his wagon train.[46] After a twenty-three-mile march, he found the raiders one mile south of Iuka,[47] Mississippi, on May 29, lined up for battle behind a forested area. Cornyn ordered Benteen to dismount the 10th Missouri, divide his men and capture the hilltop positions on both sides of the road. As Benteen led the charge up the first hill, three of the men around him were killed; but he continued until both positions were taken. The brigade was then able to move artillery into place and disperse the enemy. One of Benteen's captains described the battle as "the hottest this regiment has ever been engaged in."[48] Four men in the brigade were killed, all from the 10th Missouri.

In his official report, Cornyn said of Benteen: "Major F. W. Benteen commanding the Tenth Missouri Cavalry was where a leader should be in the front, and by his coolness and great tact and skill did much towards gaining the day."[49]

The regiment was pleased to receive the new Gibbs .52 caliber breech-loading carbine, which could be loaded on the run. The rapidity of fire made a distinct impression on the enemy.[50] Earlier, the Colt revolving percussion carbine had been enthusiastically welcomed by the regiment but was soon shown to have a distressing tendency to discharge all rounds simultaneously ("sympathetic firing").[51] Both carbines used linen or paper cartridges, which could malfunction in the rain.

The animosity between Cornyn and Bowen reached its climax on August 10, 1863. Both had been under arrest, and while the two were in the same room, Cornyn struck Bowen, whereupon Bowen pulled out his revolver and killed Cornyn with four shots.[52] Cornyn had a somewhat abrasive personality and was thought to have provoked the fight. A court martial later heard the evidence and limited Bowen's sentence to dismissal from the army. Not much is known of Bowen before or after he left the army.[53]

Major Benteen became acting regimental commander of the 10th Missouri Cavalry and was later confirmed in rank. He immediately set about diffusing tensions within the regiment. He earned the respect of his men by attending to their welfare, without allowing discipline to slacken.

With the fall of Vicksburg came a further consolidation of the cavalry units. Benteen's 10th Missouri was ordered to proceed to Vicksburg, there to join a cavalry brigade, under Colonel Edward Winslow, a twenty-five-year-old railroad construction engineer, who had commanded one of the few cavalry units that served with Grant at Vicksburg. Benteen would serve in the Winslow Brigade until the end of the war.

On October 14, 1863, two divisions, among them Winslow's 1,500-man cavalry brigade, set out for Canton, Mississippi, on a shake-down sortie. At Brownsville,[54] Mississippi, halfway to Canton, the brigade came under heavy cannon fire. The 10th Missouri took up a defensive position to allow the brigade to withdraw. For six hours the regiment drew heavy fire and suffered two deaths. The expedition returned to Vicksburg without capturing Canton.

Benteen was cited in Winslow's report as a gallant and valuable officer, compared to others "who fled to the rear when the situation became uncomfortable."[55]

Upon returning to Vicksburg, Benteen went on urgent leave at half pay for eighteen days, to visit his wife and gravely ill three-month-old daughter. He overstayed his leave, and the local provost marshall had to come knocking on his door.[56]

In the early part of December, the brigade prepared for a raid on Meridian, Mississippi, 130 miles east of Vicksburg.

Meridian was Sherman's choosing. As a prerequisite for his forthcoming Atlanta campaign, Sherman needed to interrupt the Confederate supply line. He chose Meridian, since it was the last remaining Confederate rail hub in Mississippi, at the intersection of two important railroads.

Sherman's army was composed of an infantry corps under General James B. McPherson and a cavalry division under Grierson, which included Winslow's Brigade. Plans called for the army to be reinforced before reaching Meridian, by another large Union Cavalry column, marching southeast from Memphis.

Winslow set out from Corinth on February 3, 1864, and got off to a good start. The second day, near Bolton, Mississippi, the 10th Missouri had a minor skirmish with the enemy. The following day, Jackson,[57] Mississippi, was reached, which was defended by a large enemy force. Winslow set up artillery on a hill outside the town and secured it with dismounted cavalry. Benteen and his regiment were sent galloping through the enemy breastworks into town, and they seized an important bridge before it could be destroyed. The enemy fled the city. Thereafter, Canton and Morton fell with only light skirmishing and on February 14, Meridian,[58] Mississippi, was almost effortlessly captured. After the infantry arrived, Sherman sacked the city, in a presage of what he would later repeat in his Georgia campaign. The 10th Missouri fully participated in the pillage, with the Quantrill outrages in Missouri fresh in their minds.

Winslow's Brigade was then sent north to determine the whereabouts of the column that had failed to reinforce Sherman. It was learned later that the column had been halted at Okolona, Mississippi, after a sharp encounter with Nathan Forrest, who had half the Union strength. While his brigade was searching for the lost column, Winslow became ill, leaving Benteen in command. On the way back to Meridian, the brigade was attacked on February 8 by three brigades of Forrest's Cavalry at Canton,[59] Mississippi, but succeed in driving off the enemy. Upon learning of Benteen's action, General McPherson, the corps commander, is said to have declared: "Splendid Benteen! You never get sick and I always know where to find you."[60] Benteen is the authority for the quotation.

Without the reinforcements from the other column, Sherman was compelled to turn back. Thus, with a force of only three thousand men, Forrest had succeeded in frustrating the advance of twenty-seven thousand Union soldiers. Upon his return to Vicksburg, Benteen was promoted to lieutenant colonel, replacing Bowen, who had been discharged from the army.

On May 1, 1864, the brigade was moved to Memphis, Tennessee, where it was incorporated into the cavalry corps of Brigadier General Benjamin Grierson. The following day the brigade engaged the rebels at Bolivar, Tennessee, drawing praise, according to Benteen,[61] for its skill in capturing earthworks.

With the Mississippi River firmly under Union control, and Chattanooga safe in Union hands, Sherman could now begin his Atlanta campaign—provided that his supply lines were secure. The Confederates, in turn, believed that unless those supply routes were interrupted, Sherman would be free to ravage the heartland of the Confederacy. Neither side envisioned, at this point, a campaign drawing exclusively on the countryside for provisions.

Benteen set out from Memphis to retrieve the regimental records in Vicksburg, where they had been taken by the major in preparation for his court martial. In Benteen's absence, the regiment participated in two battles, which would bring it little credit.

General Nathan Bedford Forrest had been an unshakable menace to Sherman's supply line. A large Union force of six thousand men had been assembled in Memphis, under the command of Brigadier General Samuel Sturgis, of Wilson's Creek repute, and whom we will meet again in the west. Incorporated into Sturgis' army was Grierson's Cavalry Corps, including Winslow's Brigade and the 10th Missouri, now reduced to two hundred men, since the rest of the regiment had accompanied Benteen to Vicksburg. Sturgis is reported to have prayed for an opportunity to meet Forrest.

His prayers were soon answered. His army met Forrest at Brice's Crossroads, a partially wooded area in north central Mississippi on June 10, 1864. The muddy road hindered the mobility of the Union infantry, and the Confederate artillery meted out savage punishment. The result was a bitter Union rout with the capture of 1,500 Union soldiers and 250 wagons. A court martial was held at Sturgis's request, but Sherman wryly concluded that Forrest had whipped Sturgis "fair and square." Moreover, since the purpose of Sturgis's campaign had been to occupy Forrest and to prevent him from attacking Sherman's supply lines, the object had been accomplished. There were no kudos for the Union officers, and Benteen lost nothing by his absence.

Winslow's Brigade, still without Benteen, participated in an expedition led by Major Gen. Andrew J. Smith. On July 14, they encountered Forrest near Tupelo, Mississippi, and, after several days of bitter fighting, both sides broke off the engagement. A standoff with Forrest was considered a thundering victory for the Union army. Despite his severe losses, the irrepressible Forrest continued his marauding and even raided Memphis in August, in the early hours of the morning, almost capturing the commanding general.

Benteen returned to Memphis, having at long last retrieved the regimental papers, only to have them irretrievably lost when the steamboat that was transporting them struck a snag and sank, drowning ten soldiers of the 10th Missouri. Since the three-year enlistments in his regiment were about to expire, and since there were no records available to detail their military service, Benteen received permission to return to St. Louis to present their case to the state mustering officer.[62] The detachment departed August 1, and on reaching St. Louis, the soldiers were mustered out.

Benteen set about to recruit replacements. The 10th Missouri had authorization for 1,200 men, but by late summer of 1864, it numbered no more than three hundred, including the soldiers recuperating from wounds and illness. This was not an unusual occurrence during the Civil War. The state, rather than the federal government, provided replacements, and a governor was more willing to form a new regiment than provide replacements for a regiment already in existence, since he would have greater opportunity for patronage.[63]

An officer with position, money and reputation might have spurred enlistments, but an ex-sign painter had little to offer, although the six-hundred-dollar bounty did manage to attract a few recruits. Among the newly commissioned officers of the regiment was Kate's younger brother, First Lieutenant Leslie R. Norman.

Benteen returned to Memphis and began training the recruits. The soldiers had been issued the new Spencer seven-shot .52 cal. repeating rifle, which was to be the definitive Union carbine for the rest of the war. It used rimfire metallic cartridges, impervious to weather. A lever below the trigger guard brought the cartridge into the chamber. By the end of the war, 250,000 repeating rifles and carbines were issued to most cavalrymen in the 260 Union cavalry regiments.[64]

Meanwhile, General ("Old Pap") Price was again collecting an army to carry the war into Missouri. His objective now was to inflict sufficient damage to bring the North to the bargaining table. Northern voters were preparing for the approaching 1864 Presidential election. What Old Pap's army lacked in arms, it made up in horses—twelve thousand of them. The weapons, he hoped, would be obtained along the way, perhaps in St. Louis.

As news was received of Price's advance through Arkansas, Union reinforcements were rushed to St. Louis. Two infantry divisions of General A. J. Smith were diverted to the city, and General Alfred Pleasonton was ordered to take command of a cavalry division, which was to include Winslow's Brigade.

The Winslow Brigade hurriedly left Memphis and was ferried across the Mississippi to Arkansas. It then marched north, in the wake of Price's army, without a proper wagon train. Fodder was scarce, since the pick had already been garnered by Price's troops. Soon, the brigade soon found itself in desperate straits. Compelled to abandon 1,300 horses, Winslow halted the pursuit and embarked his brigade on riverboats for transport to St. Louis.

Price's army crossed into Missouri on September 19, 1864. Carefully avoiding the fortified strongholds that had been prepared to halt his progress, he advanced his mounted army towards St. Louis, with a speed that caused increasing concern. At the outskirts of the city, a hastily assembled Union defense had been assembled. A. J. Smith's infantry were rushed to the earthworks, as quickly as the companies disembarked. Price spent three days assaulting the Union line and sustained 1,500 casualties. In the meantime, he learned that Union General Alfred Pleasonton would soon be arriving. Price wisely decided to halt his headlong assault on St. Louis and to move his cavalry toward the state capitol at Jefferson City.

Pleasonton, the former cavalry commander of the Army of the Potomac, had a creditable list of victories, including Brandy Station, Virginia, the largest cavalry engagement of the Civil War. General Ulysses Grant, newly arrived in Washington, had arbitrarily replaced him with Philip Sheridan, long a favorite of Grant.

Upon debarkation in St. Louis, Winslow's Brigade was hurried to Benton's Barracks. There the men were hastily refitted and issued fresh horses. Benteen had little time to see Kate or to comfort her on the death of their daughter.

Pleasonton assembled a force of seven thousand cavalrymen, including Winslow's Brigade, and set off in pursuit of the enemy; closely followed by the eight thousand infantrymen of A. J. Smith. With Pleasonton threatening his rear, Price was compelled to forego an attack on Jefferson City, the capital. His army swept south through Lexington and Independence, Missouri, unwilling to engage the Union forces. Along the way, he conscripted local guerrillas, cut telegraph lines, destroyed Union property and replenished his supplies. He turned towards Kansas City, Missouri, where Major General Curtis awaited him with a small body of improvised Kansas militia. Curtis stationed his troops in Westport,[65] Missouri, south of Kansas City and prepared a holding action, pending Pleasonton's arrival.

On October 23, Pleasonton's troops suddenly appeared and immediately struck at Price's rear. A total of seventeen thousand horsemen fought in this battle, the second largest cavalry engagement in the Civil War.[66] An important hilltop position protected Price's rear. Orders went out to take the position, and Winslow led several charges, until he sustained a thigh wound and had to relinquish command of the brigade to Lieutenant Colonel Benteen. After a furious six-hour battle, the 10th Missouri and another regiment were able to secure the hilltop, forcing the Confederates to abandon their line and retreat southward. The battle was called "the Gettysburg of the Transmississippi."[67] One soldier in the Winslow Brigade died; at Gettysburg, 3,155 Union soldiers lost their lives.[68] The brigade closely pursued the Confederate forces, frustrating their attempts to mount a defense.

Price quickly moved his army into Kansas, since the roads could better accommodate his wagon train. He retreated south in incessant rain, with the forces of

Pleasonton and Curtis in close pursuit. Feed was scarce and the horses jaded. On October 25, Price came to a small stream, Mine Creek[69] ("Battle of the Osage"), Kansas, where the Confederate army took up a strong defensive position. The Confederate artillery was spread thin, according to Benteen, and had large gaps in their fields of fire.

Winslow's Brigade repeatedly assaulted the enemy position, with Benteen leading the attack. Despite Benteen's fiery exhortations, the brigade faltered one hundred yards from the rebel line. Benteen rode in front of his men within pistol shot of the enemy, waving his saber and crying *Charge!*[70] Suddenly the 4th Iowa Cavalry swept around the stalled brigade and continued on toward the rebel line, followed by a chastened Winslow's Brigade. The Confederate line was broken! A fierce hand-to-hand struggle ensued, involving thousands of combatants. Mounted on his thoroughbred mare, "Bess,"[71] Benteen jumped over a rebel cannon and was shot through the hem of his overcoat but escaped unscathed. The Union army lost one hundred men; the Confederates, three hundred. Benteen's Brigade had seven deaths. Benteen was cited in the General Orders #11 for capturing five artillery pieces and carrying an important segment of the line.[72] The light Spencer repeating carbines of the Union cavalry had markedly outperformed the long rifles of the Confederate horsemen, which were difficult to load.

Gradually, as the tide of battle turned against them, the rebels began to flee across the swift Mine Creek River, abandoning many cannon. The weary Union troops followed in pursuit, but when the Marmaton River[73] (Kansas) was reached on October 25, they found the rebels too well entrenched for a direct attack. Instead, they set fire to the enemy wagon train. The completely spent Confederates continued their retreat, crossing back into Missouri.

With men and horses exhausted, Winslow's Brigade was withdrawn from the chase and sent to Fort Scott, Kansas, for refitting. Meanwhile, Major General Samuel R. Curtis had succeeded Pleasonton in command. He notified Benteen that the pursuit would continue, "as long as the horses can stand on their feet."[74]

Winslow's Brigade resumed the chase, pursuing Price's army through the Missouri Ozarks and over the Boston mountains of Arkansas into the Indian Territory. There, the rebels scattered, and the pursuit was abandoned. The weary brigade was ordered back to St. Louis.

Benteen parted on good terms with General Curtis, who praised him in a letter to the governor of Missouri: "I have had the cooperation of a brigade of cavalry commanded by Lieutenant Colonel F. W. Benteen of the 10th Missouri Cavalry, who has exhibited the most fearless and distinguished success in the field of battle." Curtis requested that the governor help to obtain for Benteen a brigadier's commission, "which he well deserves and is most competent to fill."[75]

The governor of Missouri made Benteen a Brigadier General of the Missouri Enrolled Militia, an honorary title, and urged the President by letter to promote him to brigadier general.[76] Not only was Benteen not made a brigadier general, he was not even promoted to colonel. Perhaps the promotion to brigadier general was denied him because a brigade command was not immediately available. He may not have received the colonelcy promotion because of the small size of his regiment.

The brigade marched to Rolla and boarded trains for St. Louis, where they arrived on November 30, bone-weary after a 1,800-mile expedition. Their sick and injured mounts were replaced with 1,100 new horses. The brigade was immediately assigned to a new cavalry division led by Major General James H. Wilson, Division of the Mississippi, for an operation in Alabama and Georgia.

After no more than a week of rest, the brigade set out for Memphis by river steamer, but along the way, the *Maria*, carrying Benteen's brigade, exploded, killing twenty-five men and two hundred horses, including Benteen's own two mounts. When news reached St. Louis, the grateful citizens took up a collection to replace his personal horses. Benteen conveyed to them his florid thanks by letter: "To me a poor devil of a soldier 'tis indeed a surprise, not knowing I had a friend in this world and so suddenly found myself surrounded by them."[77]

Because of the ice, the riverboats could proceed no further than Cairo, Illinois. The brigade then made its way by march to the staging area on the Tennessee River in northwestern Alabama, where it was met by Colonel Winslow, who resumed command. Benteen, of course, reverted to regimental commander of the 10th Missouri Cavalry.

Wilson had drawn up plans for a raid into central Alabama with three divisions. If all went well, it would be the greatest cavalry foray of the war,[78] effectively destroying the industrial resources of the Confederacy.

Throughout the winter, Wilson's Army underwent extensive training. His men were issued the celebrated seven-shot Spencer repeating rifles. In the months that followed, Captain Charles F. Hinricks of the 10th Missouri kept a personal diary, which supplements the official record. Hinricks was born in Germany, enlisted as a private in the Union army and had risen to command L Company.

The fortunes of war had been steadily favoring the Union army. Everywhere in the deep South, armed resistance was disintegrating. Atlanta had already fallen, and by the end of December 1864, Savannah, Georgia, too, had been captured.

Wilson's Cavalry Corps set out March 22, 1865, after the spring rains had subsided. It took three days for his three hundred supply wagons to cross the Tennessee River. The pack train carried rations for fifteen days, but wherever possible, the soldiers lived off the land. Wilson separated the three divisions to make foraging easier. Winslow's Brigade had been assigned to Brigadier General Emory Upton's division.

After six days of march, Upton's division reached Jasper and two days later on March 28th, they arrived at Elyton (Birmingham),[79] Alabama, where they destroyed an important iron works. The next day they reached

Biersfield, Alabama. There, Benteen and his three-hundred-man regiment were met by a vastly superior Confederate force of six- to seven thousand men. Confronting them, Benteen said, was the boldest act of his life.[80] The enemy apparently did not mount a spirited defense, so that Benteen and his men managed to destroy the Bibb Naval Furnace on March 31 and retire to Montevallo, Alabama, where they hoped to rest up with the rest of Winslow's Brigade. No sooner had the regiment unsaddled, when they were attacked by the same Confederate commander whom they had met at Biersfield and who now reappeared with additional forces and had to be repulsed.

The march resumed with two divisions advancing by the Selma road, while Upton's Division was deployed east of the road to thwart a flank attack. At Ebenezer Church, Alabama, on April 1, the advancing divisions were halted by the determined defenses set up by Nathan Bedford Forrest, but at a crucial moment of the battle, the Winslow Brigade outflanked the rebels. The enemy lost one hundred men, and Forrest himself received a saber slash to his arm. There were no deaths in the 10th Missouri Regiment.

Back east, great events were overshadowing the Wilson campaign. On April 1, 1865, Sheridan had pierced the Confederate line at Five Forks, Virginia, making Lee's position in Petersburg untenable. Sherman already had swept through Georgia and was moving into South Carolina, with the South in despair.

General Wilson marched south toward Selma,[81] Alabama. His corps by now was reduced to two divisions, having scattered men to such collateral duties as guarding bridges, train lines, prisoners, etc. He had the good fortune to capture an English civil engineer, who furnished him with plans for the defenses at Selma. The city was a huge industrial arsenal, renowned for its foundries and factories. It was defended by seven thousand men, under the command of Nathan B. Forrest, half of whom were veterans and the rest with little combat experience but well able to man the parapets.

On April 2, Wilson sent one division on a diversionary attack to the northwest of Selma, and Upton's division was ordered to make the frontal attack. Forrest had had ample time to reinforce the well-prepared defenses of the city. There were strong breastworks, surrounded by ditches and walls, with artillery commanding the approaches. To a captain in Benteen's regiment who was waiting for additional support, Benteen replied dryly that they would have to "depend on our stout hearts and our Spencer carbines."[82]

The Union diversionary attack in the northwest failed, when the division was itself attacked from the rear by a small force of Forrest's cavalry, newly arrived at the scene. Notwithstanding, Upton's division immediately began an attack on the Confederate breastworks. At the appointed hour, the dismounted 10th Missouri, led by Benteen, rushed forward to scale the works. With furious resolve, they attacked the parapets and mounted the walls. Once over, they waved their hats in triumph.[83] The mounted cavalry poured in, followed by the rest of the division. The swiftness of the victory left the Union forces incredulous.[84] The 10th Missouri had not lost a single soldier! Forrest narrowly escaped by swimming across the Alabama River, but one thousand of his dispirited troops were captured. Confederate factories were torched, but an effort was made to spare the civilian homes.

With Selma now in Union hands, many of the Union troops took time to inspect the Cahaba Prison, fourteen miles from the city, where two thousand hapless Federal captives had been lodged. Cahaba had been built originally to accommodate eight hundred prisoners in an abandoned cotton warehouse on the Alabama and Cahaba Rivers, but the numbers grew to a high water mark of three thousand. Conditions were appalling. The prisoners slept on the floor or on the ground and drank from a contaminated well. Hunger, lice, rats, dysentery and disease all claimed their toll. The Union prisoners had difficulty in adjusting to the heat and to the daily corn rations, intended to match those issued to the Confederate soldier. Surprisingly, the prison mortality was less than other Confederate prisons, due, it is said, to the humanitarian efforts of the prison director, who was a caring Methodist minister.

Tragically, hundreds of the liberated prisoners died on the way home when the riverboat *Sultana*, on which they were being transported, exploded, burned and sank near Memphis on April 27, with the loss of 1,700 lives.

Although Wilson's soldiers were convinced that Selma was a great Union victory, the battle was anticlimactic. It was fought on April 2, 1865, with the surrender at Appomattox Court House only a week away. Word of the fall of Richmond was received indirectly, when a captain in the 10th Missouri overheard a slave repeating his master's anguish: "Selma gone, Richmond gone too."[85]

Wilson halted his men for a week, while he sent out parties to destroy the rebel factories. On April 8, Benteen's brother in law, Lieutenant Leslie Norman of L Company, became intoxicated and threatened to shoot Colonel Winslow, the brigade commander. A court martial was held that same night, with Benteen serving as a member of the court. Norman was allowed to resign, for the good of the service.

Wilson's army crossed the Alabama River and marched unopposed twenty-five miles a day, sweeping through Montgomery. At Tuskegee, they were astonished at the friendly reception given by the white ladies, who waved their handkerchiefs and hurrayed for Lincoln. Not all the Alabama men had been sympathetic to the Confederate cause. In the north Alabama hill country, thousands of southern draft evaders had fought Confederate cavalry and killed officers sent to arrest them.[86]

Columbus,[87] Georgia was reached on April 16, a major manufacturing center, almost as productive as Selma. It was defended by three thousand rebel militia. Three of the five bridges spanning the Chattahoochee River had been destroyed. The 10th Missouri was ordered to take a remaining footbridge after dark, but the regiment met violent resistance and was forced to scatter. Benteen yelled at one of his captains, who allowed his men to wander into an area raked by enemy cannon fire.[88] The footbridge was finally captured by another regiment, and the troops entered the city. The last great Confederate asset lay firmly in Union hands. Benteen had one death in his regiment; the two brigades lost five men. Benteen was cited by General Wilson: "I would also request that Lieutenant Colonel F. W. Benteen, Tenth Missouri Cavalry, be brevetted brigadier-general for gallant and meritorious services."[89] Benteen would dearly have loved the brevet of brigadier general. For the rest of his life he would be addressed as "General," and the title would have opened for him many opportunities in civilian life.

Later generations may question the necessity of devastating the southern industry, since its destruction did little to shorten the war, yet caused untold hardship to the South in the months following the end of hostilities.

On April 9, Lee surrendered to Grant at Appomattox Court House, and eight days later Sherman arranged an armistice in North Carolina with General Johnston, who commanded the last Confederate army in the field.

Wilson reached Macon, Georgia, on April 20, where a message from Sherman awaited him, ordering that hostilities be suspended pending conclusion of negotiations for Johnston's surrender. Sherman's terms of surrender were even more generous than those proposed by Grant but were promptly repudiated by the Secretary of War, who imposed his own terms. A full surrender followed on April 26. The war had ended.

Discipline quickly became a problem. Since the Missouri soldiers had enlisted only for the duration of hostilities, they demanded a speedy return to St. Louis for demobilization. With the army no longer permitted to live off the land, supplies became irregular. Pillage was rampant. When the officers conducted a surprise inspection of the soldiers' packs, they confiscated an enormous collection of booty.[90]

By this time, Benteen had given deep thought to his post-war career. He wrote to General Wilson expressing his desire to join the regular army with a rank of captain, which would correspond to the rank held in peacetime by a West Point graduate of similar age.[91] Nothing came of the letter. The army had no plans for the future and had to await Congressional direction.

The brigade remained in Macon until May 5, when it received orders to search for Jefferson Davis, who was rumored to have absconded with one million dollars in gold. Davis was eventually captured by Wilson's Cavalry Corps, and $3,500 in gold was confiscated from one of his aides. The 10th Missouri ended its service outside of outside of Atlanta, hungry and without rations. Tempers flared within the regiment, and the blame for their privations fell on the shoulders of their senior officer. "Hardtack! Hardtack!" the soldiers shouted impatiently. Captain Hinricks protested to Benteen about conditions. "It didn't do any good," he complained in his diary. "The Gentl. was busy reading a 20 cent novel and couldn't attend to the wants of the men what had made him a man."[92] Benteen wisely seems to be avoiding an argument with a company commander who brings complaints, instead of solutions.

On June 23, Benteen led a detachment of soldiers back to Nashville for demobilization. He could have remained with the 10th Missouri, which was being incorporated into the 2nd Missouri Cavalry ("Merrill's Light Horse"), but chose instead to be assigned to a regiment then being formed. Benteen was given command of the 138th USCT (United States Colored Troops, Infantry), composed of liberated slaves who had followed in Wilson's wake. The army had by now come to value the services of the black soldier. Of the 187,000 black soldiers who had served in the Civil War, 37,000 had died in line of duty; and in the last year of the war, they comprised ten percent of the Union enlistments.

The regiment was enrolled in Atlanta on July 1, 1865,[93] and two weeks later Benteen took formal command, with the rank of colonel. He began recruiting his officers from among those in Winslow's Brigade who were being discharged. Initially, his regiment lacked officers, but by September, the empty slots had been filled. Training and drill were immediately begun, and the regiment was assigned constabulary duties in Atlanta, with Benteen the post commander.

By September, having heard nothing about a promotion, Benteen applied for a brigadier general's brevet in the volunteer army,[94] enclosing several recommendations. He requested that the original documents be returned to him, if his application were not approved. The application reached the office of

President Johnson,⁹⁵ who referred it to the General of the Army. General Grant personally rejected the application on October 12, 1865, on the grounds that it did not contain the recommendation of Benteen's immediate superior.⁹⁶ It is not likely that the reason was made known to Benteen, who continued to believe that the brevet was denied him because he was not a West Point graduate.

Benteen had no complaints then about his black soldiers, and the reputation of his regiment very much concerned him. It is certain that discipline in the 138th USCT was considerably better than it had been in the 10th Missouri after hostilities had been concluded. When a woman complained to the editors of the *Atlanta New Era* that an officer from the 138th USCT had assaulted her and robbed two other civilians, Benteen replied angrily that the said person was no longer in his regiment nor in the army, having earlier been court-martialed for conduct unbecoming an officer.⁹⁷

Predictably, word was received on January 6, 1866, that his regiment would be disbanded. Benteen made a quick assessment. Sign painting had long ago lost its allure. Since there was no immediate opportunity for a commission in the regular army, he decided to settle in Atlanta and become a farmer. Before leaving the service, he bought a large tract of 114 acres of farmland three miles south of the city in what came to be South Boulevard and McDonough Road, in South Atlanta, Fulton County. The land had been a part of a plantation, and one may presume that Benteen bought it at an advantageous price, real estate conditions in the South then being what they were. He called the farm "Hermitage Heights," an allusion to Andrew Jackson's estate. On January 6, 1866, his regiment was formally disbanded, and Colonel Benteen became farmer Benteen. He engaged several black workers to help him get the farm started.

Although born and raised in a city, Benteen had a deep love of nature, which made dirt farming and horse breeding all the more pleasant. Judging by the newspaper clippings he had accumulated over the years,[98] he was particularly interested in the cultivation of potatoes, grass, flowers and celery, as well as in orchards and trout farming. Above all, he loved horses and was exceedingly knowledgeable about their management and breeding.

Construction of the outbuildings began in winter, and by spring, the stables and a corral had been built. He and his men lived in tents, and when Catherine arrived from St. Louis, she too moved into a tent.

Around ten o'clock on a Sunday night, May 6, 1866, while he and Kate were in their tent, he heard a shot. Grabbing his revolver, Benteen rushed out and saw four outlaws, perhaps demobilized Confederate soldiers, who had come onto his property. "Who goes there?" he called out. Receiving no answer, he threw his watch and wallet behind a bush and opened fire. The outlaws shot back, striking Benteen in his right hip and left calf. Four men pounced on him and relieved him of his revolver, pocketknife and an empty money belt. They ordered Benteen to lead them to his stables. Behind a locked door lay his wounded farm hand. The robbers broke down the door with an ax and made off with four valuable horses and a choice leather saddle, disappearing into the woods. Benteen had gone through four years of Civil War with hardly a scratch, only to be shot twice on his own property.[99]

Benteen and his farm worker recovered, but the bullet remained in Benteen's thigh.[100] He offered a reward of four hundred dollars for the return of the horses, but they were gone forever. Unable to work, Benteen sent for his father to help on the farm. Like his son, Charley Benteen was no farmer, but his canny talents soon brought the farm into production. He even won a prize for his corn, which was reported in the newspaper.[101] Charley must have had sufficient farm hands to help him, since at least on one occasion, he left the farm for a trip to St. Louis.[102]

Benteen took stock of his situation. Farming 114 acres was going to quickly consume whatever capital he had put aside. A wiser choice might be to rejoin the army, when the opportunity presented itself, and to use his pay to help get the farm started. Besides, although farming had its attractions, he looked forward to "a more congenial atmosphere and pursuit."[103]

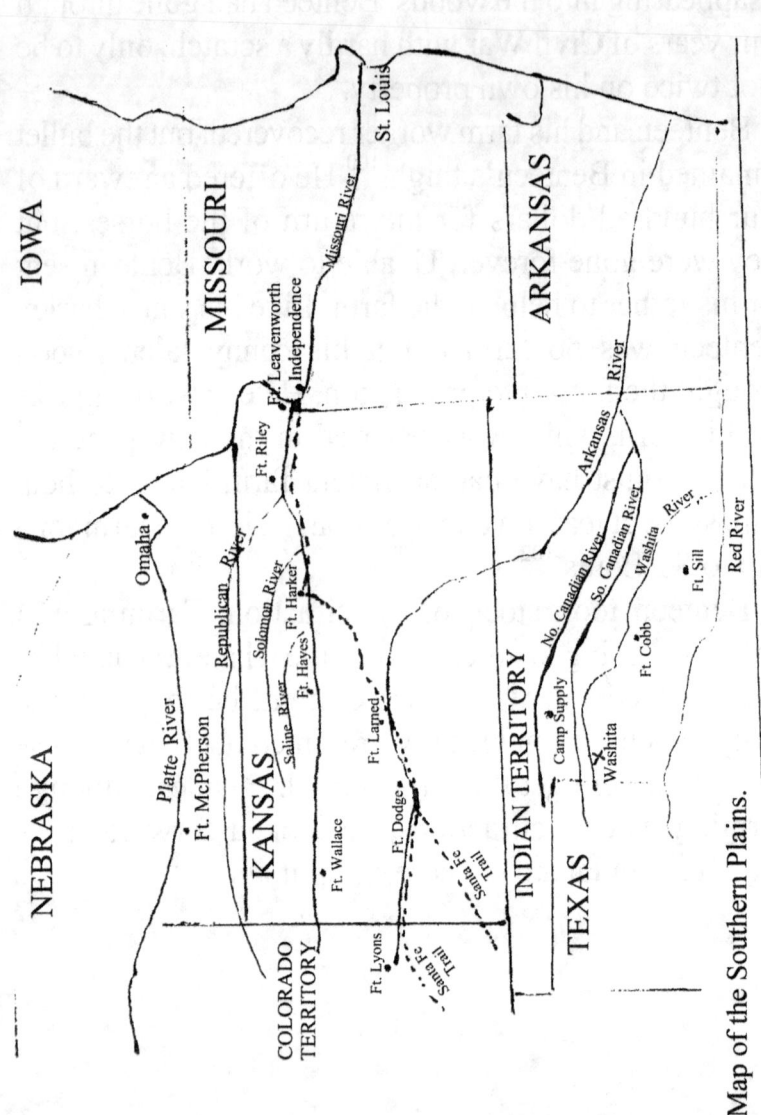

Map of the Southern Plains.

THE SOUTHERN PLAINS

Congress was not enamored of a standing army, but confronted with the requirements of reconstruction and frontier protection, it created thirty new regiments in July, 1866, four of them cavalry, for service on the plains. Two of the new cavalry regiments would have black soldiers (9th and 10th Cavalry), and the other two, (7th and 8th Cavalry) white soldiers. Two-thirds of the vacant cavalry appointments of captain and above were to be filled by volunteer officers who had served during the last two years of the Civil War. The appointments were being allotted by states.[1] This was the opportunity Benteen had been waiting for.

With his wounds well on the mend, Benteen applied in September 1866 for a commission in the regular army. He gave Missouri as his home state and the First Congressional district of St. Louis as his voting residence. He wrote to General Grant and President Johnson in quest of support[2] and submitted impressive letters of recommendation from Generals Upton,

Pleasonton, Curtis and Rosencrans, as well as from the mayor of St. Louis and the governor of Missouri. The application was sent by way of the politically important General Frances (Frank) P. Blair, Jr. of St. Louis directly to the General of the Army, U. S. Grant.[3]

On November 24, 1866, Benteen was tendered a captain's commission in the 7th Cavalry, subject to successful completion of a physical examination and a proficiency test. His annual salary would be $2,000-2,600. He traveled to Washington, and notwithstanding his six-month-old gunshot wound, he passed the physical exam.[4] Next, he underwent the competency test given by the Board of Cavalry Examiners; and was found to be "proficient."[5] Many years later, Benteen stated that the army had offered him a major's commission in a black regiment (10th Cavalry), which he refused, but there is no evidence to support this assertion, nor is it reflected in the material in his personal file. Benteen's claim may be true, but he was more than capable of inventing some harmless fabrication to support a fancy. On his way back to Atlanta, he stopped off in Petersburg to visit the grave of his mother on Christmas Day, 1866, taking from the gravesite a sprig of ivy, which he pressed and preserved for the rest of his life.

Benteen was ordered to report for duty to Fort Riley, Kansas, one hundred miles west of Kansas City, Missouri. Here, on the southern plains, he was to remain for four and one-half years. He departed Atlanta in January 1867, leaving behind his wife, now six months pregnant, who would join him after the delivery.

The Southern Plains 67

Photographs taken around this time show him to be tall and clean-shaven, with rather grim features. In those days his hair was dark brown.

Ever since the administration of President James Madison and until the Civil War, the plains had been regarded as "one big reservation."[6] In the southern prairies dwelled the Cheyenne, Arapaho, Comanche, Kiowa and Kiowa-Apache nations, who, like the Sioux to the north, had come onto the plains after acquiring the feral horse, which enabled them to hunt buffalo. During the Civil War, volunteer troops had expelled the tribes from the Kansas plains between the Platte and the Arkansas rivers, but the warriors returned after the war and immediately came into conflict with the white man.

Traffic had been increasing along the Santa Fe, the Smoky Hill and Great Platte (Oregon) trails. On the heels of migration came settlements, telegraph lines, railroad construction and sporadic and organized mining.

Settlements in Kansas had begun in the 1850's, not because the territory was prepared to receive them, but because of the encouragement given to the prospective homesteaders by the northern free soil societies and the southern slave interests, each desirous of promoting their respective causes, thereby gaining additional votes in Congress. By 1868, the white population in Kansas was larger than that of Vermont but was largely concentrated along the Missouri River. Elsewhere in Kansas, settlement was sparse and isolated.

The activities of the white man took a heavy toll on the buffalo and wild game, and, in step, engendered fiery hatred among the warriors. In the first half of 1867, the depredations against the white settlers in Kansas included 157 killed, 57 wounded or scalped, 14 women raped and murdered, and four women and twenty-four children taken into captivity.[7] The country was outraged.

To protect against warrior attacks, four forts had been built along the Smoky Hill Trail and four along the Santa Fe Trail, each 75-150 miles apart, separated by two to four days of cavalry march.

Benteen arrived by train at Fort Riley January 29, 1867. The fort was in tall-grass prairie on the Sandy Hill River, four miles east of Junction City, soon to be a stop on the Kansas-Pacific Railroad.[8] It had been built in 1853 by masons and carpenters from Cincinnati and St. Louis, who were paid a daily wage of two dollars.[9] Sandstone was used in its construction, obtained from nearby quarries. The site was chosen so that Fort Riley could be supplied three months of the year by riverboats coming up the Sandy Hill River,[10] but the advent of the railroad made water travel unnecessary. Like in other forts, the barracks and officer quarters were both situated around a parade ground.[11] Off to the side were several stone stables, each with stalls for one hundred horses.[12]

At the time of Benteen's arrival, six cavalry companies and one infantry company were stationed in the fort. As in most forts, a lively rivalry had sprung up between the two branches. Dozens of insults were regularly exchanged. The cavalry sneered at the infantry field officers, who had no personal mounts and were obliged to ride in ambulances. The infantry ridiculed the cavalry carbine, which, because of its short range, gave the warriors little concern.[13]

Benteen reported to the regimental adjutant, First Lieutenant Myles Moylan, and was told of his assignment to H Company. Moylan was a hard-bit character. He had enlisted the regular army in peacetime, received a battlefield commission during the war, only to be cashiered from the army for absenting himself from his unit without permission. Undaunted, he reenlisted in Custer's regiment (5th Cavalry), regained his former rank and was breveted major. After the war he enlisted as a private in the 7th Cavalry. Custer promoted him to sergeant-major and helped him apply for a commission. Moylan had enormous difficulty with the proficiency examination. After its successful completion, he was commissioned first lieutenant and made a regimental adjutant by Custer. An adjutant never wins friends, especially in the case of Moylan, who was regarded by the West Point officers as coarse and ill-bred.

The acting commander of the 7th Cavalry was George Armstrong Custer. He was born in Ohio, graduated from West Point and entered the army in 1861 as a second lieutenant. His rise was meteoric. Whatever his assignment, he poured heart and soul into it: balloon observer, staff officer, cavalry commander. His superiors soon came to appreciate his fierce, almost rash, will to succeed, no matter the cost (to his men). Promotion came quickly. In one day, he went from captain to brigadier general, through the gift of General

Alfred Pleasonton. "Custer is the best cavalry general in the world," said Pleasonton. Sheridan agreed: "Custer is the ablest man in the cavalry corps." At Gettysburg, Custer held off Jubal Early from an attack on the Union rear and might have halted Lee's retreat at Williamsport, had he been given sufficient support. He ended the war at the age of twenty-five as a brevet major general in the volunteer army (and brevet brigadier general in the regular army), but reverted in peacetime to the substantive rank of captain. Sheridan and other friends recommended him for advancement to the second in command of the 7th Cavalry, carrying with it the rank of lieutenant colonel, well knowing that the senior commander, Colonel A. J. Smith, would not often be around to manage the regiment. A. J. Smith was the commander, who, with General Alfred Pleasonton, had pursued Price in Missouri during the Civil War.

Custer had married Elizabeth Bacon Custer, who ran his household and presided over the social structure of the regiment. Quick to claim whatever advantages her husband's position gained for her, Libby had met and mingled with presidents, senators, generals, industrialists and actors; and had a deservedly good opinion of her social talents. She had received a fine education for the time, having studied French, German and the classics.[14] She presided with correctness over the army wives, but had no scruples about favoring the wives of her husband's allies and snubbing those of his enemies. At Fort Riley, she was immediately faced with a small problem. Some of the officers had been enlisted men in the Civil War, before being commissioned. These required special handling,[15] as in the case of Lieutenant Moylan, who initially was ostracized by the young officers, but made welcome by Libby,[16] especially after his marriage to the sister of one of the officers who had married Custer's half sister. Marriages reinforced the close bonds between the officer families.

The Custers had been quite busy prior to their arrival at Fort Riley. In September 1866, they had accompanied President Andrew Johnson on a tour, intended to win public approval for the President's lenient southern policy. The tour turned into a political disaster, but Custer managed to slip away before it ended. He reported to Fort Riley on November 3, 1866, but had to leave immediately for Washington. He returned to Fort Riley at the end of December 1866.

In his absence, the training program had been conducted by Major Joel H. Elliott. Elliott had risen through proven ability from private to captain during the Civil War. In fact, Elliott served as company commander in the brigade Benteen had temporarily commanded.[17] After the war, he had been given a major's commission in the regular army, as a result of an unusually high proficiency score, political intervention by the governor of Indiana and a succession of bureaucratic errors. Although outranked, Benteen respected him and became a close friend.

Elliott had no easy task. Much needed to be done to prepare the regiment for the field. Even the former Civil War soldiers had no experience with Indian fighting. Many recruits could not even ride a horse, let alone master the "hurricane seat," as the saddle was called. Fresh from the city streets, they had to learn the most elementary skills. The novice was first made to ride his horse around the corral, with stirrups tucked under the saddle. The pace was increased to stiff walk, trot and then to canter. He was then permitted to use stirrups when jumping his mount over a series of ever-higher hurdles. After, he was ready for simple escort duty. More than half the new officers also lacked riding skills and were given similar instruction. How the stable sergeants revelled in their assignment! The penalty for an officer falling off the horse was a basket of champagne. St. Louis champagne was acceptable.[18]

Benteen made a courtesy call to Custer at his quarters on January 30, 1867. "General" Custer and "Colonel" Benteen[19] each tried to size up the other.

Quickly Benteen's background emerged: not a West Point officer, no college, no profession, "artist" (whatever that meant), Wilson's Raid and a black regiment. Clearly, not an impressive resumé.

Custer produced a Civil War scrapbook and boasted of his role in the great battles in the east. He showed his guest a copy of his farewell address to his troops, which Benteen found cloying. When Benteen impishly offered to produce Wilson's fairwell speech for comparison, Libby Custer quickly intervened to head off a clash. And so the meeting went. All in all, not an auspicious beginning.

In late February 1867, Benteen was invited to Custer's home for an evening of five-hand poker, with dime ante and table stakes.[20] As the evening wore on,

Custer, Benteen and a Lieutenant Thomas Weir remained in the game; and by mutual agreement, the ante was raised to $2.50. Suddenly the game became serious. By dawn, Benteen had won a considerable amount, including $150 from Weir, which, according to Benteen, was never paid. Perhaps, but it is difficult to imagine an officer's gambling debt within the regiment going unpaid, unless the creditor released the debtor. Custer was an inveterate gambler and lost considerably at the gaming tables, so much so that he promised Libby in 1870[21] that he would never again gamble at cards. That did not prevent him from gambling at the racetrack or in stocks.

Thomas Weir, the officer who had lost a month's salary at poker, was born in Ohio and left the University of Michigan during wartime to enlist in the cavalry. He was later commissioned and rose to the rank of captain, finishing the war as brevet lieutenant colonel. After peacetime service in Texas, he was appointed first lieutenant in the 7th Cavalry and promoted a year later to captain.

For six months in 1867, Benteen was the only officer in H Company. This gave him a superb opportunity to imprint his character on the company. Benteen had a knack for training soldiers. He treated his men with respect and insisted that his non-commissioned officers do the same. Benteen detested bullies, no matter their rank. Once his men learned their duties, he expected them to perform. Woe to him who did not![22]

General Hugh Scott, later Adjutant-General of the Army, better expresses Benteen's gift for command: "I found my model early in Captain Benteen, the idol of the seventh Cavalry...who governed mainly by suggestion. In all the years I knew him I never once heard him raise his voice to enforce his purpose. He would sit by the open fire at night, his bright pleasant face framed by his snowy-white hair, beaming with kindness and humor and often I watched his every movement to find out the secret of his quiet steady government, that I might go and govern likewise. For example, if he intended to stay a few days in one camp he would say to his adjutant, 'Brewer, don't you think we had better take up our regular guard mount while in this camp?' And Brewer always thought it 'better' and so did everybody else. If he found that his kindly manner was misunderstood, then his iron hand would close down quickly, but that was seldom necessary, and then only with new-comers and never twice with the same person."[23]

In March 1867, Benteen received the joyous news from his Atlanta farm that his wife had given birth to a son. The boy was named Frederick Wilson Benteen, the middle name for General James H. Wilson, whom Benteen greatly admired.

Two great trails ran through southern Kansas. The Smoky Hill Trail led to Denver, Colorado, along which from east to west were Fort Leavenworth, Fort Riley, Fort Harker, Fort Hays and Fort Wallace. At Fort Harker, the Santa Fe Trail branched off to the southwest, along which were Forts Zarah, Larned, Dodge and Union. These posts were invariably undermanned and severely underofficered. Given an opportunity, warriors did not hesitate to attack the forts. Army horses grazing outside the forts received their special attention.

In early spring, while the regiment was being formed, Benteen received his Civil War brevets in the regular army—a major's brevet for Mine Creek, Kansas (October 25, 1864), and a lieutenant colonel's brevet for Columbus, Georgia (April 16, 1865). One brevet was often given in the volunteer army at the end of volunteer service, but usually not for a rank above colonel. Officers doted on these brevets. They pored over the published lists. There were no medals for officers in the post-war years, so these brevets represented the ribbons and medals that are worn today. An officer was addressed by his brevet rank. If two officers held the same date of rank in the regular army, the one with the higher brevet took precedence in housing, seating arrangements and courtesies. For example, Benteen had the same date of rank as Captain Myles Keogh, and they both had lieutenant colonel brevets (as did Thomas Weir), but when Benteen received his colonel brevet, he became the senior.

Brevets did not just happen. The officer had to make a time-consuming application for each brevet and enclose endorsements by his superior officers for the battle cited in the request. In Benteen's case, the endorsements were furnished by Generals Pleasonton and Wilson. The application was then sent to Senator B. Gratz Brown of Missouri, who forwarded it on January 19, 1867, to the Secretary of War.

Benteen was disappointed with the brevets he received. He believed that at the very least he should have been awarded a colonel's brevet, which was his discharge rank in the Civil War. Secretly, he had hoped for a brigadier general's brevet. He wrote to the Hon. Tom Noell,[24] requesting his help in the matter. When the colonel's brevet was finally awarded,[25] it was not through the intercession of the congressman, but because of Benteen's role in the forthcoming Saline River battle.

During the month of February 1867 all twelve companies were stationed in Fort Riley. Then, four were retained at Fort Riley and the rest distributed to other forts in Kansas or the Colorado Territory. Preparations were begun for the spring campaign.

General Winfield Hancock commanded the Department of the Missouri from his headquarters at Fort Leavenworth. He had been given the task of maintaining peace on the southern plains. Above all, he wanted no repetition of last year's Bozeman disaster, where the army suffered ignominious defeat on the northern plains, because of its inability to protect the sattelite forts. Hancock felt it imperative to show his strength to the tribes in his command. He assembled 1,400 men, by far the largest collection of infantry, artillery and cavalry heretofore gathered in the region, and even managed to procure pontoon trains to ford the rivers.

Late in March, with the first appearance of the new grass, the companies at Fort Riley took to the field, against the advice of Edward W. Wynkoop, the Indian agent, who maintained that the tribes were essentially peaceful and should be left alone. Custer led four companies from Fort Riley and was joined by another four companies from the other forts. For the first time, the 7th Cavalry campaigned in strength. Hancock accompanied the column, riding in an ambulance.

They marched one hundred miles to Fort Harker and a similar distance to Fort Larned on the Santa Fe Trail, where they set up camp. General Hancock sent word to the Cheyenne chiefs to meet him for a pow-wow, at the same time ordering them to immediately surrender their white captives. As he awaited the arrival of the Cheyenne chiefs, a severe snowstorm struck the camp. To keep the horses from freezing, the soldiers fed them extra rations and whipped them during the night to keep them moving.[26]

The Cheyenne tribes were camped forty miles west of Fort Larned, across the swollen Arkansas River. Believing that their villages were safe from army attack, the chiefs begrudgingly obeyed the summons but did not bring the white captives. At Fort Larned, they were treated to a meal of hardtack, bacon and coffee, and similar fare was given to the Indian women accompanying them. The chiefs tried to discourage Hancock from approaching the Indian villages, fearful of another massacre, similar to what had befallen them at Sand Creek, Colorado, three years before,[27] where 150 Cheyenne had been killed and scalped by the Colorado militiamen.

Hancock made clear that he would accept nothing less than total submission, which, in his mind, would come only after the villages had seen his army, surrendered their captives and agreed to his terms. He crossed the swollen Arkansas River on a pontoon bridge, put together by a detachment of engineers, and on April 14 drew up his column in sight of a three-hundred-lodge Cheyenne encampment. The chiefs were stunned. Fearing harsh punishment, they asked to parlay. That night Hancock ordered the village surrounded to forestall an escape. To his consternation, the scouts reported that the Cheyenne had fled under cover of darkness, abandoning their tepees and their goods. Hancock ordered the 7th Cavalry to hunt them down.

Custer set off in hot pursuit, even abandoning his supply wagons. Soon, the trail divided and then it ended, as the tribes scattered. Custer could report seeing a burning stage station with three dead bodies, but not a single warrior. He sent word to Hancock.

Hancock was furious. Against the advice of the Indian agent, he ordered the village burned and the tons of chattels destroyed. As the agent had predicted, the Cheyennes viewed this as a declaration of war.

Low in supplies, Custer had no choice but to march his eight companies to the nearest post, old Fort Hays on the Smoky Hill Trail. Built originally as a shelter on the banks of Big Creek, a branch of the Smoky Hill River, the primitive buildings were constructed of sod and log, with mud chinking and dirt floors.[28] Two barracks and two officers' quarters[29] bordered the parade ground, along with a tent hospital, a quartermaster storehouse and a guardhouse. Stables were dug into the ground with the opening facing south.[30]

The regiment arrived at the fort on April 19, in desperate need of supplies. Instead of provisions, they found a bare cupboard.

Camp was set up a half-mile from the fort. Since neither grain nor fodder was on hand, the horses had to graze on early prairie grass.[31] Officers and soldiers shared beans, hardtack and bacon. Some seventy-five men came down with scurvy.[32] Slowly, supplies began to trickle in, but it took a month for the horses to regain their strength.

No sooner had tents been raised, than men began to desert. Within a week, seventeen men were gone.[33] Custer kept the soldiers from entering the fort. He did this, Benteen claimed, because Custer had not been paid a bribe by the post trader.[34] Surely there is a more plausible explanation. With men deserting in droves, Custer would want to keep them from buying liquor, which was being sold by the post trader inside the fort. The going price was for whiskey was ten cents a "shot"; for beer, fifty cents a quart.[35] In any event, the soldiers soon found another source of supply, when civilians set up shop in a nearby canyon.[36]

In early May, Hancock visited the fort. He was anxious that the 7th Cavalry take to the field, since warrior attacks had again started up. The regiment organized a festive program to welcome him. The soldiers ran a foot race, with the winner relieved of guard duty for a month; and his company excused for a week.[37] In the horse race, H Company ran one of their mounts against a "celebrated quarter horse" belonging to an infantry officer; and the company horse won. For the grand review, Benteen lent his private mount, "Midnight," to Moylan without disclosing that the mare shied when the rider wore a saber. To Benteen's delight, Moylan could barely remain in the saddle.[38]

Hancock's incessant prodding irked Custer, who passed on his anger to his officers. They withstood Custer's pique as best they could. To avoid having to deal with him, Benteen and some other officers reported sick whenever they had the duty as officer of the day. Custer seemed to have become unhinged by Hancock's unrealistic expectations. One captain wrote: "things are becoming very unpleasant here. General Custer...is the most complete example of a petty tyrant I have ever seen."[39]

Soon after Hancock's departure, Libby Custer arrived. She had come part of the way by ambulance, since the railroad had not yet reached the fort. Custer installed her in a cone-shaped Sibley tent inside the fort. The Sibley has one pole twelve feet high, with the sides of the tent extending obliquely outward. During her first week, she was awakened three times by bullets flying through the air, as sentries exchanged fire with deserters. To add to Custer's woes, the Cheyenne were again raiding settlements along the Smoky Hill Trail,[40] and Hancock kept insisting that the 7th Cavalry take to the field.

Benteen was relieved of the stresses in Custer's command, when he was ordered in May to bring five witnesses to Fort Riley, where a court martial was being held for several deserters from his company. Trackers were paid thirty dollars to retrieve each deserter.[41] The usual penalties for desertion were two to five years for the offense and two additional years for the theft of a horse, as well as a "bob-tail" (dishonorable) discharge.[42] Men had been deserting at a rate of fifty a month. Between October 1866 and October 1867, 512 men deserted, taking with them horses and equipment. Officer's mounts were preferred, since some did not carry the "US" brand. Benteen himself was to lose seven of his own horses during his service in the 7th Cavalry.[43]

The goal of the deserter was to join the miners in Colorado, or the railroad workers or the outlaws.[44] If caught, the soldier had half his head shaved and was marched around camp to the tune of "The Rogue's March." He was then court martialed, in which case his services were permanently lost to the regiment; or, if he were a first offender and apprehended near the fort, he might be given company discipline, which would include any of several highly disagreeable extra-legal punishments. He could spend nights in a hell hole dug into the ground,[45] and days with ball and chain, shackles, buck and gag or made to endure any other discipline that the company commander might chose to assign.

Benteen remained at Fort Riley for more than six weeks and did not accompany Custer on his inglorious Nebraska scouting expedition.

By late May, marauding was reported along the Platte Road (Oregon Trail) in Nebraska. At the express wish of General William T. Sherman, Custer was ordered to halt the attacks and to expel all hostiles found between the Platte and the Republican rivers.

Not until June 1, 1867, was the regiment ready for the field. Custer left old Fort Hays with six companies on a six-week scout that would take him into Nebraska, Colorado and back into western Kansas. The regiment would never return to old Fort Hays.[46] Four days after Custer and his men left, the river flooded the fort, rising thirty-five feet in a few hours and drowning six men. The army wives were terrified. The army ordered a new fort built fifteen miles away, along the proposed railbed of the Kansas-Pacific. With the cavalry gone, warriors seized the opportunity to threaten old Fort Hays. The wives were rushed to Fort Harker, and temporarily lodged in two rooms;[47] then sent further east to Fort Riley.[48]

From the start, Custer's march was ill fated. The heat was fierce, the dust choking and the provisions vile. Men drank from creeks, water holes and buffalo wallows. Soon troopers came down with dysentery or scurvy, and the sick had to be carried in the ambulances. The dead were buried along the march with the company commander performing the rites. One drunken officer committed suicide.[49] To make matters worse, Custer took out his frustrations on the men. When the party reached the Platte River (Oregon) Trail, desertions began again. In one night, thirty-four men deserted. All this in a command of less than three hundred![50] Officers were ordered to patrol the company streets after *Taps!*[51]

One day, twelve men deserted, taking with them seven of the best horses. Furious, Custer ordered them pursued, blurting out that he wanted none of them brought back alive. Three deserters were shot, one of whom died. Custer drove his men relentlessly, but was unable to find the warriors. Arriving at Fort McPherson, Nebraska, two hundred miles north of Fort Hays, he had a pow-wow with the notorious Sioux war chief, Pawnee Killer, who convinced Custer of his peaceful intentions and was even given rations! General Sherman, himself, faulted Custer for allowing Pawnee Killer to slip from his grasp. Within days, five hundred of Pawnee Killer's warriors attacked Custer's train and Pawnee Killer, under a flag of truce, had the effrontery to demand additional supplies. The warriors were everywhere and nowhere, striking swiftly and avoiding engagement. For five weeks, the regiment cut a wide and unproductive swath, finally ending up at Fort Wallace, Kansas, 125 miles west of Fort Hays, with lame horses and bitter, weary men. The warriors had eluded them and were continuing their attacks on all fronts. Mail and stagecoach traffic had been brought to a halt. A train had been derailed. The 1867 sweep had been a failure, and there was vast dissatisfaction with Custer's performance.

To add to Custer's woes, the other forts were in perilous condition, drained of cavalry and plagued by cholera, officer shortages, desertions, inadequate provisions and warrior attacks. At Fort Dodge, the warriors had made off with all of A Company's horses.[52]

While at Fort Wallace, Custer somehow convinced himself that his wife needed rescuing. He had been told of the flood at old Fort Hays and heard rumors of a cholera epidemic. Heedless of his orders to remain at Fort Wallace, Custer set out for Fort Hays, 150 miles distant, with an escort of seventy-five men. They kept the tired horses to the brisk pace of fifty minutes walk and ten minutes rest. Along the way, he met Benteen, who was leading a supply train to Fort Wallace. More than likely, Benteen informed him that his wife was safe at Fort Riley. Later, the possibility was raised that Benteen might have also brought cholera to Fort Wallace.[53] Benteen had with him four half-inch Gatling Guns, which he had been ordered to deliver. Benteen had a poor opinion of the Gatling Guns and had tried to persuade his superiors that "those guns were worthless against Indians as they were then constructed." Black powder quickly fouled the barrel, causing the gun to overheat and jam. Even against stampeding buffalo the Gatling Gun was not as effective as mounted solders firing carbines.[54]

Upon learning that Libby Custer was not at old Fort Hays, Custer rode by ambulance to Fort Harker, where he obtained permission by a ruse to travel by train to Fort Riley. There he found her, safe and overjoyed to see him. Of his seventy-five-man escort, twenty had deserted along the way, and two had been shot by warriors. The horses were lame.

Custer was arrested and tried by court martial for disregarding orders, deserting his command, causing men to be shot and refusing medical care for the wounded. After a lengthy and well-publicized trial lasting nearly one month, he was found guilty of the charges and suspended from command for one year without pay. He was also arraigned before a civil court on murder allegations, but the charges were dismissed. He spent some of his sentence at Fort Leavenworth in quarters reserved for General Sheridan, where he began his Civil War memoirs. "We are free of Custer!" Benteen gloated, when he learned of the outcome of the court martial.

Custer was away from his regiment for fourteen months, from July 1867 to September 1868. In the meantime, great changes came to the plains, brought about by the Chisholm, Western and Goodnight-Loving trails, which brought four million head of cattle up from Texas; and by the Kansas-Pacific Railroad, which took the beef away. Almost overnight, Hays City sprang up, and new Fort Hays grew with it.

Benteen rejoined his company at Fort Wallace and returned with it to new Fort Hays. In October 1867, Major Elliott, the acting regimental commander, escorted a party of treaty commissioners to the Medicine Lodge Creek, Kansas, seventy miles from Fort Larned, where an important pact was being negotiated.

The eastern Indian Territory was inhabited by the exiled "Five Civilized Tribes"—Creeks, Seminoles, Chickasaw, Choctaw and Cherokee. Now, the western Indian Territory was about to be offered to the tribes of the southern plains.[55]

An offer was made for the Kiowa and Comanche to settle on a three-million-acre reservation in western Indian Territory between the Red and Washita rivers. A week later, a similar offer was extended to the Cheyenne and Arapaho, to settle the western Indian Territory between the Cimarron and Arkansas rivers. North of the Arkansas River, the territory was reserved for white settlement and railroad construction.

Although the treaty was discussed with the chiefs, the terms were never read to them. Enticed by gifts, threats and promises, the older chiefs made their mark on the treaty document, but from the start, the younger warriors (dog soldiers) scorned the offer.[56] The young braves watched with growing fury as the railroad tracks stretched ever-farther westward, over lands that once had been prime warrior hunting grounds. Further, the great buffalo massacre by the white hunters was now underway, following the discovery of a new method of tanning that rendered the buffalo hide commercially marketable.

For the remainder of the fall and through the cold months (1867-8) the fighting subsided, as expected. In November 1867, H Company was assigned a "permanent" station at Fort Harker. Major Joel Elliott commanded the garrison, with a complement of two infantry and two cavalry companies.

Fort Harker was situated on the banks of the Smoky Hill River, two miles west of Elsworth City, a stop on the Kansas Pacific Railroad and a railhead for the Chisholm Trail.

Barracks and quarters were constructed with logs.[57] Two log stables housed the horses, and a large corral accommodated the mules and the unfit mounts. The soldiers spent a dreary winter in patrol, escort duty and interminable drill. Regardless of the depths of the snow drifts, discipline and dress were resolutely maintained. Hair had to be cut once monthly and the face shaved twice weekly by the company barber.[58]

In February 1868, Catherine Benteen and eleven-month-old Freddie joined Benteen at Fort Harker. Together, they began their army life in the "splendid isolation" of a frontier fort deep in winter. Kate was new to army posts. Her reaction to the ramshackle quarters, the bone-piercing cold and the ever-oppressive stench from the piles of manure and the frozen privies and latrines are best left to the imagination. Soon after her arrival, Kate again became pregnant, with an expected delivery date in December 1868.

Benteen was joined by First Lieutenant William Cooke, a twenty-one-year-old, Ontario-born, who had moved to Buffalo, New York, received a commission in the 24th New York Cavalry and served in the Union cavalry during the war, finishing with a brevet of lieutenant colonel. Cooke was six feet, six inches tall, with long Dundreary sidewiskers and was accounted the best shot in the regiment, although Custer and Benteen privately aspired to the honor.

Also at Fort Harker was another company commander, Lieutenant Owen Hale, who had risen from the ranks during the Civil War and who ended up with a captain's brevet. Hale's second lieutenant, Donald

McIntosh, was half Six-Nations Indian, born in Canada, who was joining the regiment on his first assignment. He had no wartime experience and was later accused uncharitably of being inefficient and indifferent. The four officers messed together and developed a cordial friendship, which would continue until Cooke agreed to become Custer's adjutant.

With the coming of spring, 1868, General Philip H. Sheridan assumed command of the Department of the Missouri. Sheridan toured the forts along the Santa Fe Trail and was immediately confronted by the complaints of the warrior chiefs who were awaiting the goods and weapons promised them under the terms of the Medicine Lodge Treaty.

Major Elliott was ordered on May 3 to march six companies to Fort Larned, one hundred miles southwest on the Santa Fe Trail, to calm the hoard of twelve thousand Cheyenne, Arapaho and Kiowa camped around the fort, who were clamoring for their rifles and supplies.

While Major Elliott was in the field, Benteen was left in command at Fort Harker. When a herd of horses arrived, intended as replacements for the exhausted mounts of the 10th Cavalry, Benteen exchanged the best of the new horses for the weaker horses in his command. Unfortunately, Benteen's mounts had already been branded with the company letter, so that when the horses reached the 10th Cavalry, this rather brazen deception became immediately evident. Months later, General Sheridan is supposed to have told him, pointing to the horses: "Benteen, this is the best mounted

The Southern Plains

squadron of cavalry I have ever seen."[59] Benteen took this to mean that the general had heard of Benteen's scheming and was prepared to ignore it. There would come a time in later years when Benteen would learn firsthand what good horses mean to a black cavalry regiment.

In July, Benteen was ordered to march his two companies to Fort Larned, where the warriors were still waiting for their promised supplies. Camp was set up outside the fort. There was great excitement when a rabid wolf entered the fort and bit six people, before being shot by a sentry. The post surgeon cauterized the bite wounds with silver nitrate, but when he tried to amputate a finger that had been severely mauled, the soldier refused to allow it. A month later, the soldier was dead. According to Benteen, all the others, but one, also died of "hydrophobia."[60] An officer was spared, since the thickness of his trousers prevented the virus from infecting the skin. The usual incubation period for rabies is one to three months, with one week to one year as the outer limits.

Benteen drilled his men and conducted mounted target exercises, an uncommon practice at the time.[61] Finally, without direct authorization, since the treaty had not yet been ratified by the Senate, E. W. Wynkoop, the Indian agent, began releasing the long-awaited arms and supplies. The rifles and revolvers were outdated; and, moreover, had been issued too late to satisfy the angry warriors.

Frightening news was received of large bands of marauders along the Saline and Solomon rivers to the north. Fifteen settlers had been killed, five women raped, houses burned and stock driven off. The homesteaders were desperate. Warriors on the warpath were easily identified, even from the distance. They wore eagle feather war bonnets and painted their bodies with black and yellow stripes. The horses' tails were unbraided and smeared with paint.[62]

Benteen reacted promptly. He ordered H Company to force-march to Fort Harker, and he himself completed the trip in one day by express ambulance. On arrival, he sent a sergeant and a guide to scout the far side of Saline River. To his disgust, the pair reported that the river was too high to be forded.

Benteen left Fort Harker on August 13, with forty men and pack mules. They forded the river without difficulty. An hour later, they encountered a party of Cheyenne braves, thought to be Black Kettle's dog soldiers.[63] After first setting a ten-man guard on the mules, he galloped after the warriors with the remaining thirty men.[64] The braves had just raided a ranch house on Elk Horn Creek, raped a woman and abducted two small girls.[65] Soon, the party of braves swelled to two hundred warriors, as others joined them. Believing that Benteen's men were only a small part of their pursuers, the warriors were bluffed into abandoning the girls. Benteen continued the pursuit for another ten miles. His men were armed with the seven-round Spencer repeating rifles, and six-round Colt revolvers. The soldiers galloped, then dismounted to rest the horses and to fire their carbines. They then reloaded, mounted and continued the pursuit, always guarding their flanks.

Benteen and his men managed to kill three warriors and wound ten others, but had to abandon the chase at nightfall. The girls were returned to their kin, who long remembered the heroic action. "I struck the first blow in the Indian war of 1868 & 69," Benteen proudly noted.[66] He sent word to Fort Larned to watch for warriors intent on exchanging musket loaders for repeating rifles, since they were sure to have been impressed with the performance of the Spencer carbine.

Elk Horn was the first victory for the 7th Cavalry and was later to earn Benteen a brevet to colonel, one of the last awarded before the practice was obviated. It is not known who signed the endorsement, but it was certainly not Custer. The brevet superseded the "adjustment" he had been seeking through the congressman.

Benteen and his men patrolled the Saline River, but the warriors had flown. Another company joined them, and the men spent their free time playing baseball, with sentinels posted in the outfield. They competed for the on-site championship, with "losers to set up the liquids when we got to where it was to be had."[67] H Company won two games. Benteen was captain of his team and an active player, so it is likely that H Company had brought along the equipment.

On his return to Fort Harker, Benteen met General Sheridan, who was on an inspection tour. Sheridan was anxious to recoup his public image, which he had lost in Louisiana, after he had made himself unpopular with the white community by vigorously enforcing the reconstruction laws. President Johnson, himself, had insisted that Sheridan exchange commands with Hancock, to get him out of Louisiana.

Benteen had last seen Sheridan in 1862 when the latter was a captain and acting assistant quartermaster-commissary officer. After their first meeting, Sheridan became involved in a dispute with General Curtis and was sent to St. Louis under arrest. At the time of his arrival, General Halleck was in desperate need of a qualified officer to command a regiment of volunteer cavalry; and Sheridan got the job.[68] Sheridan's progress thereafter was spectacular. When Sheridan inquired about Benteen's Civil War career, Benteen replied dejectedly that the best he could achieve was colonel. "I had no political influence to forward me in rank or assist me in anyway whatsoever," he declared.[69] Sheridan is supposed to have told Benteen: "I saw chances; in fact sought them, got the opportunities and well, I did the very best I could with them; and here I am, God Bless You! Let's have a drink!"[70]

Sheridan had given careful thought to the situation. Unless the Cheyenne could be stopped, the attacks along the Saline were but a prelude to what lay ahead. Meanwhile, he had a steep learning curve to master.

In September 1868, Sheridan sent a large detachment of six hundred men under Lieutenant Colonel Alfred Sully, including nine companies of the 7th Cavalry, to engage the Cheyenne and the Arapaho along the Canadian River in the Indian Territory, hoping to draw the warriors away from Kansas. Despite his many opportunities, Sully accomplished little. In the same month, Sheridan sent another party under Major G. A.

Forsyth to protect the Kansas-Pacific Railroad workers, but it barely escaped annihilation on Beecher Island. Only the arrival of a detachment of 10th Cavalry saved them.

Sheridan began to see that his main problem was the warrior pony. Not only could it easily outrun an army horse, it needed neither grain nor tack nor shoes. Lacking a bridle, the pony was guided by a long strip of buffalo skin, which was fastened by a slipknot around its lower jaw.[71] The rider directed the pony by leaning to the side.[72] The pony can stand for hours without moving or neighing.[73] It required no shoes, although on occasion rawhide moccasins were made for it. More often, the warrior toughened the hooves by exposing them to the smoke and heat of burned wild rosemary.[74]

Moreover, it would seem that the best time for a campaign would be during the cold months. The pony was then skin-and-bones and had to paw snow to find a few mouthfuls of graze, while the army horse throve on its wholesome ration of grain. In spring and summer, the advantage reverted to the warrior, unless the villages could be attacked when the warriors were away on the hunt, leaving only the women and the aged to defend the tepees.[75]

According to Benteen, Sheridan's adjutant confided to Benteen that Sheridan intended to give Benteen command of the 7th Cavalry during the forthcoming operations, but Benteen declined the offer, recommending instead that Custer be released from detention to take command.[76]

Lieutenant Colonel George A. Custer in civilian dress.
[U. S. Military Institute]

Lieutenant General Philip Sheridan. [Hargrett Rare Book and Manuscript Library, University of Georgia]

Only an innocent would believe this. At any rate, on September 24, Sheridan released Custer from detention two months before the expiration of his sentence. Custer rushed to Fort Hays, eager to repair his sullied reputation. Arriving September 30, he examined the plans that Sheridan set before him.

Sheridan had devised a three-pronged attack on the wintering tribes. One column would start out from Fort Hays, driving south; another from Fort Lyon, Colorado, would drive east; and the third from Fort Bascom, New Mexico, would sweep north.

The post traders greeted the news of a winter campaign with great enthusiasm. According to the cynical Benteen, they could now charge nine dollars for flannel shirts, one dollar for a pair of plain cotton socks and everything else in proportion; "and no one caviled at prices."[77]

Only two of the 7th Cavalry companies were then stationed at Fort Hays. The remainder, including Benteen and H Company, were at Camp Forsyth, thirty miles from Fort Dodge on the Arkansas River, where they had been camped since the end of Sully's failed campaign in September. After hurried preparations, Custer marched the Fort Hays companies one hundred miles to Camp Forsyth, joined along the way by a volunteer cavalry regiment. The entire column came under the nominal command of Lieutenant Colonel Alfred Sully, who had earlier failed Sheridan and whom Sheridan would shortly replace with Custer. He could do this because although both had the same active-duty rank, Custer was a brevet major general and Sully, a

The Southern Plains

brevet brigidier general. Warrior outriders showed their contempt for the column by taunting it with insults, while remaining outside of carbine range. They kidnaped two soldiers.

After their arrival at Camp Forsyth, Custer sent Benteen to Fort Harker 150 miles away, "with a fair chance of getting scalped,"[78] to fetch additional horses and recruits. Benteen was also asked to wire one hundred dollars to Libby Custer, since Benteen was known to keep cash on hand. He was allowed to take with him his orderly, a soldier-friend from his Petersburg days,[79] who had been a major in the Confederate army. The two moved quickly and safely along the Santa Fe Trail.

Benteen reached Fort Harker without difficulty and on November 4th set out for Camp Forsyth with the recruits. Ahead of them on the Santa Fe Trail was a Mexican wagon train, laden with guns and ammunition. Benteen and his detachment overtook the train, just as it was about to be attacked by a large band of warriors. Despite their inferior numbers, the detachment drove off the raiders. Benteen then proceeded on to Camp Forsyth and delivered the recruits, arriving November 10. The track left in the snow by the raiding party was shortly to be of some importance, according to Benteen.[80]

Meanwhile, Custer had been hard at work reorganizing the regiment. He personally took charge of the training. The companies spent long hours in drill, which included twice-daily target practice. At walk, trot and gallop gait, the horseman fired his revolver at a stack of hardtack boxes. When dismounted, he fired his carbine at a twenty-six-inch bullseye target at distances of one hundred to one thousand feet.[81] Buffalo coats, buffalo overshoes and two-finger buffalo mittens were issued to the men. Unlike the soldier's uniform, which was owned by the soldier, winter clothing belonged to the regiment and later had to be returned.

Gradually, by diligence, patience and example, Custer began to instill in the 7th Cavalry an esprit which had hitherto been lacking. Within a month, the regiment had been transformed into a fighting command. Custer adopted the French practice of "coloring the horses,"[82] i.e., assigning to each company horses of similar color. Actually, six of the companies ended up with light bay horses. This new arrangement infuriated some company commanders, who had been diligently attempting to procure for their company the very best horses, regardless of color. H Company was assigned light bay horses. All Benteen's efforts to swindle the 10th Cavalry had been in vain.[83]

On November 12, Custer set out in freezing cold with his eleven companies. After a six-day march, they reached the North Canadian River in the Indian Territory. Here, they established a staging area, which came to be called "Camp Supply." This well-constructed depot was surrounded by a stockade and had blockhouses to shelter the supplies and to lodge the officers. The soldiers were camped outside the stockade. To protect themselves from the cold, the soldiers lined their buffalo overcoats with discarded blankets and made leggings from canvas.[84]

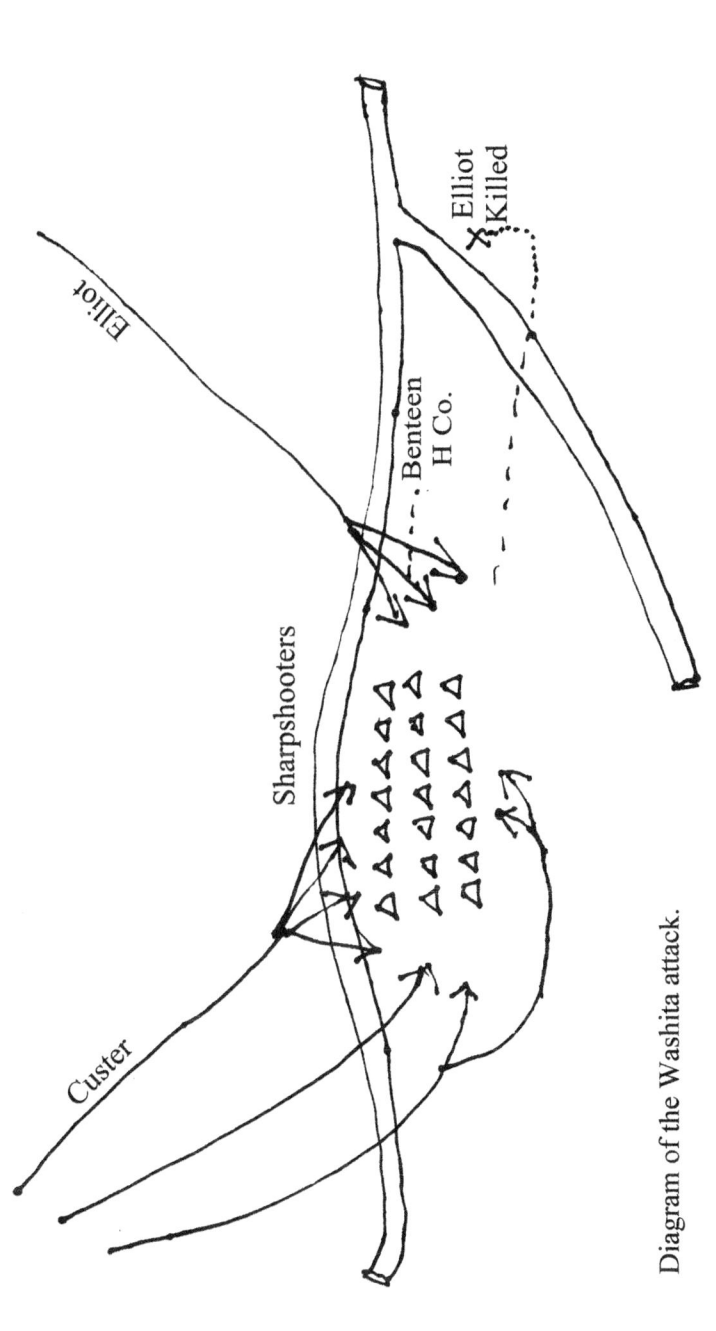

Diagram of the Washita attack.

[Benteen Photo Collection, Hargrett Rare Book and Manuscript Library, University of Georgia]

General Sheridan joined them in Camp Supply. Grimly, he made known that he had no interest in peace treaties, but wanted the warriors punished. Custer need not distinguish between treaty-abiding and hostile warriors, since in Sheridan's mind, there was no distinction. He ordered Custer to precede to the Washita River, where the tribes were reported to be wintering, and "destroy their villages and ponies...kill...all warriors and bring back all women and children!"[85]

Sunrise, on November 23, *General Call!* sounded, the call to strike tents. This was followed by *Boots and Saddles!*, the order to prepare to depart. Custer set out in a foot of snow with his six hundred men. Incredibly, he took with him the regimental band. Also, he had organized a party of forty sharpshooters under Lieutenant Cooke, selected from the best shots in the command. The regiment rode due south, often guided only by compass, into a region unfamiliar to their Osage guides, with the supply train lumbering behind them.[86] Some of the saddles split open from the moisture. On the second day, the sun shone briefly, and men began to complain of "snow blindness." Benteen owned a pair of colored glasses but, in a moment of generosity, had lent them to the surgeon. He later attributed his myopia to the Washita campaign. Benteen and his company were detailed to protect the supply wagons. When the regiment made camp, the horses would not eat until the snow had been cleared and their forage laid on the ground. The soldiers pitched pup tents on a cleared patch or wrapped themselves in blankets and lay beside the fire. Boots were often burned, as soldiers tried to warm their feet. Some soldiers heated the ground with burning embers, then kicked away the embers and spread their horse cover, saddle blanket and pup tent. Bridle, bits and guns were kept under the blankets.[87] Horses were picketed along the supply train to a line threaded through the rear wheels of the supply wagons.

The following day the regiment came to a ford in the South Canadian River. After detaching his supply train, Custer ordered Major Elliott to take a battalion upstream to search for recent tracks. Elliott sent back word that his Osage scouts had sighted a trail made by a war party, which could be identified by the absence of dogs' tracks. Benteen surmised that it was the same party that had attacked the Mexican wagon train and was now returning to its winter encampment.[88]

Custer and his companies reached Elliott's battalion at 9 p.m. and, after an hour's rest, the reunited regiment pushed on in the dark. Custer rode well ahead with the scouts until they heard a dog barking and the tinkling of bells. Some warriors put bells on their ponies at nighttime.[89] Three hours later, the regiment caught up to Custer. Behind a ridge lay the fifty-one-tepee Cheyenne village of Chief Black Kettle, on the south side of the Washita River. The chief had been an innocent victim of the infamous Sands Creek massacre in 1864, while flying an American flag and a white flag from his tepee. He was now supposedly on peaceful terms with the white authorities, having been ordered by the Superintendent for Indian Affairs to return to his Washita village to await the arrival of General Sheridan's soldiers. The contraband later found in his village would seem to belie his peaceful intentions, but chiefs were sometimes blamed for the misdeeds of their dog soldiers—young braves who did not always follow the counsel of the elders. Black Kettle's dog soldiers were thought to have been responsible for the Saline River raids.

During the night, the troops took their positions in the freezing cold, with orders to keep from stamping their feet.[90] Officers removed their sabers.[91] When his dogs began to bark, Custer ordered them killed.[92]

Custer divided his 720 men into four detachments. He would lead a frontal attack on the village with four companies and the sharpshooters. Elliott, with three companies, including H Company, would swing wide and attack from the northeast; two companies would attack from the south; and an additional two companies would attack from the west.

At the dawn of November 17, as the band began the first notes of their regimental song, the troops began the charge. The music so unnerved the musicians' horses that they too were carried along.[93] Sharpshooters picked off the warriors running outside the tepees and the women holding rifles. They also shot many women who had no weapons. With shrill yells, the soldiers galloped into the camp. Benteen led his company at the canter, when his path was blocked by a fourteen-year-old warrior. Benteen tried to sign that he did not want to shoot, but the warrior fired at him three times. With the third shot, Benteen's horse was hit, dumping Benteen. As the boy warrior prepared to fire again, Benteen shot him. Custer later mocked Benteen over this incident, but when he wrote his book, Custer described Benteen's dilemma with respect.[94]

In fifteen minutes, the battle was over. While the soldiers were rounding up the thousand ponies, Major Elliott, with a party of nineteen men, dashed off in pursuit of some fleeing warriors. Unknown to Custer, Black Kettle's village was only a small part of the six hundred lodges extending east for twelve miles along the Washita valley, sheltering several thousand Arapaho, Kiowa and Cheyenne.[95] Summoned by the gunfire, the warriors from the other villages raced to the scene of the fighting. Major Elliott encountered the first of the advancing braves two miles outside of Black Kettle's camp and after a fierce two-hour battle, Elliott and his men were killed. He might have retreated to the village, but apparently had decided to fight it out.[96]

The arrival of a few forward wagons detached from his supply train brought much needed ammunition and supplies. Soldiers eagerly scooped up the cartridges.[97] Custer then ordered an inventory of the booty, taken from the twenty-hide commissary tepees and the twelve-hide family tepees. The tally of the saddles, buffalo robes, and other goods was conducted by Lieutenant Edward Godfrey. His figures seem rather extravagant for a fifty-odd tepee village. Godfrey also found photograph albums, unopened mail and other possessions unmistakably belonging to white settlers, which presumably had been seized by the dog soldiers in their rampages.

Custer kept two hundred ponies and four mules[98] and gave orders to kill the remaining eight hundred ponies and burn the tepees and goods. The surviving women and children were taken as hostages. Meanwhile, hundreds of warriors from the other villages began closing in. They seized the high ground and began firing down on the soldiers. An attack was launched on the warrior position but was beaten back. Custer then ordered Benteen to attack. Benteen divided two companies into four platoons and stormed the heights. "I have never seen troops in an engagement act in such a manner or keep their line in such a fire as these troops did," wrote one sergeant.[99] Benteen continued the attack, until *Recall!* sounded, meanwhile having given the regiment ample time to prepare for a withdrawal. Benteen also claimed that he shot Chief Black Kettle, who had retreated to the high ground and was shouting encouragement to the warriors. Others say he was shot escaping.[100]

Custer sent an officer, Captain Edward Myers, to report on the whereabouts of the Elliott party, but the officer turned back before he reached the bodies of Elliott and his nineteen men. Why the officer could not follow the tracks of twenty shod horses in the light snow for two miles, is difficult to understand. With the warriors now arriving in increasing numbers, Custer ordered his men to withdraw from Washita. Instead of a direct retreat, Custer ordered the band to strike up a tune, while he marched his regiment in the direction of the other lodges, throwing fear into the warriors, who rushed back to their villages. On the way, he put out flankers, without success, to search for Elliott and his men.[101] When night came, Custer changed direction and countermarched toward his supply train, which was guarded by only eighty men. Fortunately, they had not been troubled.

It was a costly victory for the capture of a fifty-odd tepee village, undertaken with the advantage of complete surprise. Two officers and nineteen enlisted men had been killed and three officers and eleven enlisted wounded. Custer claimed that his men had killed seventy-five warriors and about the same number of women and children.

Although Washita was celebrated as a victory by a country appalled by reports of warrior brutality, there was some dissent. The *New York Tribune* on December 5, 1867, questioned whether in fact the tribe had committed any offence. After all, Washita was in the Indian Territory, and the Cheyenne had not been told why they were being punished. Other articles critical of the "army massacre" followed. Caustic remarks were delivered in Congress, fueled by criticisms made by E. W. Wyncoop, the former Indian agent, and General W. B. Hazen, Superintendent of Indian Affairs for the Southern Superintendency. Wyncoop maintained that the trail Custer had followed to the Washita was made by Kiowas, returning from combat with the Utes in Colorado. For the Cheyenne, the effects of the Washita were far-reaching, since it demonstrated that the army could wage war in winter, when the tribes were most vulnerable.

At the first bivouac after the battle, Custer prepared his report. He informed his company commanders, to their astonishment, that he did not require a written account but would take a verbal statement. In his final narrative, Custer cited two officers, one of whom had been killed, the other seriously wounded. He made no mention of the other officers, except to note that Benteen had had his horse shot from under him. These omissions were deeply resented by his subordinates, who believed that they, too, should share in the glory.

The regiment returned to Camp Supply to replenish equipment and supplies. Benteen, an avid outdoorsman, used his spare time to hunt turkey, which were abundant in the area. He also tried to learn the Kiowa tongue and invited a Kiowa chief to dinner, only to have him refuse to eat turkey "since it would make a coward of him."[102]

After General Sheridan arrived, the regiment set out for Fort Cobb, deep in the Indian Territory, revisiting the Washita battleground along the way. The bodies of Major Elliott and his party, including three men from H Company,[103] were found two miles from the village, unspeakably mutilated by the warriors and scavenged by wolves, coyote and birds. Benteen, who had a genuine liking for the enthusiastic Elliott, was shocked at the terrible mutilations and lost no time in assigning the blame to Custer. Unjustly so, perhaps, since Custer did send an officer to search for Elliott, and it is difficult to imagine what other reasonable actions Custer could have taken to save Major Elliott and his men, although a more aggressive search might have found the bodies. Historians have wondered why Benteen did not fault the officer initially sent to search for Elliott. Perhaps it was easier to blame Custer, since the officer in question,

Captain Edward Myers, was known to have an explosive temper and given to dueling.[104] But there lingers a faint suspicion that Benteen may have been right. After all, he was present at the scene and never ceased to believe that Custer had failed to make a meaningful effort to support Elliott.

Not far from the Elliott battle site, they found the bodies of a white woman captive and a white child disemboweled or clubbed to death.[105] The regiment followed the tracks of the Kiowas for seventy-five miles leading from the Washita battleground, and on December 18, it reached Fort Cobb, high up the Washita River. General Hazen was there to meet the regiment and made known that the Kiowas, whom they had been pursuing, were peaceful, and that they need not be forced onto their reservation, since in fact they were on it.

Benteen reported sick, with complaints of "chronic rheumatism." This usually meant severe back pain from hours in the saddle and sleeping on the ground. Bad news arrived from Fort Harker. Kate had given birth to a baby girl, named Catherine Norman Benteen, who died a week after delivery, leaving Kate weak and profoundly depressed.[106] The baby was buried in the post cemetery and later reburied at Fort Leavenworth.

Benteen too was dispirited, not only by the death of his baby, but also by the awful fate of his friend, Major Joel Elliott. He asked a scout if he would attest that Custer made no attempt to save Elliott, but the scout refused.[107] On December 22, 1868, while at Fort Cobb, Benteen wrote a letter to a Civil War comrade, now living in St. Louis. In it, he described Elliott's sortie and defeat at the hands of the large warrior force. He accused Custer of wasting his time inventorying the booty, slaughtering ponies and burning the captured chattels, without giving a thought to the missing Major Elliott and his party. "No, they are forgotten," he wrote. "Over them and the poor ponies, the wolves will hold high carnival, and their howling will be their only requiem..."

Benteen steadfastly maintained that he intended the letter only for his friend's information. Surely this cannot be true, judging from the rhetoric:

"Ah, 'tis only to intercept the wily foe, A grey troop goes on in the direction again. One more short mile and they will be saved. Oh, for a mother's prayers. Will not some good angel prompt them?"[108]

The letter was published anonymously on February 8 in the *Missouri Democrat* and reprinted in the *New York Times* on February 14. This is the first of other occasions where Benteen used the press to advance his own purposes.

By January 1, 1869, the Kiowa chiefs had agreed to the government terms,[109] which, according to General Hazen, they had already fulfilled. The campaign now took on a different aspect. Heretofore, it had been a punitive expedition; now, the goal was to drive the remaining tribes onto their reservations. This left the Cheyenne and the Arapaho still to be dealt with.

General Sheridan wanted the regiment resited farther within the Indian Territory. On January 4, 1869, it left

Fort Cobb for the Medicine Bluff Creek, thirty miles to the south, near the Texas border, which would later become Fort Sill. Among the hostages taken at Washita was a seven-month pregnant women called "Mona" (Mo-nah-se-tah). Benteen reported decades later that Custer consorted with the comely woman.[110] According to Benteen, these and other Custer peccadilloes were told to Libby Custer, who was "as cold-blooded a woman as I ever knew, in which respect the pair were admirably mated."[111] For whatever one cares to make of it, Libby Custer mentions Mona with respect in her book, *Following the Guidon*. Also, Custer is said to have invited his officers to take their pick of the Indian maidens, again according to Benteen.[112] It is difficult to sift embellishment from the truth, but one is justified in observing that if Benteen did not "take his pick," there is no compelling reason to believe that the other officers did so either.

Custer left camp in late January 1869 with forty chosen men, mounted on the best of the serviceable horses. They pursued the Arapahos in hellish marches that crippled half the cavalry mounts. The detachment finally stumbled on a sixty-five-lodge Arapaho village and, through patient persuasion, Custer induced the warriors to report to Fort Sill for enrollment in their agency. All this Custer accomplished without bloodshed.

After returning from patrol in February, Benteen was shown a copy of the *St. Louis Democrat* by Lieutenant Tom Custer, George Custer's brother. It contained an extract of Benteen's letter, published without his signature. "Why, Tom," Benteen artlessly exclaimed, "I wrote that myself." That night Custer assembled the officers inside a tent and, with a riding crop in hand, asserted that if he ever learned the identity of the author, he would hidewhip him. Benteen heard this from outside the tent and after cocking his revolver so that all could hear it, he entered the tent and informed his commanding officer: "General Custer, while I cannot father all of the blame you have asserted still, I guess I am the man you are after, and I am ready for the whipping promised." To this Custer blustered, "Colonel Benteen, I'll see you again, sir!"[113]

That was Benteen's version. One can only imagine how Custer felt about being held up to public ridicule by a subordinate officer, coming so soon after the unfavorable publicity Custer had received during his court martial.

Benteen claimed that he later related the incident to a reporter, who happened to be in camp. The reporter is supposed to have taken Benteen with him to see Custer in order to verify the facts, which, according to Benteen, caused Custer to wilt. The reporter is said to have later discussed the matter with General Sheridan, who had previously been a friend to Custer, but thereafter grew distant.[114] The stories sound wishful. It is highly unlikely that Sheridan would have become estranged from the man who had just won for Sheridan his first victory on the plains. Sheridan liberally praised Custer in his General Field Orders Number Six.

The regiment spent two months at Medicine Bluff Creek, helping to construct the new fort. It was later named Fort Sill, for a Civil War general.

Custer now turned his attention to the free-roaming Cheyenne who were still resisting settlement on their prescribed lands. On March 2, he led the regiment (and the 19th Kansas Volunteer Cavalry) in a wide loop through the Indian Territory, on the lookout for Cheyenne villages. Always short of grain, he started with half rations, then issued quarter rations and finally had no grain at all to feed the horses. His men ate mule meat, which according to Benteen, "had the odor of saddle blanket."[115] Several of the soldiers had to walk, after their horses died. Custer and his men followed a narrow trail and watched it become larger. On March 15, after a grueling march, they found a two-hundred-tepee Cheyenne village along the Sweetwater Creek in the Texas Panhandle, not far from the Washita battlefield.

With great courage, Custer entered the camp to parlay, accompanied by only the army surgeon and Lieutenant Cooke, whom he had borrowed from H Company. When it became apparent that the chiefs were dallying in order to prepare the village for flight, Custer sent word to Benteen to surround the tepees of the important chiefs, with two companies. Benteen brought up the troops at slow walk, taking care to conceal from the warriors any suggestion that the horses were exhausted from the march.

Custer then informed the chiefs that they were his prisoners, [116] whereupon the warriors and their families scattered, leaving behind the tepees and the four chiefs. Custer sent one of his prisoners to a Cheyenne camp fifteen miles away with the message that he was holding the hostages, in return for the release of two captive white women. The next day, the second village vanished. Custer sent word that if the white women were not delivered to him, he would hang the hostages on a nearby cottonwood tree. Eventually, the women were released in pitiful condition, after the payment of a sum of money equal to the amount paid for them by their owner.[117] Unlike Hancock, Custer spared the two-hundred-tepee village from destruction, to allow time for the tribes to move onto their reservation.[118] One by one, the bands agreed. To insure compliance, Custer had the hostages brought to new Fort Hays, along with the Washita women and children. The late winter campaign had fulfilled all of Sheridan's goals, without the firing of a single shot; but at a frightful cost to the health of the soldiers and their mounts. Regardless of the conflicting opinions about the Washita battle, Custer's brave actions in the late winter campaign merit the highest praise.

Other Cheyenne were later subdued by the western prong of Sheridan's attack. Major Eugene A. Carr and the 5th Cavalry defeated the western Cheyenne on July 11, in a savage blood bath (some call it a massacre) at Summit Springs, Colorado, while Custer was back in new Fort Hays. The southern prong served chiefly as "herders," to keep the tribes from scattering.

Custer set out March 22 on a five-day return march to Camp Supply, along the way meeting up with his sorely needed main wagon train. The regiment set up tents outside the stockade. According to Benteen, Custer again kept his men from entering Camp Supply until the trader had agreed to pay him $3,500, in return for which Custer allowed entry into the fort and gave the trader an ambulance, four mules and horses.[119] Perhaps, but the reader will later discover that Custer almost wrecked his career by reporting dishonest practices among post traders.

After the Civil War, the sutler was chosen by the regimental commander, with whom he often had a "private arrangement." During Custer's service on the southern plains, the post trader was selected by a committee of administration composed of three senior officers of the post, subject to approval by the post commander.[120] This arrangement also placed the trader under the control of the commanding officer.

The regiment arrived at Fort Dodge, 125 miles due north on April 4. Here, Benteen received payback for the Washita letter. Custer had a gloating Moylan inform Benteen that he was to remain at the fort, knowing that Benteen was anxious to return to his ailing wife. Also, Custer ordered Lieutenant Cooke to be detached from H Company and made his adjutant. Benteen was angered because Cooke left without saying a word and without settling his mess bill. Officers have a long tradition of dwelling on mess bills, often involving trivial amounts. Also, Custer chose to repay in spot cash the money he owed Benteen. Custer had obtained the money, according to Benteen, from a notorious "jaywalker" (a Union irregular during the Civil War), who was employed at Camp Supply and who ran a gambling operation on the side. Not quite all the money, since Benteen had lost nine dollars in a poker game.

Benteen soon found himself in command at Fort Dodge,[121] when the senior infantry officer was recalled during the great army reorganization of 1869, which reduced the infantry from forty-five to twenty-five regiments. Benteen used his new authority to grant himself a week's leave and set out for Fort Harker.[122] He made arrangements for his wife and son to depart for St. Louis, where Kate could recuperate in the care of her family.

Upon his return to Fort Dodge, Benteen was visited by the Inspector General of the Department. Benteen told him the reasons for his banishment and showed him the letter he had written to his friend in St. Louis. According to Benteen, the Inspector General saw to it that Benteen and H Company were recalled from their exile and sent to new Fort Hays, which would be their station for the next two years. Benteen also learned that Colonel A. J. Smith had resigned his commission.

Custer and the regiment had earlier arrived at new Fort Hays and were jubilantly welcomed as heroes. The post had recently been completed and families were beginning to settle in. The hostages were deposited in a large enclosed stockade within the fort, with walls fifteen feet high. The regiment then went into camp two miles from the fort.

Horses were turned out to graze on the open prairie, reducing by a third their need for fodder. Nearby, buffalo roamed the plains, occasionally providing the camp with juicy rump steaks and tongues.¹²³ Benteen was not fond of buffalo hunting. He found it a "very tame sport, too hard on horse flesh and...too, too simple."¹²⁴ Custer, on the other hand, thought buffalo hunting as exciting as hunting warriors.

The camp was situated on somewhat soggy ground, bounded by Big Creek on the north, and by a deep ravine to the south. Officers' tents were pitched along a bend in the creek. Nearby, the companies were bivouacked in long rows of A tents, with the first sergeant at the end. "A tents" have two upright poles connected by a ridge pole, with the sides of the tent sloping obliquely to the ground.¹²⁵ The Custer compound lay to the east end of the campground. Libby chose to live in camp, rather than with the other families inside the fort. The Custer quarters consisted of eight Sibley tents, which served as bedroom, sitting room, guest room, dining room, and coachman's room. There was also a tent for Eliza Brown, their black cook.

The trader's hut was situated south of camp. It had two billiard tables, for the use of the men and the officers. Nearby, a log theater had been built for amateur entertainments, which included concerts, minstrels and clog dancing. But the soldiers' thoughts were elsewhere. After *Taps!* a guard was posted around camp, to keep the soldiers from slipping away to Hays City.¹²⁶

New Fort Hays was an improvement of sorts over the decaying buildings of the old fort, but it was not a cheerful place. Scarcely a tree grew inside the post, and even the grass was stunted. Here the Benteens took up residence. Two officer families were assigned to each of the seven frame houses.

Quarters had to be furnished anew with each change of station. Common household articles were costly, whether purchased from the trader or through the mail. At times, a soldier might be prevailed upon to make an item of furniture. The wives fashioned rugs from discarded government blankets, bureaus from packing, and tables from boxes covered with calico.[127] The walls were adorned with pages from *Army and Navy Journal* and pictures from *Harper's Weekly*. Since the quarters were unplastered, the occupants could easily overhear the conversations of the other family sharing the building, as well as the cries of the children.

Soldiers were recruited to help with the chores, in return for a monthly stipend of five to ten dollars and exemption from guard duty. These "strikers" fetched water, fed the chickens, tended the officers' horses, and made themselves useful in the kitchen. They were especially conspicuous around mealtime. In the field, the striker would set up the officer's tent and care for his horses. While the company was in the field, the wife was left to her own devices. Knitting, stitching, painting, guitar playing and gossip[128] helped pass the lonely hours, while she waited anxiously for her husband's return.

The officer was allowed to purchase two government horses, for which he was issued grain and fodder at government expense.[129] His salary was adequate for the necessities of daily living, but was insufficient when his family required special medical care, or when his children were sent off to private boarding schools.

Women were confined to the fort, unless accompanied by an escort. Danger lurked even in the two miles between the fort and the camp. Every wife knew the tragic story of the Box woman and her three children who had been taken captive.[130] Rarely did the women get to see a warrior, apart from the hostages brought back from Washita and kept inside the stockade. The women were warned that if they saw a brave, he was either friendly or there were many others hidden from view.[131] At times, an adventurous woman might be taken onto the plains, riding sidesaddle. One woman visitor was amazed to see 100,000 buffalo grazing peacefully.[132]

A mile from new Fort Hays was Hays City, a wild, one-street town, where the Kansas Pacific Railroad stopped on its way to Denver, Colorado. The buildings were mostly frame, some with canvas roofing. The roofs of the shacks were fashioned from flattened tin cans.[133] Dance halls and gambling places abounded, and music played throughout the night. So often were the soldiers drugged and robbed, that they visited the town in groups of three or four. There was an active market in horses and goods stolen from the fort.[134] Since no suitable trees were on hand, hangings were conducted from the nearest railroad bridge. The sounds of gunfire from town carried over into camp, so that every day seemed like the Fourth of July. A special cemetery was started for the men who died in gunfights. The year

1869 was the most violent in Hays City's wild existence.[135]

The tall, handsome Wild Bill Hickok made his mark in Hays City as gambler and sometime marshal. According to one story (and there were many) Lieutenant Tom Custer had once crossed him and narrowly escaped with his life, but two of his soldiers were killed, and Tom Custer had to stay away from town for a few days.[136]

Libby often visited the train station in Hays City to meet visitors, who were appearing in ever-increasing numbers. Many had come west to see the famous "Wild Bill" Hickok, familiar to the readers of the dime novels. Others came to shoot a buffalo. Railroad passengers were encouraged to fire their rifles at the buffalo herds through an open window of their railroad car. P. T. Barnum and Grand Duke Alexei, son of Alexander II, Czar of Russia, were visitors to Hays City, as were senators, financiers and journalists. As many as 150 excursionists might arrive in one day, and Libby would make a valiant attempt to entertain them.[137] Meals, races and buffalo hunts were arranged for their pleasure. Officers' wives were enlisted to help, improvising as best they could.

A young woman on an officer-shopping mission during the "beau season" visited Fort Hays and wrote of her experiences.[138] She later married a 7th Cavalry officer. Kate Benteen and the other wives took her on a shopping trip to Hays City, entertained her and prepared refreshments, which included champagne punch, cake and ice cream, the latter made from condensed milk and canned fruit.[139] The Benteens kept a cow so that their son, Freddie, could have fresh milk. The Benteens also kept chickens. The ingenious Benteen once tried to hatch game eggs by setting a hen over the clutch.[140] If he had succeeded, no doubt we would have heard about it. The visitor complained that Benteen's son misbehaved during church services. Freddie could be dreadfully mischievous at times. At the age of twelve, he rode out alone from a fort to pick plums. The following day a huge grizzly was shot in the vicinity.[141]

Among the new officers at Fort Hays was Second Lieutenant Charles C. De Rudio, two years older than Benteen. De Rudio had led an extraordinary life.[142] Born in Belluno, Italy, then under Austrian rule, he was educated at the St. Luca Military Academy in Milan, but left the Austrian service during the Revolution of 1848, to fight for the liberation of Italy, under Giuseppe Garibaldi. With the failure of the Revolution of 1848, he became a conspirator in the vast network controlled by Giuseppe Mazzini. Exiled to England, he married a fifteen-year-old English girl and became embroiled in an attempt to assassinate Napoleon III, who the conspirators believed was hindering Italian unification. The plan misfired and, after narrowly escaping the guillotine, he was exiled to French Guyana, from where he escaped in an astonishing set of adventures. Returning to England, he was encouraged by Mazzini to emigrate to the United States. He enlisted in the army and was commissioned in the United States Colored Troops, later serving in Florida. After the war, he obtained a commission in the regular army and served in Kentucky in an infantry unit, before being transferred to the 7th Cavalry.

Like many other officers in the regiment, De Rudio was no horseman and had to learn to ride the army way. Even later, he was never quite at ease in "the hurricane seat." Most probably, he was foisted on Benteen, for Custer had little use for a man with an assassin's credentials. In the beginning, De Rudio was not popular in the regiment, since most officers took their prompt from Custer. Benteen defended De Rudio; encouraged him; taught him and watched him grow into a competent officer. Fortunate for De Rudio, his English wife became a close friend of Kate, and his daughter, Roma, played with Freddie Benteen.

Also newly arrived to the regiment was Major Marcus Reno, who reported in March 15, 1870. The thirty-six-year-old Reno was born in Carroltown, Illinois, and graduated from West Point in 1857, after having been suspended twice for accumulating excessive disciplinary demerits, which today do not seem particularly earth-shaking. He served in the Civil War, rising to become chief of staff for Sheridan's cavalry, then regimental commander of the 12th Pennsylvania Cavalry. A brigadier general's brevet in the volunteer army was conferred June 11, 1865, together with a colonel's brevet in the regular army. For some unaccountable reason, he was addressed as "Colonel Reno" and never as "General Reno." Perhaps there was no room for two generals in one regiment. Reno had married a wealthy Philadelphia woman, who completely detested army life. He used every opportunity to seek detached duty, away from the frontier fort.

Benteen and Reno did not quite hit it off. Around this time, the army was replacing the single-shot trapdoor .52 caliber Sharps carbine with the Spencer repeating carbine. The former was a more powerful weapon with greater range; the latter, rapid-firing but with a rather weak muzzle velocity. This exchange engendered much controversy among the officers. Reno was scheduled to serve with the small arms board and already may have had strong convictions.

Soon after his arrival at Fort Hays, Reno brawled with Benteen in the trader's post. According to Benteen, Reno had tried to bully him, so Benteen called him a "dirty S.O.B." and slapped his face, offering to give him satisfaction.[143] Perhaps the quarrel happened as Benteen described it twenty years later, but there were many, many fights in the officers' bar, most of which were forgotten by the next morning. At any rate, the incident, if indeed it did occur, did not prevent the two officers from performing their duties away from the trader's post, and it was Benteen who alone stood by Reno when all the others turned their backs to him.

The regiment had long since split into Custer-friend and Custer-foe camps, with Benteen foremost among the foes. There were important advantages to being in the Custer clique. Not only might your wife be welcomed into Libby Custer's social circle, but you might receive preferential assignments.

George Custer hoped to be appointed regimental commander when Colonel A. J. Smith retired in May

Captain Benteen [Benteen Photo Collection, Hargrett Rare Book and Manuscript Library, University of Georgia]

Major Marcus Reno, 7th Cavalry. [U. S. Military Institute]

1869, but, instead, the assignment went to Colonel Samuel D. Sturgis, who arrived at Fort Leavenworth to assume command. Sturgis was no admirer of Custer. After the Civil War had ended, Sturgis reverted to lieutenant colonel in the regular army and for a brief time had served under Custer, who was then Major General of Volunteers, before reverting to his permanent rank of captain in the peacetime army.

Custer's adversaries compiled a long roster of stories about Custer chicanery, and Benteen was an avid scribe. For example, Benteen later wrote that Colonel Sturgis confided to him that while in Texas after the Civil War, Custer fiddled with the quartermaster contracts,[144] etc. There is no record of any action being taken against Custer, so we cannot distinguish fact from fiction.

The summer seemed to bring no respite from the warrior attacks. Eleven warrior raids were recorded. Within a month of the Washita battle, small bands of Cheyenne dog soldiers were back harassing settlers, railroad workers and soldiers. Custer sent off small detachments to halt the incursions, giving the junior officers an opportunity to command. Happily, the attacks subsided after the hostages were released from the stockade and returned to their tribes.[145]

As autumn 1869 approached, seven companies were distributed to the other forts in Kansas and the Indian Territory. H Company remained at Fort Hays, and three fortunate companies accompanied Custer to Fort Leavenworth. Two miles from the fort was Leavenworth City, more than just a prairie town, and renowned for its well-constructed streets and attractive stores.[146] In November 1869, Custer left for Monroe, Michigan, to inspect a property adjoining his parents' home, stopping off along the way to visit the Audubon Club in Detroit and General Sheridan in Chicago.

Custer returned to Leavenworth in the spring of 1870 and began a successful literary career, writing articles for the sportsmen's magazines. Some insist that Libby Custer wrote the stories, but no one who has read Custer's descriptive and fluent letters to Libby can deny his unmistakable literary talents. He arrived back at Fort Hays on May 18.

Benteen, too, had a brief respite from garrison life. He was sent to St. Louis in the spring of 1870 for three months of temporary duty, to inspect horses.[147] Doubtless, his family accompanied him. When he returned to Fort Hays, the regimental encampment outside the fort had been renamed "Camp Sturgis." The name change had little effect on the desertions.

Hostile activity by now had greatly diminished, although rumors and false reports still required dozens of "Indian chasings." A visit to Hays City seemed more perilous than a trip on the plains; but random warrior attacks did not altogether disappear.

Benteen served in Colorado from July to October 1870[148] with few difficulties, thanks in large measure to his Delaware scouts. The hunting was excellent. Accompanied by his setter, he brought down ten canvasback ducks with his ten-gauge double-barrel shotgun, using a number six "chilled" lead load.[149] A "chilled" load contains more than one percent antimony to increase hardness. Upon his return to Fort Hays,

The Southern Plains

Benteen, as usual, harvested the Custer gossip. Custer is supposed to have compelled an officer to resign for consorting with a Leavenworth prostitute. This, Benteen asserts, was sheer hypocrisy, since Custer had done the very same thing.[150]

Officers came and went, leaving their mark on garrison life. Some resigned to quit the plains; others to seek better opportunities in civilian life. Many officers were only nominally assigned to the 7th Cavalry, since they had staff duties elsewhere but were required to be carried on the regimental rolls. Officers were shuffled about within the regiment, sometimes arbitrarily. Captain Thomas H. French was a late replacement. A short, somewhat pudgy officer, he had been commissioned from the ranks during the Civil War and had remained in the regular army as a commissioned officer, rising to captain two years before his transfer to the 7th Cavalry. From the start, he was a heavy drinker, but Benteen had deep respect for his courage.

To add to the uncertainties of army life, the army had convened review panels ("Benzine Boards"), to weed out the inefficient officers. Colonel Sturgis submitted the names of Lieutenant Donald McIntosh and Captain Thomas Weir; but Custer came to their rescue. Also named was Lieutenant Edward Godfrey, a West Point graduate, but Colonel Sturgis was persuaded to withdraw his submission,[151] perhaps at Custer's insistence. Several other officers were also reported. One of them, a Custer ally in H Company, was forced to resign. Benteen made no effort to support him.

In October 1870, Custer departed for Fort Leavenworth, taking with him several companies and leaving behind at Fort Hays H and M companies, with Benteen in command. Benteen moved the companies inside the fort, in preparation for winter. When Lieutenant Tom Custer of M Company requested a transfer to his brother's headquarters at Fort Leavenworth, Benteen refused the request on the grounds that he could not dispense with his services; but granted him a short leave.

Custer went on leave in January 1871, first visiting Monroe, Michigan, where he left Libby. He then traveled to New York, to explore the opportunities in civilian life. He frequented Delmonico's, the opera, the theater and dinner parties. He also cultivated wealthy New Yorkers, whom he tried to interest in a silver mine near Georgetown, Colorado.[152] The undercapitalized mine never prospered, and Custer was left with a promissory note for $13,000. Thoughts of entering civilian life were deferred.

By February 1871, Kate Benteen was fed up with army life and left for Atlanta, much to Benteen's annoyance. She was persuaded to return only after Benteen had received a new assignment and had threatened to give away the furniture.[153]

In accordance with the army policy of rotating troops whenever possible (except for the black regiments), the 7th Cavalry was ordered south for two years of constabulary duty. Union troops were distributed throughout the former Confederate states, where they were received by the disenfranchised white community with thinly concealed hostility. At the time, the southern states were governed by discordant legislatures, predominantly white, except for South Carolina; composed of an aggregate of venal and hopelessly impractical politicians. Their laws—some good, many bad—were scorned by the white population. Violence replaced order, and law enforcement was daily challenged by such secret organizations as the Ku Klux Klan, the White Camellia and the White Brotherhood. The military struggled to maintain order by exercising the authority granted it by the Enforcement Act of 1870, which authorized martial law in many southern districts.

Benteen established his battalion headquarters in Louisville, Kentucky, and remained there for almost two years. Another battalion under Major Reno was sent to Spartanburg, South Carolina, where it succeeded in suppressing the activities of the local Klan. Benteen was visited by Colonel Custer and his adjutant, Lieutenant Cooke, now very much a Custer man. They tried to induce Benteen to have Tom Custer transferred from South Carolina to Elizabethtown, Kentucky, where Colonel Custer was stationed. Benteen artfully referred the matter to Colonel Sturgis, who erupted when he heard the story. George Custer later grumbled to Kate that Benteen always did the opposite of what he wanted.[154]

Louisville was also the headquarters of Brigadier General Alfred H. Terry, newly appointed to the Department of the South. His previous station had been in the Department of the Dakotas. Terry was a former lawyer who had steadily advanced in rank during the

Civil War. For his gallant capture of the almost impregnable Fort Fisher, North Carolina, which guarded Wilmington, the last great Confederate seaport, he had received from a grateful Congress a commission of brigadier general in the regular army.

Louisville was the largest city in Kentucky, renowned for its elegant residences and excellent hotels. While at Louisville, Terry saw a great deal of Benteen and formed a favorable impression of him and the 7th Cavalry.

Benteen gave his junior officers and NCO's an opportunity to demonstrate their talents. He divided the companies into small units, which assisted the U.S. marshals in enforcing writs, collecting taxes, destroying illicit distilleries and suppressing Klan activities.[155]

While in Louisville, Benteen was inducted into the International Order of Odd Fellows. The society had found its way to American shores from England in the early nineteenth century. Its benevolent purposes were "to visit the sick, relieve the distressed, bury the dead and educate the orphan." The membership steadily grew, so that by the 1890's, it surpassed the Freemasons.[156] Benteen remained an active member, permanently enrolled in the St. Louis Lodge # 5 I.O.O.F.[157] Custer, Reno, De Rudio and Charley Benteen chose the Freemasons. Benteen let little interfere with Odd Fellow duties. In his second letter home after the Little Bighorn Battle, he mentions lodge business.

Benteen used his stay in Louisville as an opportunity to purchase some fine Kentucky horses for the regiment and for himself. Since the Civil War, Kentucky had become the preeminent horse breeding state, having supplanted Virginia and North Carolina, whose pastures and stables had been ruined.[158] New recruits arrived to increase company strength to the authorized sixty men, but the number was not maintained. Among the new arrivals was a young German immigrant, Charles Windolph, who was greatly impressed with Benteen. "I thought he was about the finest looking soldier I had ever seen," he later wrote.[159] Another recruit was Joseph McCurry, a young Pennsylvanian, who, to Benteen's delight, turned into a fine baseball pitcher.

It was in Nashville where the Benteen Base Ball Club was formally organized. Fifty men enrolled, and the club purchased eighteen baseball bats and a dozen baseballs.[160] At the time, bats were of different sizes and made of various woods, but were restricted to a diameter of 2.5 inches. The baseball was stuffed with rubber and was pitched underhand. The players did not use gloves, except for the catcher, who sometimes wore a leather, fingerless mitt.

In April 1872, Catherine gave birth to a baby girl, Fanny Benteen, in Louisville. Later that summer, First Lieutenant Francis (Frank) Gibson was transferred to H Company from Moylan's A Company. His wife's sister was married to Lieutenant Donald McIntosh of G Company. Gibson tried hard, but was not an outstanding officer. He had been commissioned from civilian life without previous military service, which may have been the reason that Custer had him transferred to Benteen's company.

Custer was stationed in Elizabethtown, Kentucky with two companies. He and Libby first boarded in a fine townhouse, then settled into a furnished cottage. He passed the time visiting breeding farms and racing horses, mostly without success. In the course of his stay in Kentucky, he lost $10,000 buying, selling and betting on horses.[161] His debts were a further incentive for Custer to write articles for the sportsmen's magazines.

In January 1872, at the request of General Sheridan, Custer accompanied Grand Duke Alexei, third son of Czar Alexander II, on a buffalo hunt lasting several weeks. Afterwards, the party went by rail to Louisville, where Libby Custer joined them. A grand ball was held in the Grand Duke's honor, before the group proceeded by boat to New Orleans. There is no mention of Benteen being introduced to the royal entourage.

THE NORTHERN PLAINS

The Fort Laramie Treaty of 1878 had been concluded with the Sioux the year following the Medicine Lodge Treaty. By the terms of the accord, the Lakota Sioux were given the western part of what would later be South Dakota, including the Black Hills; and also hunting rights in "unceded lands" north of the Platte River and east of the Bighorn Mountains. Unceded lands are territories occupied by those Sioux and Northern Cheyenne whose chiefs had not been signatories to the Fort Laramie Treaty.

The Lakota, one of three great branches of the Sioux, occupied the northern plains. They numbered more than thirty thousand and lived in harmony with the five thousand Northern Cheyenne.[1] Most of the Lakota Sioux and Northern Cheyenne lived on the Great Sioux Reserve, but left it from spring to autumn to hunt with the three thousand Lakota and four hundred Northern Cheyenne who roamed the unceded land.

Around 1871, the Northern Pacific Railroad began survey operations along the Yellowstone Valley, in preparation for the construction of a railroad west to the Pacific. The Yellowstone country lay in unceded land, occupied by the roamers. Retaliation by the Lakota and Northern Cheyenne was immediate. An infantry expedition was sent in 1871 to protect the surveying parties, and another in 1872; but their efforts were insufficient.

Upon his return in 1873 to the Department of the Dakotas, General Alfred Terry concluded that he could better protect the survey parties with cavalry, and, remembering Benteen, he arranged to have the 7th Cavalry transferred to his command. The Department was based in St. Paul, Minnesota (Fort Snelling), and included Minnesota, and the Dakota and Montana territories.

In April 1873, the 7th Cavalry were ordered to the northern plains to garrison the forts along the Missouri River and its branches, and two to four forts elsewhere in the Dakota Territory. During the summer, the regiment was expected to protect the Northern Pacific survey party and also to provide an escort for a government team surveying the Canadian boundary.

The regiment assembled two miles outside of Memphis, where it awaited transportation. Nathan Bedford Forrest was then a resident of Memphis, but it is not known if he visited the encampment, since by then he was a very busy railroad executive. The townspeople flocked to the regimental drills. The officers were popular with the ladies, and the troops with the public, especially after payday. Ever the recorder of Custer gossip, Benteen states that he learned from De Rudio that Custer had helped a tavern owner obtain a trader's concession, in return for a gratuity of $1,100.[2]

Three steamers finally arrived, and the regiment was transported to Cairo, Illinois. There, they boarded a train and began an exhausting trip, interrupted by frequent stops to exercise, groom and water the horses.[3] After a week of travel, they reached Yankton, Dakota Territory, and the regiment set up camp a mile from town. Yankton was described by an army wife as consisting of "a few houses built of cottonwood or fresh pine, some rutted dirt roads and a frame hostelry called a hotel."[4] The town had first drawn settlers at the end of 1868, lured by the advertisements of land-speculating companies. With the coming of the Illinois Central Railroad to nearby Sioux City, a veritable "Dakota Boom" erupted, and ten thousand settlers arrived to break sod.[5]

Throughout their stay in Yankton, the soldiers were made to feel welcome. The Odd Fellows were organizing a lodge, which must have interested Benteen. The army notified the officers that henceforth they would be required to purchase their own horses. Several had been using government mounts and feared that the horse dealers would now drive up prices.[6] In March 1873, a public ball was held for the regiment, and the army wives drank "their last drought from the bowl of dissipation and festivity."[7] The next month a fierce spring blizzard struck the camp, dumping two feet of snow. The soldiers were hurried into town to seek shelter in whatever structure was available, narrowly escaping the ravages of the storm.

Word reached the wives that the officers' quarters at Fort Rice and Fort Abraham Lincoln were not ready for occupation. The women were furious, but most were resigned to finding temporary accommodations elsewhere.

With the first appearance of the new grass, the ten companies set out on the five-hundred-mile Yellowstone expedition. Baggage and supplies went by riverboat, which kept pace with the regiment and tied up nightly near the camp.[8] When snags or sandbars interrupted travel, the boats used a small donkey engine to pull the riverboat over the obstruction. One end of the rope would be attached to the donkey engine and the other end to a firm object beyond the obstruction.[9] A few wives came with the riverboat, huddled in a little cabin behind the pilot house. They hoped "to storm Fort Rice in a body, take to tents, throw themselves on the charity of the government and the 'inns' at that post."[10] In other words, they wanted to see for themselves. When the boat reached Fort Rice, one glance at the unfinished quarters convinced the women of the futility of their trip and off they went to join the other wives in the squalid hotels of Bismarck and Yankton or the more acceptable one in St. Paul.

The regiment left Fort Rice on June 20, 1873, marching west cross country. With them went the Northern Pacific surveyors and engineers and nineteen infantry companies, under the over-all command of

Colonel David Stanley, 22nd Infantry, a heavy drinker. Also accompanying them were two English milords, along for the adventure, and a bevy of journalists, to keep the public informed.[11] The order of march was strictly followed: cavalry, surveyors, infantry, train, cavalry. Custer rode ahead with eight cavalry companies, and the other two cavalry companies flanked the wagons and brought up the rear. Camp was laid out in a parallelogram with the company and officers' tents pitched on the long sides and headquarters on the small side, facing a river or creek. Along the way, Custer worked feverishly, at times well into the night. He sent fossils to the University of Michigan,[12] animals to the Bronx Zoo, and, having mastered the rudiments of taxidermy, sent mounted specimens to the Detroit Audubon Club.[13]

Benteen added to his store of Custer tales. One story involved Custer's gift of an H Company horse to the civilian brother of a captain in the Custer clique.[14] Benteen made Colonel Stanley aware of the matter, and Stanley resolved to take stern action against Custer. Before that happened, Stanley drank himself into an alcoholic stupor, and the matter was forgotten. When he recovered his senses, Stanley had a cache of liquor destroyed, but not before Benteen and several of the officers, each managed to salvage a quart.[15] Other liquor supplies were soon broached, and there continued to be much drinking and gambling among the officers.[16]

Also, from his inexhaustible trove of Custer stories, Benteen relates that Custer had sex with his black female cook, which, according to Benteen, he had also done during the late war. The charge is most unfair. The woman who had served him during the Civil War and until recently, was Eliza Brown Denison, a loyal servant and a beloved companion to Libby Custer. She is affectionately mentioned by Libby in her books. Eliza later married a small town lawyer and visited Libby in New York in 1886, where Libby accommodated her at the Fifth Avenue Hotel and showed her the sights.[17] Eliza had left the Custers' employ before the Yellowstone Expedition and had been replaced by an elderly black couple, Mary and Ham. Mary had accompanied the expedition and cooked for Custer on an iron stove.

After a few days' march, the column reached the badlands, an area ninety-five miles long and thirty-five miles wide, the site of a smoldering subterranean coal deposit or an ancient lava bed.[18] The procession passed single file through precipitous defiles and wild cactus, with the ever-present threat of needles, which could pierce the horses' fetlocks. Innumerable rifts in the baked clay surface, some twenty feet deep and four feet wide, made wagon traffic perilous.[19] Soldiers scrambled to collect fossils. Benteen was assigned to the wagon train and did a masterful job in bringing the wagons through, but it took five days of brutal march and the construction of many bridges to traverse the thirty-five miles of badlands.[20] On July 31, the column reached the Yellowstone River. Here, Custer detached some companies, H Company among them, to guard a supply depot named Stanley's Stockade, twenty miles up the Glendive River before it joins the Yellowstone. The column then crossed the Yellowstone River by riverboat and proceeded along the northern bank.

Benteen wiled away the hours at Stanley's Stockade in outdoor sport. The officers hunted elk, grouse, mountain sheep, and wolves. Benteen especially enjoyed fishing for catfish, which he preferred to trout. He had brought along many yards of strong cotton line, which enabled his men to catch thousands of channel catfish.[21] Benteen wrote to his wife in his beautiful script, decorated with small amusing sketches. Not only do the letters reflect a strong family attachment, but a healthy sexual bond as well.

The Stanley expedition marched westward, and the surveyors began their measurements. Supplies were plentiful, and the band entertained at night. The column had two sharp clashes with the Sioux in which four soldiers and two civilians were killed. Warriors relied heavily on the artifices of decoy or ambush.[22] At the first encounter, Custer had been following a decoy and narrowly avoided a trap. Five days later, on the northern bank of the Yellowstone, Custer suddenly found himself caught between fire from warrior sharpshooters perched atop a bluff and others firing from across the river. General Stanley arrived in time to disperse the warriors with two rounds from the three-inch ordnance ("Rodman") gun.[23] The journalists kept the public informed.

By the time the column reached the Bighorn River, the financial crisis of 1873 had erupted, halting Northern Pacific operations. The surveyors concluded their measurements, and the column started back, along the way retrieving the detachment at Stanley's Stockade. Benteen and his men presented the column with a feast of catfish.[24]

While still in the field, Custer announced the postings of his companies. Soldiers and officers would both have preferred Fort Lincoln, because of its proximity to Bismarck, across the river. Custer stationed four companies at Fort Lincoln; four companies at Fort Rice, including H Company and an infantry company; two companies along the Canadian border and the rest in forts along the Missouri. Major Marcus Reno was assigned to Canadian boundary duty where he remained until 1874, then took a leave of absence for one year, to adjust to the death of his wife.[25]

The reunited column started out for Fort Rice on September 12. Custer avoided the badlands, but had Benteen march his company through the region, to enable the surveyors to take further measurements. This was not an unreasonable order, since H Company had been idle during much of the Yellowstone march. Benteen was delighted to revisit the badlands, especially its more verdant section, where hunting was excellent. By now he had tired of antelope meat and looked forward to hunting bighorn sheep, which were found in the region. The bighorn meat is reputed to be tender and juicy, but gamey, unless hung for a few days.[26] Because the bridges erected during the initial journey were still intact, Benteen's second trip through the badlands took but one day.[27]

Captain Benteen of the 7th U. S. Cavalry in Nashville, 1872. His hair is beginning to turn white. [Benteen Photo Collection, Hargrett Rare Book and Manuscript Library, University of Georgia]

Catherine Norman Benteen in 1872. [Benteen Photo Collection, Hargrett Rare Book and Manuscript Library, University of Georgia]

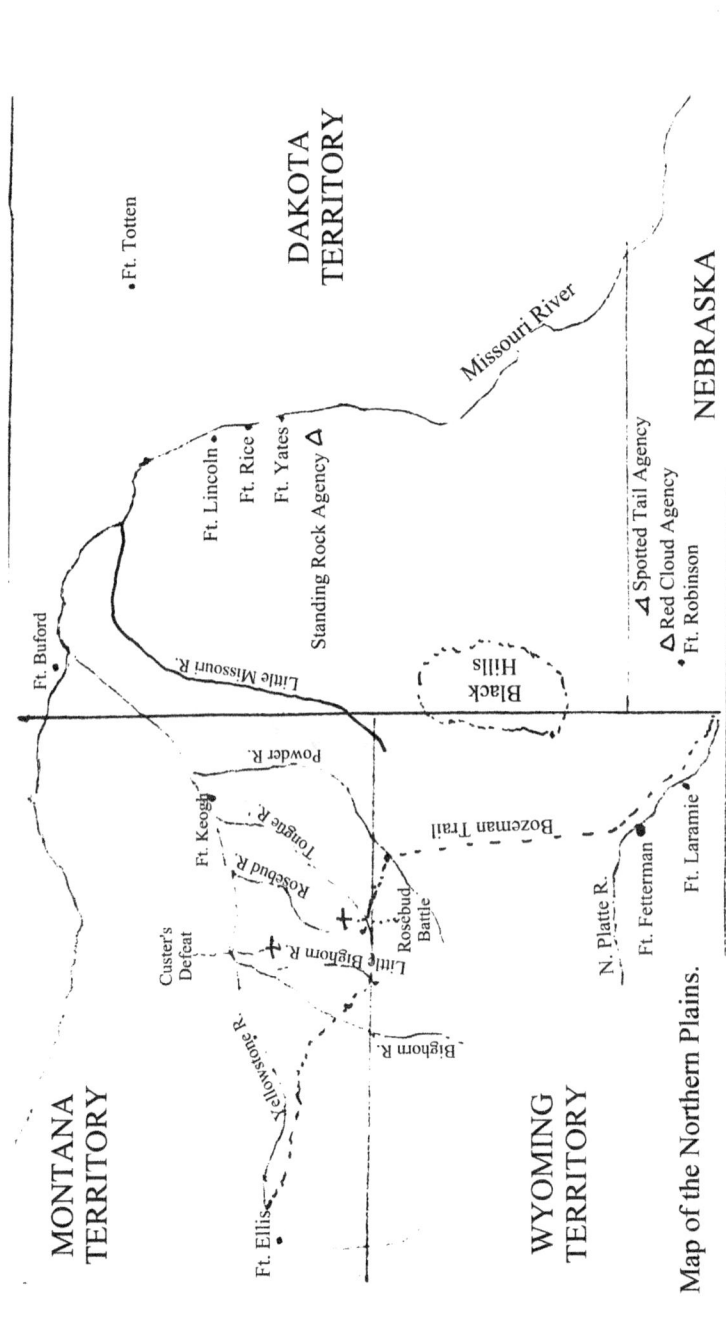

Map of the Northern Plains.

Major Benteen in dress uniform in later years.
[Benteen Photo Collection, Hargrett Rare Book and Manuscript Library, University of Georgia]

The expedition reached Fort Rice on September 22, 1873, and promptly disbanded. The Benteens would spend the next five years at Fort Rice.

The fort was stockaded on three sides, and had two manned blockhouses and two sally ports. It was situated on the west bank of the Missouri about thirty miles southeast of Fort Abraham Lincoln and thirty-five miles from the Standing Rock Lakota Agency. Unlike Fort Lincoln, which had Bismarck across the Missouri, Fort Rice was off by its lonely self. A visitor from Fort Lincoln described it as "the conception of some nightmare"[28] and "one of the most God forsaken spots on earth."[29] The fort had two barracks which housed four companies, and seven two-family officers' quarters. The log stables were inside the post, with the name of each horse inscribed over its stall. The corral, grazing grounds and garden plots were all outside the fort and readily accessible to the passing warriors.

As elsewhere, quarters were assigned by rank and had to be vacated when the occupant was "ranked out" by a senior officer.[30] A major was the nominal post commander. He detested garrison life and used every opportunity to seek detached duty elsewhere. The regiment was entitled to three majors, but seldom saw more than one. When the regular major was away, Benteen became the post commander and his wife, the chatelaine. She was tall and thin, somewhat in contrast to her clean-shaven, now heavy-set husband. The younger wives found Kate sympathetic and helpful. Her closest friend was Lisa De Rudio, the wife of Benteen's second lieutenant.

In summer, blistering heat plagued the fort, with hoards of insects adding to the misery. In the fall, when the heating stoves were started, rattlesnakes left their dens in the foundations and appeared in the quarters. During the winter, temperatures could drop to forty-five degrees below zero. A black plainsman, Isaiah Dorman, had the wood contract, but despite his well-appreciated efforts, wood was hard to come by, apart from cottonwood.[31] Dismounted drills and the manual of arms were all that could be performed during the snow months, and these only two or three times weekly.[32] Sufficient fodder and grain always had to be on hand, especially after river traffic shut down. While in garrison, the army horse required a daily ration of fourteen pounds of grain and fourteen pounds of hay.[33]

During the first winter, the Benteens were again plunged into despair, when little Fanny died. She was buried in the large post graveyard. Since the establishment of the fort in 1864, the cemetery had accumulated the graves of several hundred enlisted men and scouts, as well as several warrior scaffolds.[34] Servants were buried outside the graveyard.[35]

Maintenance within the fort was often neglected, since the post was scheduled for closure. Warping of doors and windows was especially exasperating. The quarters reeked of buffalo robes, even though the hides had been thoroughly aired and rubbed with camphor to disguise the smell.[36] Dining room tables, ironing boards, beds or benches were improvised from planks set on wooden horses. On the infrequent occasions when warriors were allowed inside the fort, wives might be startled to see five or six strange faces pressing up against the window panes of their parlors.[37]

Entertainment was held in a converted sawmill, and there was talk of raising money for a billiard table.[38] The same books and magazines were read and reread until retired from wear. Alcohol was readily accessible to soldier and officer, even inside the fort. It arrived in mislabeled bottles or in kegs pushed overboard from the riverboats. The barrels were retrieved by the traders and the contents sold in tents outside of camp.

Not all the Fort Rice officers shared Benteen's animosity toward Custer. The colonel's brother, Lieutenant Tom Custer, was stationed at Fort Rice in M Company, but was frequently called away to Lincoln on detached duty. Other Fort Rice officers in the Custer clique included First Lieutenant Edward S. Godfrey, a young West Point graduate, who managed to remain on correct terms with Benteen. On the other hand, Benteen detested First Lieutenant Edwin G. Mathey, an ardent Custer supporter, for his lack of officer qualities. The Custer-Benteen feud never waned. When a civilian brother of an officer in the Custer clique applied for a commission, Benteen declined to sign the petition. The officer was commissioned anyway, but not in the cavalry.

Thirty miles upriver from Fort Rice was Fort Abraham Lincoln, the regimental headquarters. The fort had the usual army design, but was of new construction. High up on the bluff overlooking the garrison was a forlorn infantry post, which protected the fort when the cavalry was in the field. When the cavalry wives visited the infantry station, the mules pulling the ambulance had difficulty climbing the hill.[39] Presiding over the forty women in the Fort Lincoln social circle was its doyenne, Libby Custer, who carefully guarded her husband's interests. "Instinct guided me always in detecting the general's enemies," she wrote, "and when I found them out, a struggle began between us as to my manner of treating them."[40]

Across the river from Fort Lincoln was the town of Bismarck, accessible by an hour-long rowboat trip.[41] This "wretched railhead hamlet" had a muddy main street bordered by shacks, general stores, fodder houses, laundries and saloons. There was a long-standing hostility between the citizens and the army, especially after the railroads closed down in the Depression of 1873, and the mail had to be carried by the army. Wary of the fleecing they received in town, many soldiers preferred to take their custom to a small collection of shacks, called "Whiskey Point," situated at the Bismarck ferry landing a mile outside of town. Custer quickly became estranged from the citizens and merchants of Bismarck. On one occasion he sent a troop into town to retrieve sacks of grain that had been stolen from the fort, only to discover them in the mayor's warehouse. At another time, he had forty or fifty citizens arrested for defrauding the government.[42]

During the summer of 1874, the 7th Cavalry was ordered to complete within sixty days a long-postponed expedition to the Black Hills.[43] The declared purpose of the expedition was to find a suitable site for a fort, but the real objective was to determine whether gold was present in payable quantities. The Native Americans saw the incursion as a violation of the Laramie Treaty, but the government insisted that the accord had made ample provision for government officials to enter the area on official business.[44]

The column assembled at Fort Abraham Lincoln. It consisted of ten companies of cavalry, two infantry companies and a large supply train of 110 wagons. With the expedition went miners, scientists, photographers and, of course, the all-important journalists. Custer was a gracious host to the officers from the outlying forts, but Libby Custer did not hesitate to show a frigid but correct demeanor to the officers on poor terms with her husband. Benteen described her as "penurious," adding that she put out little in the way of food to unwelcome guests.[45] A visitor to Fort Lincoln, soon to be an officer's wife, described Benteen as having "eyes of great brilliance and a precision of glance that was quietly piercing...He was compactly built, had a firm mouth and square chin, and walked with burro-sure footedness."[46] By now his hair had turned white.

The soldiers had been issued the new 1873 Springfield trapdoor .45/55 single-shot carbine, which fired a copper-alloy cartridge, having an effective range of three hundred yards, although it could reach three times farther. The army had a sizable supply of the old Springfield muskets, which it had converted to breechloaders. When the carbine was used for hunting, a seventy-grain cartridge might be substituted for the usual fifty-five grain load. Both cartridges had the same size, wadding filling the extra space in the fifty-five.

Both had an internal Benet cup primer,[47] which precluded reuse of the empty cartridge. Later, objections would be raised that the soft copper-alloy cartridge jammed when the weapon overheated, but this criticism was not voiced between 1874-1876. Also beginning to make an appearance was the six-shot, .45 caliber Colt "Peacemaker" revolver, of solid frame type, which fired metallic cartridges. Both carbine and revolver were considered quality arms.

The expedition left on July 2, 1874, in *Heavy Marching Order!* Each soldier had a rolled up woolen blanket on the pommel of the saddle, an overcoat on the cantle of the saddle, a nosebag with curry comb and brush on one of the rings of the saddle, haversack and canteen on another ring. Lariat rope and picket pin were attached to a third ring, and side lines attached to the fourth.[48] In the baggage train were tents and collapsible furniture for the comfort of the officers. While the regiment was on the usual march, the soldiers' meal was prepared by a trooper who had been designated as cook for a period of ten days. If his efforts met with the approval of the men, he might be accorded the privilege for longer periods. Each officers' mess had its own cook, usually a striker, who prepared a sit-down meal for the officers in the company.

After an unhurried three-hundred-mile march to the Black Hills, the column reached its destination. The Black Hills covered an area 150 miles by fifty miles,[49] blanketed with dark pines, which emitted a fragrant odor. The land was in full blossom, and the biologists identified fifty-two varieties of wildflowers. Soldiers decked their horses with garlands of flowers.

The miners had no difficulty finding gold in exploitable quantities. Teamsters and wagonmasters sunk numbered posts, so that they could later stake a claim when the hills were legally opened for mining.[50] Custer immediately dispatched a short message to General Sheridan by way of the nearest telegraph office at Fort Laramie, informing him of the discovery. The *New York Tribune* correspondent speculated that a miner could earn ten cents a pan and could shovel 1,500 pans a day into his sluices.[51] While the scientists were collecting specimens, Benteen's baseball team, calling themselves the "Athletics," lost a game to the Fort Abraham Lincoln team but defeated a pick-up team of wagoners.[52] Benteen celebrated the victory by opening a bottle of champagne.

After completing the survey, the expedition started back. Along the way, a soldier in H Company died, the second death since the expedition began. Custer would not delay the march, so Benteen conducted the burial service. When the column passed an abandoned Lakota campsite, Custer boasted to a scout that the 7th Cavalry could whip all the Sioux it could find. As the column neared Fort Lincoln, Custer posted a guard, to prevent the news of the gold discovery from escaping prematurely. The earlier message to Sheridan was meant to be private. After two months in the field, the soldiers arrived at Fort Lincoln, with faded hair, burned skin, unshaven faces and patched clothing.

Some of the members of the expedition, Benteen among them, had doubts about the extent of the gold discovery. Similar reservations prompted the government the following year to send another prospecting party to the Black Hills. The second expedition confirmed the presence of rich gold deposits but reported that the loads required hard rock mining and the use of sophisticated equipment. Notwithstanding, the trickle of miners progressed to a torrent.

No sooner had the regiment returned, when orders were received for six companies, H Company among them, to be dispatched to South Carolina and to the Department of the Gulf.

Louisiana had been seething with civil unrest, especially after the contentious gubernatorial election of 1872, which left the state with two governors and dual legislatures. Bands of white supporters of the Democratic governor, calling themselves Knights of the White Camellia, roamed the countryside, terrorizing the black population. On May 10, 1873, in Colfax, 160 miles from New Orleans, 150-200 blacks had been murdered outside the court house. The discord spread to New Orleans, where the Metropolitan Police, under the Republican governor's control, fought with the white militia. On September 14, 1874, at the Cabildo, the clash left twenty-five dead and 105 wounded strewn over the streets of the city.

Custer remained at Fort Abraham Lincoln, engaged in writing his *Life on the Plains*, (which Benteen called,

Lie on the Plains),[53] a compilation of the articles that had been previously published in *Galaxy* magazine.

In September of 1874, the two battalions traveled by train to St. Paul, from where they were transported by riverboat to New Orleans, since the upper Mississippi River ran high that autumn. They joined the fifteen infantry companies that had been rushed to the city. By the time the Dakota detachment arrived, the riots had subsided. Benteen was permitted to establish his headquarters in New Orleans, and the other cavalry companies were sent to Shreveport, Texas; Breaux Bridge, Louisiana and Alabama, where they set about restoring order. During its five-month stay in New Orleans, Benteen's battalion was the only cavalry in the city.[54]

New Orleans had many amenities to offer the army. The St. Charles Hotel, dubbed by some "the Army and Navy Club," was a popular meeting place for the officers. The army participated in the high life, including the Mardi Gras parade, the Rex Balls and the Washington Artillery Ball.[55] In his spare time, Benteen studied French, which the West Point officers so often injected into the conversation. The cadets were required to take two years of French at the Military Academy. Benteen spent many hours training his two fine mares, each 16 ½ hands high. He did not enter them in a race, since they had not been properly prepared. General Sheridan visited New Orleans, and when he saw Benteen, he hugged him in delight. The two went often to the races.[56]

While in New Orleans, Kate gave birth to a baby boy, Theodore Norman Benteen, in April 1875. They hired a young black man to help with domestic chores. This was a Benteen innovation. White girls lasted only two to six weeks before they married a soldier, so hiring agencies were instructed to send only the homeliest. Their usual salary was thirty-five dollars a month. Black servant girls usually lasted only one frigid winter and then were gone.[57] The salary paid to the young man is not known, but the Custers paid their black servants twenty dollars a month.

In May 1875, the detachment was ordered back to the Dakotas. It traveled by train to Yankton and marched seventy-five miles to Fort Randall. The plains were alive with golden plover, which Benteen hunted from horseback, riding leisurely through the fields of verbena and wild pansy.

Benteen was assigned a battalion and given several weeks to prepare for a trip back to the Black Hills. He was ordered to evict prospectors who were inundating the region. In its spare time, the Benteen Base Ball Club challenged all comers and generally won by a lopsided score. Since Nashville, Benteen's team had won twelve of their seventeen games.

The battalion reached the Black Hills after an uneventful march, and prepared for an extended stay. Benteen had the opportunity to closely observe the miners at work. He watched five of them sluice ten or twelve tons of gravel in two and one-half days, only to find seventy-five cents worth of gold. He tried to interest some warriors in panning, but they laughed at him.[58]

While in the Black Hills, Benteen chanced to meet Brigadier General George Crook, who commanded the Department of the Platte. Most of the Black Hills fell under the jurisdiction of General Alfred Terry, but the western portion was in Crook's domain. Crook was a classmate of Sheridan and had served under him in the Civil War. Recently promoted to brigadier general, Crook was considered by many to be among the foremost Indian fighters of the day. Certainly, he was a gifted innovator.

On Crook's advice, Benteen refrained from interfering with the miners. He permitted them to send a petition to the government and to draw up plans for a town, which would come to be called Custer City, after someone who might do them good. Benteen was given some corner lots, but did not validate the claim, although he continued to receive tax notices.[59]

In accordance with their agreement with General Crook, fifty-five miners allowed themselves to be brought to Fort Randall,[60] so that the army could demonstrate its diligence in expelling intruders. Benteen made a point of treating them "not as prisoners but as brother Americans."[61] The miners greatly appreciated the courtesy and drew up a testimonial praising Benteen. They were released without bail from the fort and most certainly made their way back to the Black Hills.[62] His mission over, Benteen left for Fort Rice, arriving in early October.

Benteen learned that he was now the post commander. His complement included an infantry company and two cavalry companies: M Company (French-Mathey) and H Company (Benteen-Gibson-De Rudio). While Benteen was on patrol in the Sioux reservation, calamity again struck the Benteen household. His infant son died. The baby had to be buried in a makeshift crate, since the carpenter had accompanied Benteen. One of the wives donated her wedding dress to line the interior of the box.[63] Lieutenant Edwin Mathey, the OOD, said a prayer, and the infant was buried in the post cemetery alongside his sister.

LITTLE BIGHORN

The discovery of gold in the Black Hills had awakened enormous interest throughout the country. The greenback had been legal tender since the Civil War, although unbacked by metal specie. With the growth of the post-war commerce and industry, the national economy desperately required an expansion of the paper money in circulation, made even the more necessary by the onset of the Depression of 1873. But an increase in unbacked paper money might result in an inflation, which in turn would harm foreign trade and the financial institutions, although, in the short run, it might benefit debtors and mortgagees. To prevent an inflation, Congress passed the Specie Resumption Act of 1875, which directed that all circulating paper money must be backed on demand by gold. Only a new supply of gold could bring relief to the economy, it was thought, since more paper money could then be put into circulation.

President Ulysses S. Grant agreed that the Black Hills must be exploited, and since the Sioux were in possession, a way must be found to extinguish Sioux title. Army patrols were withdrawn from sentinel duty in the Black Hills, and fifteen thousand prospective miners were allowed to pour in, unhindered. The next step was to drive the roamers off the unceded lands onto the reservation. This, in some way, would compel the Lakota Nation to agree to the conveyance of title of the Black Hills to the government. Accordingly, on December 6, the Bureau of Indian Affairs issued a directive that all Lakota and Northern Cheyenne must return to their respective agencies no later than January 31, 1876. The order was purely procedural, since there was no expectation that it could, or would, be obeyed. By what authority the free roamers could be ordered from the unceded lands is obscure, since they were not participants of the Laramie Treaty, nor were they assigned to any specific agency. The only reason that could be devised was that the Sioux were waging an illegal war on the Crow, in contravention of the terms of the treaty.

General Sheridan drew up a plan to dislodge the Sioux and Northern Cheyenne from the unceded lands. Crook would march north from Fort Fetterman along the old Bozeman Trail in Wyoming; Colonel Gibbon would march east from Fort Ellis, Montana Territory, along the northern bank of the Yellowstone River to cut off a retreat; and Custer would march west from Fort Lincoln, Dakota Territory, using riverboats to support his column, to reduce dependency on the supply wagons. A riverboat could carry two hundred infantrymen and three hundred tons of cargo.

Sheridan preferred that the operation be launched in winter, with chiefly the roamers to contend with. Most warriors preferred to spend the cold months on the reservation, where they received government allotments. Also, for reasons previously discussed, the warriors lose their mobility in winter. On the other hand, riverboats cannot travel before mid-spring.

Crook started out in early March 1876, in the frigid Wyoming weather. Unlike the other columns, his had mules and horses on hand, left over from his campaign in the Southwest; and skilled packers to load them. In the warmer months, Crook's mules could even forage off the land without the need for supplemental feed.[1] Crook was fascinated by the mule; he even put his infantry on mules. When his column reached the staging area at Goose Creek in northern Wyoming, he transferred his wagon supplies onto pack mules, before pushing on along the old Bozeman Trail. Each mule was loaded on packsaddles (*aparejos*) with a burden of three- to six hundred pounds. Arriving in the Montana Territory, two of his battalions found, and destroyed, a one-hundred-lodge Sioux-Northern Cheyenne village, only to be dealt a stinging riposte by Crazy Horse's warriors, who halted the column and compelled it to turn back.

Next to depart was the Montana column, led by Colonel John Gibbon, which set off on April 3 from Fort Ellis, Montana Territory, with one thousand men. Without river steamers to supply them, the Gibbon column had to rely on wagons, which necessitated the constant widening of the trails. As the column traveled slowly along the northern bank of the Yellowstone, Gibbon's scouts reported seeing tracks of enemy tribes moving from the Tongue toward the Rosebud valley. Despite the prodding of his young officers, Gibbon was in no hurry to engage the warriors, without support from the other columns.

On May 29, Crook set out again with fifteen companies of cavalry and five of infantry, following the old Bozeman Trail. At Goose Creek, Wyoming, he established a staging area and transferred his loads onto pack mules. The column proceeded north to the Rosebud valley. On June 17, while halted for a rest, Crook's column was suddenly attacked by one thousand warriors. The warriors struck, retreated, and then struck again, sometimes engaging in hand-to-hand combat over fragmented terrain. This continued in repetitive succession for six hours. Crazy Horse seemed willing to continue the battle, until Crook brought up some cavalry to the rear of the warriors, compelling them to withdraw. Crook, too, had had enough. The column had suffered twenty-eight deaths and fifty-six wounded; and expended twenty-five thousand rounds of ammunition. He returned to his camp at Goose Creek, to lick his wounds. No word of his setback reached the other columns.

The Dakota column was the last to leave. Custer had been away from the regiment for five months. Railroad fares were of no concern to him, since, as a "valued promotor,"[2] he was held in high regard by the railroad directors, who saw in him a pliable tool for the sale of their right-of-way lands in the Dakotas. When a critic denounced the land as worthless, Custer wrote a stinging rebuttal in the press. His reward was free passes, with an occasional private coach included.[3]

Custer had first visited New York, a great Democratic stronghold, where his complaints about the post traders and the Indian agents reached the attention of the publisher of the *New York Tribune*, who demanded a public investigation of the charges. During the Grant administration, the post trader no longer received his appointment from the post commander, but from the Secretary of War.[4] Evidence had emerged that these post trader concessions were being sold, resulting in charges being brought against the Secretary of War, William Belknap, who had made the appointments.

In due time, Custer was summoned to Washington, where he testified before a Congressional committee (headed by Hiester Clymer of Pennsylvania), which was investigating Belknap, who had since been compelled to resign. The committee was primarily interested in the trading practices at Fort Sill, but was willing to listen to anyone with evidence of trader dishonesty. Custer related a story of a post trader at Fort Abraham Lincoln who was angered when he viewed the contents of an officer's wagon returning from a shopping trip to Bismarck and threatened to report the officer to the Secretary of War. The Secretary, in fact, did intervene to support the trader. Also, Custer told of a post trader who bribed a sergeant to accept short-weighed sacks of corn, clearly labeled for Indian use.[5] The President's brother was named as a bag man for William W. Belknap, the Secretary of War, and a close friend of the President.

Custer testified truthfully but could only relate hearsay. Of course, he made an instant enemy of President Grant, who had him removed from command. To make matters worse, Custer had recently court-martialed Captain Fred Grant, the President's son, for drunkenness. Until then, Custer had headed the Lincoln column, but thereafter authority reverted to General Alfred Terry, the over-all commander of both the Lincoln and Ellis expeditions. Terry and Sheridan both pleaded Custer's cause, and got the President to restore Custer to the 7th Cavalry command, but not to the command of the column. This, by default, Terry would keep. Custer is said to have told someone that he was planning to "swing clear" from Terry's supervision, but the story passed through five sources before emerging after Custer's death.[6]

Custer arrived at Lincoln five days before the day of departure and immediately ordered the purchase of all available civilian horses. He divided the regiment into two wings, each consisting of six companies.[7] One wing was given to Reno, the other to Benteen. In Custer's absence, Major Reno had been doing the donkey work in preparing the regiment for the field and had even requested command of the 7th Cavalry, before it was learned that Custer would be reinstated.

Benteen left Fort Rice on May 5, 1876, with H and M Companies and arrived the next day at Fort Abraham Lincoln. Tents were set up in the usual campground two miles north of the fort. There had been a few changes in the table of organization. At long last, De Rudio had been promoted to first lieutenant and placed in Company A under Moylan, much to De Rudio's regret. Moylan would not mess with him, surly creature that he was (although some enlisted men found him "fair and just"[8]) so that De Rudio had to mess with a guide, Fred Girard. Tom Custer, the colonel's brother, was now the captain of C Company. Colonel Custer and his wife surprised Benteen with their cordiality. The reason soon became apparent, when Custer relayed regards to him from Benteen's cousin, Lawrence A. Gobright, a very influential Washington journalist and co-founder of the Associated Press. The man had evidently impressed Custer, who at this crucial stage of his career, was anxious to extend his network, even if it included a relative of Benteen.[9]

On May 17, 1876, Terry led the Dakota column out of Lincoln, while the sixteen-piece band, mounted on white horses,[10] played the favorite tunes. In the column were 1,200 men, including twelve cavalry companies and three infantry companies. In addition, it had two Gatling guns, one brass twenty-four pound Napoleon cannon, a three-inch "Rodman" gun, and thirty Arikara scouts, some of whom had Winchester rifles and metallic cartridges. The scouts were paid sixteen dollars per month and given an allowance of twelve dollars for each horse.[11] This was more than a private earned, but the scout's work was irregular. With the column were 140 six-mule teams and sixty four-mule teams.[12] The balance of the supplies was transported by riverboat.

Custer set a slow pace, to allow the 1,600 animals in the mule train to keep up.[13]

At the Hart River, the paymaster paid the troops, leaving them with no immediate opportunity to squander their money. He then rode back to Lincoln with Mrs. Custer. The U.S. Marshall, Ben Ash, rode up from Bismarck with subpoenas for some of the soldiers to appear at the trial of forty Bismarck citizens, whom Custer had accused of defrauding the government. Custer refused to release the soldiers.[14]

The march resumed. The wagon train had difficulty crossing the Hart River. Fifty men were needed to haul the wagons across the water.[15] The weather turned miserable, rain alternating with hail.[16] The column traveled thirteen to twenty miles a day across the broken plain. The infantry struggled to keep up, as did the six-mule government wagons, each loaded with 3,000 to 5,000 pounds of supplies and the four-mule private teams, carrying 1,500 to 2,000 pounds.[17] Camp was made at 2:30 p.m., to enable the wagon train to arrive by 6 p.m. Custer forbade the discharge of firearms in camp. When one of the scouts fired at a rattlesnake, Custer made him balance on one foot atop a keg.[18] The Arikara were allowed to hunt away from camp and were paid handsomely for the meat: two dollars for deer hind quarters, one dollar for front quarters and one dollar for back or saddle. One Arikara earned two hundred dollars.[19]

In the vanguard were three cavalry companies, one of which, the pioneer company, prepared the trail for the wagon train. They carried in a forward wagon axes, picks, shovels, iron bars, pitchforks and lumber for the construction of bridges. From the beginning, Terry had trouble with Custer. Custer tried to assert his independence by going off to reconnoiter, without first notifying Terry. On another occasion, Custer led the column astray while searching for a pass, which cost the column a day's march.[20]

On May 27, the column reached the badlands,[21] which from the distance looked like "a great sunken city with high spires and buildings half-hidden in the haze." Custer had the band mount a butte and play for the troops,[22] as they struggled in single file through a narrow gorge, lowering and raising the mule teams by ropes.[23]

On arrival at camp on the Little Missouri River, it began to snow. The river was swollen by spring freshets, which impeded bridge construction and compelled the animals to swim across.[24] Terry halted the column for "four sleeps,"[25] until the snow stopped. Earlier reports had the Sioux camped along this river. When the information was found to be in error, Terry realized that he was facing a long campaign.

On June 7 the column reached the Powder River. From here, Terry was escorted down the Powder to the Yellowstone River, where the river steamer *Far West* awaited him. The steamer took Terry upriver to Colonel Gibbon's camp, where they conferred. Post traders had come along on the riverboat and did a lively business filling flasks and canteens with spirits.

Three days later, over Custer's objections, Terry ordered Reno to take a wing (six companies) up the

Powder to reconnoiter; then move west to the Tongue River and descend the Tongue to the Yellowstone, where he would rejoin the other wing. Reno set out with reduced rations, burdened by a Gatling gun, which impeded the march. Rather than descend the Tongue River, he tracked the warriors farther west to the Rosebud River and followed the Rosebud down to the Yellowstone River. After a 240-mile scout, he sent word that he had seen warrior tracks leading west over the Rosebud divide in the direction of the Little Bighorn River.

In Reno's absence, Custer brought the remainder of his column to the mouth of the Tongue River. There, he met General Terry, who had arrived by boat. The six companies camped at the site of an old Lakota camp, where they found the body of a dead soldier, probably killed in the first Crook encounter. A message from Reno was received on June 19, informing the command that he was at the mouth of the Rosebud River. Custer ordered Benteen to move his wing west to the Rosebud, to unite with Reno. Across the Yellowstone, they could see Gibbon's column on the north bank.

Another conference was held aboard the steamer *Far West*, with Terry, Custer, Gibbon and Reno in attendance. Major Reno confirmed that he had seen tracks moving across the Rosebud divide leading in the direction of the valley of the Little Bighorn. This accorded, more or less, with the information supplied by Colonel Gibbon. Terry was angry with Reno for exceeding his explicit orders, fearing that Reno's impromptu march westward might have alerted the

Sioux. Custer, on the other hand, scoffed at Reno's timidity, in failing to boldly follow the tracks further. In a dispatch sent June 22, 1876, to the *New York Herald*, the reporter quotes Custer as hinting of a possible court martial for Reno.[26] Actually, Reno had done a creditable scout and provided good information. In a way, Reno was fortunate to escape unscathed, since the Sioux had been occupied with Crook.

A plan of action was drawn up. Custer and the 7th Cavalry would move west to the Little Bighorn valley. Since Terry estimated that Custer would be traveling faster than Gibbon and would therefore arrive at the Little Bighorn plain prematurely, Custer was instructed on reaching the Rosebud River, to extend his march by moving up the Rosebud to its headwaters and then south to the valley of the Little Bighorn, where the Sioux were camped. Gibbon would move along the Yellowstone to the Bighorn River and then move south to meet up with Custer. The orders were written in contemplation of a joint attack, but Terry allowed Custer some discretion, "when nearly in contact with the enemy." Controversy later arose as to whether Terry had issued an order or a directive.[27] General Nelson Miles, a rabid partisan of Custer, in later years claimed that he had letters which demonstrated that Terry had told Custer to do what he thought best, and, above all, to hold on to the wounded; but his documents were unconvincing.[28] The consensus among the parties was that there were no more than eight hundred warriors opposing them.[29]

Terry chose to accompany Gibbon. Terry was not a cavalryman, nor was he inured to the march. Until then, he had been enjoying fine cuisines with cakes and pies[30] and was in no hurry to exchange his fare for march rations. Gibbon gave Custer six of his best Crow scouts, who, unlike the Arikara, were thoroughly familiar with the region. The Crow could be distinguished even from a distance by his large bronco, compared to the smaller the Arikara pony.[31] The Crows wore tribal dress; the Arikara, odd pieces of army uniform.

The evening before their departure, Custer announced that he was discontinuing the "wing" organization. Henceforth, each company would report directly to him. During the meeting, Benteen and Custer become embroiled in a violent argument when Benteen remarked that he hoped for better support than Elliott had received at Washita; and Custer, in turn, twitted him for killing an Indian youngster. The officers had heard all this before. None of them knew that on June 17, Crook's large command had suffered a defeat on the Rosebud River and had been forced to withdraw to Wyoming.

The command was given for *Light Marching Order!* Wagon supplies were transferred to the mules, as Crook had long championed. Wagons, band, infantry, Gatling guns, three-inch "Rodman" gun, officers' tents, sabers, luxury items and Custer's dogs were all left behind.[32] The men were issued march provisions for fifteen days and reduced rations for the horses. Twelve pack mules were assigned to each company to carry their supplies.

Thousands of extra rounds of pistol and carbine ammunition were also packed on mules for regimental use. The officers conducted a careful inspection of their company mounts. Custer personally examined the hooves of the Arikara horses and where they were unsuited for a quick march, he ordered the rider to remain behind.[33]

The soldier wore two-piece underwear extending to wrist and ankle, flannel shirt, trousers, sack coat, a broad-brim hat and a pair of low bull-hide boots. He wore his short boots constantly, since, if shrunk, they could not be stretched.[34] He took an extra shirt, but without a change of underclothing and few opportunities to bathe, scabies ("cooties") became a pervasive problem on all the marches.[35] Benteen brought with him a buffalo robe, two blankets and a pillow. He left behind two horses, bedding, a footlocker and $115.04 in cash.[36] The rest of his pay he kept in his money belt. A poker player with more cash than the next man has an advantage when playing for "table stakes."

On the morning of June 22, the regiment passed in review before Terry, and then, in columns of four, it departed.

They marched the first day along the Rosebud River, crossing and recrossing it several times. Lieutenant Charles Varnum sent out scouts on both sides of the river. The scouts saw pictures of fighting buffalo inscribed on sandstone. They interpreted them to mean: "do not follow us or we will destroy you." Rocks were painted red, which to the Sioux signified "victory."[37]

Custer halted the march at 4:30 p.m., having traveled only twelve miles. Orders were given to dispense with trumpet calls and to build only small fires.[38]

The soldier unsaddled his horse, then dried, unbitted and watered it, and put it out to graze. An hour before sunset, *Stable Call!* was announced. The men again brought the horses to water, then back to camp for grooming and feeding. After the withers, back and hooves had been carefully inspected by the duty officer and first sergeant, the horse was picketed.[39] The picket rope, passed through a ring in the halter, would hold the horse securely, unless a warrior were to creep up, wave a blanket or buffalo robe and shriek wildly, causing the horse to snap the line and run away.[40]

Just after sundown, *Officers' Call!* went out by word of mouth to the twenty-eight officers and three doctors, (one regular army and two civilian surgeons). Somewhat irritated, Custer let it be known that he was willing to accept advice, but would not tolerate grumbling. He told them that he had learned that certain officers had complained to General Terry. When Benteen asked him to name the persons, Custer demurred. "I want the saddle to go where it fits," he said, avoiding an argument.[41] Benteen shared a pup tent with Lieutenant De Rudio, who, although in A Company, messed with Benteen. Mosquitoes kept Benteen awake throughout the night.[42]

The following day, June 23, Benteen was the officer of the day and was given three companies to protect the pack train. The march began before sunrise. The mules were especially troublesome. They were wagon mules, untrained to carry a pack and prone to fall behind. Moreover, the soldiers who packed them were inexperienced and kept forgetting the instructions of the civilian packers. The warrior trails grew wider, as narrower trails began to coalesce. Benteen divided his battalion, placing one company on each flank of the mule train and a half company in front and the other half in the rear.[43]

The column halted late afternoon and made camp after a thirty-three-mile march. Men scurried around trying to set up camp. Two hours later Benteen arrived with the pack train and was shown his bivouac area by Lieutenant Cooke. Benteen tried to get Cooke to recommend to Custer that Benteen's disposition of the duty battalion be made a standing order. Cooke curtly told Benteen to speak to Custer himself. Before the meal, Benteen put out a fishing line but caught nothing and had to content himself with the soldier's "SOB" (sh-t on a biscuit): bacon, coffee and hardtack. Fires were built and guards posted. After attending to his horse and his company duties, the weary soldier spreads his blanket and horse blanket and sets down his saddle, which serves as a pillow. He then toasts his ration of bacon on a stick, soaks his hardtack and steams his coffee.[44] There was always time for a yarn or a song before dropping off to sleep, provided that he did not have picket or vidette duty.

At sunrise the next day, June 24, Custer began his tour of the camp. Benteen repeated his recommendations for the mule train. Custer approved the arrangement and wanted it made a standing order.

His OOD duty over, Benteen returned to his company duties, carefully detailing to Lieutenant Gibson, his assistant company commander, the orders for the day. The column started at fast walk, but soon changed to slow walk, to better allow the mule train to keep up. Gnats and deerflies tormented the horsemen.

By midday they had come twenty miles and halted near a row of curious rocks bordering some flattened ground. Here, the warriors had held their summer solstice Sun Dance. Sitting Bull, the legendary Lakota shaman, had suspended himself for two days by sinews tunneled under his skin. At the end of that time, he had a divination that a great victory over the white soldiers lay ahead. Sitting Bull was an implacable foe of the Americans and refused to speak their language, but was kindly disposed toward French-Canadians and had some knowledge of French,[45] which he denied.[46] The Arikara examined the figures drawn in the sand around the lodge and interpreted them to mean that the Lakota knew Custer was coming. In an improvised sweat lodge, they saw figures showing the Lakota on one side, Custer on the other, and a line of dead men with their heads pointing toward the Lakota. The Arikara construed this to mean that the Lakota medicine was too strong for the army.[47]

The column continued the march, following the ever-widening trail made by the reservation warriors and their families on their way to join the roamers. The horse droppings were carefully studied to determine the age. Late in the afternoon the column made camp at

Muddy Creek, near the divide between the Rosebud and Little Bighorn valleys.

Captain Myles Keogh, the I Company commander, pointed out to Benteen a good place to set up his pup tent, which he shared with De Rudio. Benteen messed with Gibson, De Rudio and Captain McDougall, the latter a fellow baseball enthusiast. *Officers' Call!* was announced at 5 p.m. When Lieutenant Edwin Mathey, the mule train officer whom Benteen despised, complained that the mules of G and H companies had been poorly packed and were giving trouble, Benteen could scarcely contain his anger. Meanwhile, the scouts had returned and reported that the warrior trail led west over the divide. Custer decided not to follow the Rosebud River up to its headwaters, but to continue due west to the valley of the Little Bighorn.

A merry group of officers collected outside Benteen's pup tent. Lieutenant De Rudio entertained them with stories of his adventures in Europe. Benteen tried to cut short the festivities, fearing that they would be called upon to make a night march. He urged them to get some sleep. No sooner had he spoken when orders went out to prepare to march. "Second night's loss of sleep," grumbled Benteen.[48]

Custer informed his officers that he planned to rest the regiment the next day and attack on June 26, the tentative date for the arrival of Gibbon.

The regiment moved out at 11 p.m.. Custer halted the column for one and one-half hours to permit the pack train to cross Muddy Creek. Lead men guided the horsemen in the dark by tapping the tin cup attached to their saddle horn. Captain Myles Keogh was the duty officer. When he complained that he had no knowledge of how the pack train was faring, Benteen advised him to keep moving and that if anything were to fall off the mules, he could retrieve it in daylight.[49] On one occasion, Custer, who was in the lead, lost the trail, and he and his adjutant were seen lighting matches and a candle to find it.[50] At 2 a.m., the column halted after an eight-mile ascent. The men were too tired to eat.[51]

Horses were unbitted but kept saddled. Some men tried to sleep, holding the bridle reins under their arms;[52] others built fires, which could be seen from afar. Five Crow scouts led Lieutenant Varnum and a party of Arikara guides to a nearby mountain lookout, called Crow's Nest.

The exact location of the Crow's Nest is in dispute. The author has made two trips to the lookout points in the company of Willie Peters, a Crow, to whom he is indebted for the information. The author has also spoken with Bill Redfield, a local settler. A strong Crow tradition has "Crow's Nest" one-half mile further south of the usually accepted site, which the Crows derisively call "White Man's Crow's Nest." The view at "Crow's Nest" is as good, if not better; and it can be more easily mounted on horseback, especially in the dark. The Crow tradition was recorded in a land deed one hundred years ago in which the land that the Crows call "Crow's Nest" was cited as having special historic significance. An attempt has been made to legitimize "White Man's Crow's Nest" by building a concrete memorial on the land, but the validity of the marker is questionable.

At sunrise, the scouts reported seeing a large village fifteen miles away, surrounded by a huge herd of horses. The Crow and Arikara had no means of expressing numbers in excess of one hundred. Varnum, who was fluent in sign language, understood what the Crows were trying to say, but could not see the village.[53] Custer was summoned. When he arrived, he borrowed field glasses from one of the guides[54] and scanned the area. He looked in the appropriate direction but could see nothing but a cloud of smoke or mist overlying the flood plain. Mitch Bouyer, a half-Santee (Sioux) guide, was apprehensive, but Custer brushed aside his forebodings. Custer was familiar with those dire scout warnings, which always magnified dangers and discouraged action. Also, from atop the lookout peak, Custer could clearly view the small area of badland directly in front of him a few miles away. Neither he, nor any of the scouts, made any mention of warrior activity in this area.

A soldier, who had retraced the trail to retrieve some clothing that had fallen off a mule, came across a warrior examining a fallen load and gave chase. He reported the incident, and it was taken to mean that the regiment had been discovered. Custer decided to forego the day of rest and attack the Indian village that very day.

Benteen invited himself to Major Reno's early breakfast of raw bacon, hardtack and cold water.[55] At 6 a.m. the regiment set out,[56] without Custer on hand to give the order.[57] One of the guides later suggested that Custer may not have wanted the regiment to march, and intended to rest that day and attack at night,[58] but this is highly conjectural. Custer rejoined the column a mile down the trail. He had Martin, his duty trumpeter, sound *Officers' Call!*, believing that the Lakota already knew of his presence.[59] Benteen contradicts this and says that he was summoned by an orderly.[60] Custer informed the officers that he had been to the mountain top where the scouts had claimed to have seen a large village, but he could see nothing. Benteen was dubious, he later wrote, since in similar circumstances in the Dakotas, he had found the scouts completely reliable.[61]

The column marched five miles, with Custer riding well ahead. When he returned to the column, he ordered the saddle taken off "Dandy," the brown horse he was riding, and put on "Vic," his sorrel mare,[62] with white feet and legs and a face blaze.[63] The soldiers viewed this as an ominous sign. At 11:30 a.m. *Officers' Call!* was announced and Custer made known his intention to attack the enemy encampment, now fourteen riding miles away, as soon as they got there. He told the officers to make final preparations for the attack and reminded them that an NCO and six men from each company were assigned to the company mules. The officers were also to insure that each soldier had one hundred rounds of carbine ammunition and twenty-four rounds of revolver ammunition. Additional ammunition, of course, was carried on the regimental mules. He added that the first company to announce its readiness would have the honor of heading up the march. Benteen walked fifty yards, turned around and reported that his company was ready.[64]

After an hour of march, Custer complained to Benteen that his pace was too fast. Custer himself took the lead, accompanied by his adjutant, chief trumpeter, and sergeant-major. The column crossed the Wolf Mountain divide and halted on the western slope. After a fifteen-minute conversation with his adjutant, who busied himself with a scratch pad,[65] Custer sent for Benteen and ordered him to march a battalion—H Company (Captain Benteen), K Company (Lieutenant Godfrey), and D Company (Captain Weir)—left oblique from the trail to a series of buttes off to the southwest. Benteen was to designate an officer and six men to climb the first butte and scan the region for hostiles. If warriors were encountered, he was to engage them; otherwise, he was to rejoin the column. Custer offered no explanation for his order, nor could Benteen or the other officers discern any reason. Custer had had an excellent view of the designated area while atop Crow's Nest and had said nothing about warrior activity. None of the scouts had seen warriors in the assigned area, nor had any seen tracks leaving the trail, which might have indicated that warriors had gone off to this area.[66] Varnum and a few scouts could just as well have been sent to investigate an area having a low probability of hostile presence. Lastly, as to Custer wanting to cut off an escape, why would he send a battalion to the east bank to block the escape of warriors camping on the west bank? One is justified in wondering whether Custer's order might have been a ruse to move Benteen to the rear of the column. After all, Benteen had been the first to enter the Washita camp. Why give him a similar honor?

Benteen was dubious about the order. "Hadn't we better keep the men together?" Benteen asked, according to one of the privates.

"You have your orders," Custer replied curtly.[67]

Benteen had started out toward the bluffs, Lieutenant Gibson in the advance, when they were overtaken by a messenger from Custer ordering him to continue south, past the first ridge. The terrain was especially difficult and demanding. "To say that the country...was rough, is but putting it mildly," wrote Benteen.[68] The terrain is irregular, pockmarked with mounds, hills and trenches all hindering linear movement. Gibson climbed the first ridge and saw nothing. Soon, another messenger arrived, ordering Benteen to continue to the second valley, even if nothing were seen from the first ridge.

Gibson climbed the second ridge and again reported to Benteen that he saw nothing. The terrain was too rugged and chopped-up for warrior travel, hunting or camping.[69] Benteen had earlier caught a glimpse of the Custer column galloping along the trail. Galloping suggests that an attack had been initiated. His immediate thought was that the column had "struck something."[70]

Having marched five miles in two to three hours without seeing an Indian or traces of Indians, Benteen ordered his battalion to make a "right oblique," to rejoin the command, not wishing to be left out of the fight.[71] In his narrative of July 7, 1876, to the subsequent adjutant of the 7th Cavalry, Benteen states that Custer had earlier instructed him "that if in my judgement there was nothing to be seen of Indians in the direction I was going, to return with the battalion to the trail the command was following."[72] The battalion reached the Custer trail ahead of the mule train and came upon a small spring, which had turned the adjacent ground into a morass. There, Benteen halted the battalion to water the horses and fill the canteens, which, as fate decreed, would have to last them for twenty hours. Custer, too, had watered his column here. Reno watered his horses when he reached the Little Bighorn River, since his horses were so desperately thirsty that they would not cross the river until after they had drunk.

Benteen was riding "Dick," a U.S. horse, and he had another U.S. horse available in case of need.[73] He tied up his tired mount and rubbed off the sweat, before allowing it to drink. The horses had not been watered since 8 p.m. of the previous day. The watering lasted fifteen minutes,[74] during which time the men filled their pint canteens.

In the distance the battalion heard gunfire, and it became uneasy. Captain Weir was anxious that he not miss out on any of Custer's battles. He set off with D Company without waiting for an order, and Benteen immediately started up the march with his other two companies at a "stiff walk" pace,[75] just as the first pack mule arrived. Benteen overtook Weir but did not chide him, although he would have been justified in doing so. Soon they passed a messenger sent by Custer to the pack train commander, bearing an order for the pack train to join Custer. At the moment this order was written, Custer apparently saw no urgent need for Benteen. The messenger showed the order to Benteen, who informed the messenger that the train was a mile behind them.

The battalion started out again. They came to a burning tepee, which had been set afire by one of Custer's scouts. According to Crow oral tradition, the location is in a level field fifty yards from what would have been the trail leading to the Little Bighorn. Two miles from the river, a messenger from Custer arrived, with an order for Benteen to come quickly and bring up the pack train. The messenger was an Italian named Martin (Giovanni Martini), who tried to answer Benteen's questions as best he could. Martin was in H Company, assigned for that day to Custer as duty trumpeter. Benteen's later opinion of the young Italian, poorly versed in the English language, who rode under fire on a wounded horse, is vintage: "The trumpeter who brought this dispatch was a thick-headed, dull-witted Italian just about as much cut out for a cavalryman as he was for a king."[76]

From the messenger, they learned that Custer was three miles away. Benteen had the choice of either helping to speed the pack train or hurrying to join Custer.[77] He elected to join Custer and let the packs catch up.

The battalion resumed the march at a quick trot until the trail divided, one trail leading west to the river, the other north. Some Crow scouts suddenly appeared, driving a small herd of Sioux ponies.[78] They directed

Benteen to the northern trail parallel to the river atop the bluffs, along which Martin had come. As they moved along the trail, the battalion could hear gunfire from across the river. At first, Benteen thought that the firing had come from the whole regiment.[79] Martin could have told him about Reno, whom Martin had seen while on his way to deliver the message, but the trumpeter was not asked, nor did he volunteer the information. Soon Benteen saw cavalrymen, mounted and dismounted, climbing the bluff, pursued by large numbers of mounted warriors, who were firing at them. Benteen formed his battalion into a single column, and led them forward with the command: *"Draw Pistols, Charge!"*

* * *

After issuing his orders to Benteen, Custer led the column a short distance, then sent his adjutant to Reno with orders to take command of three companies: A Company (Captain Moylan), M Company (Captain French) and G Company (Lieutenant McIntosh), a total of 125 men, in addition to the guides, scouts, two civilian surgeons, etc. Reno led his battalion along the left bank of a small, dried stream, now called "Reno Creek," while Custer continued along the right bank with five companies, totaling perhaps about 250 men, as well as guides, scouts, a regular surgeon and supernumeraries. The ridges and trees obstructed their line of vision, so that they could not yet see the Little Bighorn River. After eight miles, the trail along the left bank ended, and Custer allowed Reno to cross over onto the right side of the creek, ahead of him.

Custer saw smoke up ahead, and prepared for a charge. The soldiers quickly discarded their overcoats and haversacks to make themselves as light as possible. The order *Charge!* was given, and the column galloped to the source of the smoke.[80] This may have been the galloping that Benteen had observed. They found a dead warrior in a lodge ("lone tepee"), which the Arikara scouts had set afire. The fire caught the attention of some forty Lakota warriors in the vicinity, who galloped back toward the river.

The column chased the fleeing warriors for a mile. Custer then sent his adjutant to Reno, who was up ahead with his battalion, with orders to continue the pursuit into the village, promising to support him: "General Custer directs you to take as rapid a gait as you think prudent and charge the village afterward, and you will be supported by the whole outfit."[81] Since Reno's and Custer's battalions were both engaged in the chase, it is plausible that the order was brought to Reno by an intermediary (Lieutenant Cooke), rather than given in person by Custer. Custer well knew that Reno's horses could not overtake the warrior ponies. It is likely Custer intended that Reno enter the village on the heels of the fleeing warriors, before the encampment could be alerted to the danger. Meanwhile, Custer's five companies would be attacking from across a ford (Ford B) a few miles to the north, which the Crow scouts had described to him. These seem the best premises on which to base the events that followed.

* * *

Little Bighorn

After Reno left, Custer continued forward at a slower pace. The trail divided, and Reno took the path leading to the river, disappearing from Custer's view. Custer detailed Lieutenant Cooke and Captain Keogh to accompany Reno to the river, at which point they left Reno and returned to Custer.

Custer turned off the trail onto a path that led north along the bluffs parallel to the river. It must have been a well established trail, since it would eventually lead to "Ford B," across which lay the splendid camping grounds used for decades by both Crow and Lakota. The trail must not be confused with the paved road now existing, which runs on the top of the bluffs. Lieutenant Cooke, whom Custer had sent to watch Reno cross the Little Bighorn River, reported to him that Reno had encountered warriors. This information had been conveyed to Cooke by Girard, one of Reno's scouts.[82] Soon, Custer arrived at a bluff overlooking the river (Weir Point, according to Crow tradition). From atop a hillock, an obvious observation site, he scanned the area with borrowed binoculars.

He may have caught a glimpse of the Reno battalion across the river before Reno was hotly engaged by the warriors, although John Martin, the duty trumpeter and only white survivor who was at Custer's side, states that Custer did not see Reno. Martin himself had seen Reno only later while carrying Custer's message to Benteen,[83] when he reached a point three miles from Reno Creek and near a large ravine leading one mile down to the Little Bighorn River (Reno Hill?).[84]

To Custer's amazement, he now saw from atop the hill a huge warrior village across the Little Bighorn River, but because of the topography, only a third of the encampment was visible. He immediately sent word to the pack train.

Custer then proceeded north along a trail, now called Cedar Coulee, which dips down behind the bluffs for one mile. It then joins another trail called Medicine Tail Coulee, which turns west for a mile slowly rising to the crest; then slowly descends to a ford on the river (Ford B). As he came up onto the crest of the trail, Custer suddenly saw the entire encampment. This was no fifty-tepee village like the Washita. Here were one thousand tepees and wickiups and thousands of horses grazing on the flood plain. A wickiup is a cone-like structure made from cottonwood poles and covered with thatch or buffalo robe. Each wickiup lodged two or more young braves, each tepee two or more warriors. The total number of warriors has been variously estimated from two thousand to seven thousand. Nothing of this dimension had ever before been seen in North America!

As the full, gigantic size of the encampment became evident, he dispatched the duty trumpeter to Benteen, with a message ordering him to come quickly and bring up the mule train. The warriors must already have begun to threaten the column, for the trumpeter was told that he need not return immediately if he saw danger but could come back with Benteen.[85] Moreover, the trumpeter's horse was subsequently wounded by gunfire. Along the way to Benteen, the trumpeter passed Boston Custer, a civilian with the wagon train, who had left the train to join brothers George and Tom. Boston Custer had also passed Benteen, so that Boston could furnish his brother with knowledge of the relative location of Benteen and the pack train. The Crow scouts, who had been scanning the countryside from a vantage point high up on a ridge, now reported to Custer that Reno was in full retreat.[86]

From the point where Medicine Tail Coulee begins to descend, Custer sent some men to inspect the trail going down to the river. The tracks of two shod horses were later found on the riverbank. Why did he do this? One can see the ford and the encampment well enough from where Custer stood on the Medicine Tail, perhaps only 125 yards from the ford. Sending men to the riverbank may have been, perhaps, a token gesture so that Custer could later say that he explored ways to relieve Reno. The huge size of the village and the numbers of warriors streaming across the river would surely have discouraged Custer from attempting a crossing.

Cheyenne women who had crossed the river to get a better view of the Reno battle from the east bank had been the first to see the approach of Custer and sounded the alarm.[87] A Lakota witness, Mrs. Spotted Horn Bull, reported that at the first warning many warriors had crossed the river and were stalking Custer.[88] Warriors did not have to cross at the ford, but could cross the river at many other locations. The ford was required chiefly for the women and the travois.

At this juncture, Custer was in full possession of all the information needed to make a decision. He knew of the huge enemy encampment; Reno's retreat; the locations of Benteen's battalion and the pack train; the enemy horsemen fording the river and the warriors maneuvering around his position. Should he halt and wait for Benteen and the pack train? Should he turn back, consolidate with Benteen and go to Reno's rescue? Or should he advance and trust to "Custer's luck"? With the Custer party was a journalist who had been taken along against Terry's orders, to insure that Custer would get proper coverage in the press.

Custer and his men advanced north along the bluffs. The men who had gone down to the ford returned by way of a different gully, Deep Coulee (not Deep Ravine), and rejoined the march two-tenths of a mile from where Medicine Tail dips down to the ford. Two and one-half miles north of the Medicine Tail, the march came to Calhoun Hill. Here, Custer may have halted three companies and marched the other two companies in the direction of the Custer Battleground; or he may have been marching all five companies north, with the lead company reaching the Custer Battleground and the rear companies at Calhoun Hill, separated by a distance of only one mile. Three companies were strung out along a march for three-quarters of a mile, and Custer had five companies. Custer sensed, as can be discerned from his instructions to Martin, that the enemy was in the vicinity.

Warrior accounts seem to indicate that a large party of warriors, perhaps led by Crazy Horse, crossed the river north of the encampment and encircled Custer's two companies from the north.[89] The theory that Custer marched his two companies north beyond the Custer

Battlefield to look for another ford and then turned back, seems improbable, since that would have placed him squarely in the midst of Crazy Horse and his warriors. And surely he would not have split his battalion after seeing that huge enemy encampment! The three rear companies had halted or were on the march behind Custer, when they were encircled by warriors, said to have been led by Chief Gall. The word "led" can be misleading, for warriors, for the most part, acted independently, waiting only for the final signal to attack in concert. The warriors had been protected by hollows, ravines and four-foot-tall grass, as they moved abreast of the column. Warriors often dismounted to fight a stationary foe, but kept their ponies nearby for the final spurt.[90]

The attack was probably made simultaneously, since all of Custer's men were within a one-mile distance— from Calhoun Hill to Custer Battleground. Warrior custom often began with riders rushing in, waving blankets to spook the horses[91] followed by sorties by the young braves, eager to make a coup, and by the suicide braves. Finally, the leader of the band cried "Hi-yi-yi!" and the braves rushed forward, slapping the rumps of each other's horses, to speed them.[92] Warriors fired until their ammunition was exhausted, then used bow and arrow.[93] They later reported that they swarmed over the soldiers "so thickly that scarcely half of them [the soldiers] could fight, for fear of killing each other." In the course of a half hour or sooner, Custer, his 220 men, officers, guides, nephew, brothers, surgeon and supernumeraries were annihilated. Two hundred and eight bodies were counted at the first tally. More were later found and some remain to be discovered.

Where considerable black gunpowder has been spent in a battle, a large cloud of smoke overlies the battlefield, lasting, in the case of black powder, as long as fifteen minutes. Since this was not observed from Weir Point,[94] it is possible that Custer was overcome more by the momentum of the large warrior numbers, than from sustained gunfire.[95] On the other hand, an eighteen-inch-thick tree trunk was later found on the battlefield, hewn down by bullets.[96] If a cloud of spent gunpowder hovering over the battlefield had not been seen from Weir Point, it may be that the Reno party had looked after the cloud had blown away, i.e., later than fifteen minutes after the firing had subsided.

Benteen later reported that he saw no evidence of a skirmish line, suggesting that there had been a complete rout. "There was no line on the battlefield," he stated. "You can take a handful of corn and scatter it over the floor and make such lines." By his estimate, the battle lasted fifteen to thirty minutes.[97] Moylan later testified that he saw the bodies of the soldiers in one company in the familiar position of skirmishers,[98] but this may have been an attempt to extol the ineffectual defense. A score or more of soldiers tried unsuccessfully to flee the battlefield down a cut leading to the river. Only three officers died with their respective companies; the rest fell beside Custer, suggesting that Custer had sounded *Officers' Call!* immediately before the warriors struck.[99] If the battalion were on the march, officers would have been summoned by trumpet call; if separated into two detachments, word arguably might have been sent to the officers of the other detachment by messenger. Mrs. Spotted Horn Bull states that she had heard trumpet calls.[100] The warriors used tomahawks to finish off the soldiers and propped up some bodies for bow-and-arrow and lance practice.[101]

The warriors collected the rewards of battle, especially ammunition, and then directed their attention to the remaining two battalions.

* * *

After receiving his orders to pursue the warriors, Major Reno led his men toward the Little Bighorn River. The fleeing warriors remained in sight of Reno's battalion and seemed to be inviting pursuit.[102] By the time the battalion got to the river, the braves were no longer visible. At the river, ten of the twenty-three Arikara refused to ago further, despite the exhortations of Lieutenant Varnum, the chief scout.[103] The Arikara were more fearful of being shot by soldiers in the heat of battle than they were of being shot by the Sioux.[104] The river was about twenty-five feet wide and in full flood. Its banks were very steep, so that the horses slid and rolled into the river.[105] Reno watered his horses and then crossed to the other side. They started out north on the plain bordered by a densely wooded area with cottonwood trees, bullberry thickets and willows along the west bank, Lieutenant Varnum in the van.[106]

Some of the soldiers caught a glimpse of Custer's battle flag on the bluffs.[107] This strongly suggests that

Custer's trail was along the bluffs, from Reno Hill to Weir Point, rather than, as is usually depicted, higher up along Sharpshooter Ridge, where the battalion would be less visible from across the river. The battalion marched three miles, and then began to see the outskirts of the tepee village. Reno saw warriors pouring out of the encampment and knew immediately that he had lost the advantage of surprise. He sent two messengers back to Custer, reporting his position, no doubt to remind him of his promise of support. No response was received from Custer. Reno's orders had been to pursue the warriors into the village, but not without the assurance of support. He had assumed that Custer would be following behind him, not having spoken directly to Custer, and not knowing of Custer's probable intention to attack from across Ford B.

Ordering the men to *Draw Pistols!* (revolvers), Reno led them forward towards the encampment, two to three miles ahead. More and more warriors streamed out of the village.

Reno could see immediately that a six-round revolver load would not get his battalion to the encampment, let alone through the encampment. He knew that there would be no opportunity for the soldiers to reload, while mounted.

Reloading the 1873 Peacemaker revolver requires the use of two hands. For a right-handed person, the weapon is grasped in the left hand. The right hand opens the loading gate and half-cocks the hammer to allow the cylinder to spin. The cylinder is rotated until an empty cartridge is aligned with the loading gate. The shooter ejects the empty cartridge by means of an ejection rod lying alongside the barrel. This is repeated for each of the six charge holes. The revolver is then reloaded by inserting each new cartridge through the loading gate into the charge hole. The gate is then snapped shut, the hammer fully cocked and the revolver is then ready to fire. The reloading cannot be performed while the cavalryman holds the reins, especially if the mount is frightened by the scent of the ponies, the shrill cries of the warriors and the sounds of the bone whistles. One of the companies had Smith and Wesson top break .44 caliber revolvers which eject their cartridges automatically when the cylinder is unhinged from the frame, but their numbers were few; and the weapon still required two hands. A soldier summed up the situation: "To attack the village would have been be suicidal."[108]

Warriors, who had acquired their skills while hunting buffalo, were able to fire their carbines from a galloping pony (and sometimes from under the neck of the pony), but firing the single-shot Springfield while mounted was not a part of the troopers' training. Cavalry tradition had long held that the charge was meant to be used only for initial shock, thereby permitting the cavalry to choose its ground for dismounted battle.

With hundreds of warriors racing toward him, Reno ordered the battalion to dismount and form a skirmish line. Two companies were placed on the line and one company held in reserve. To the left of the line were eight Arikara and two Crows.[109] Five of the other Arikara scouts galloped up to the warrior herd. They killed a Lakota woman and her children, later found to be the family of Chief Gall.[110] After cutting out some ponies, they led them towards the river but were forced to abandon them when pursued by the warriors.[111]

Informed that the warriors were moving along the east bank in an attempt to spook the horses, Reno sent the reserve company into the woods to protect the mounts. If the horses were stampeded, the battalion would be cut off. Meanwhile, as the warriors swept around the flank to the rear of his skirmish line, Reno swung his line clockwise, so that the backs of the soldiers would now border the timber belt. The Arikara abandoned their position on the line but remained with Reno throughout the battle.[112]

The soldiers, a quarter of them with less than a year of service, fired as quickly as they could load and were rapidly exhausting the fifty rounds of ammunition in their belts. With soldiers firing two to three rounds a minute, the one hundred rounds of ammunition would last no longer than fifty minutes, assuming that the soldier could fetch the ammunition from his horse and that the horse had not been stampeded. Otherwise, twenty minutes of normal fire would exhaust the supply of cartridges in his cartridge belt. Some of the carbines jammed when the locks overheated, causing the soft, copper-plated cartridge to expand and resist ejection. This strongly suggests that a few of the soldiers in panic may have been firing more rapidly than three rounds a minute; or, perhaps, that the cartridges somehow had become soiled with verdigris or dirt. "I thought we were about to meet our end, every one of us," later wrote one of the scouts.[113] He may not have been a soldier, but he knew the odds.

Reno saw that his position was untenable. In short order, the warriors would occupy the east bank and present an additional danger front. According to one of the non-commissioned officer veterans, "If Reno had remained in the timber a short time longer, not a man would have made his escape. The Indians were about ten to one of us."[114] After consulting with Captain French,[115] a respected brawler, Reno ordered a withdrawal. The troopers ran for their horses. In the melee, some grabbed whatever mount they could find, others took wounded mounts, and some without mounts had to be abandoned. Fourteen men, three scouts, Lieutenant De Rudio and the dead and wounded were left behind; but the rest escaped, or at least were able to leave the trap.

Reno began the withdrawal at a gallop. He realized that the battalion could not possibly reach the original ford with the nimble warriors in pursuit. When the scouts indicated a crossing a half mile distant from their skirmish line, Reno led his disorganized battalion towards it.

The new crossing had steep embankments on both sides of the river. Amid frightful confusion, thrashing horses, screaming men, hand-to-hand combat and general chaos, they managed to cross the river. Men rode two and three on a horse, some crossed on foot, holding a horse's tail.[116] Captain French is said to have been the last person to ford the river, bravely protecting the rear of the fleeing battalion.[117] In point of fact, several Arikara also remained behind and continued fighting until they had an opportunity to withdraw.[118] Thus far, Reno had lost twenty-nine men and had three officers killed and seven soldiers wounded. Two Arikara scouts had been killed and one Arikara and one Crow wounded.[119] The rout had one other consequence. It helped the warriors replenish some of the badly needed ammunition, which they took from the slain troopers and their horses.

Reno and the remnants of his three companies scrambled up the bluff following an old buffalo trail, with the warriors close behind. In the climb, one officer, one surgeon and three enlisted men were killed. Atop the bluff, they came to a horseshoe-shaped elevation with the open edge facing west. Enemy fire had begun to slacken, as warriors rushed off to attend to Custer. When Reno discovered that his adjutant was missing, he borrowed a carbine and went down the bluff to search for him. He found the body near the river and removed the West Point class ring to give to his family.[120]

Returning to the crest of the bluff, Reno ordered the wounded and the animals to be placed in the meadow-like depression in the center of the horseshoe. There was a total of sixty-six wounded in the entire engagement, not all with serious injury.[121] The soldiers took up defensive positions. Some had only five cartridges remaining.[122] Their situation was desperate. At about 4:30 p.m., Captain Benteen and his three companies rode into view.

Reno rushed out and implored Benteen to help him defend his position. Benteen noted that Captain Moylan was "blubbering like a whipped urchin."[123] Reno read the order Benteen had received from Custer and dispatched an officer to hurry the mule train. Benteen ordered his men to share their ammunition with Reno's battalion, which they did begrudgingly.[124]

The besieged soldiers were soon joined by five Crow scouts; two of Reno's and three of Custer's.[125] Some remained with Reno, others left to find Terry. The Arikara had also returned to Reno Hill. Two of them actively participated in the defenses; the rest remained, but did not participate.[126]

During a lull in the fighting, Captain Weir and his lieutenant rode off with D Company, again without permission, to discover the whereabouts of Custer. Benteen followed behind with his other two companies, as did Reno, with French's company. Reno's remaining two companies were left behind with the wounded. Reno kept ordering his trumpeter to sound *Halt!*, intended for Weir.[127]

The party arrived at a site one mile from the redoubt, now called "Weir Point," where, to their horror, they caught a partial glimpse from atop the hillock of the encampment across the river. [According to Crow tradition, this was also the observation point that Custer and Martin had mounted.[128] The author has seen riders easily mount this hillock on horseback. The Custer Battlefield is not visible from the base of the hillock at Weir Point]. They also saw three miles upriver what looked like ants moving around a field.[129] There was no mention of an overhanging cloud of smoke, merely dust kicked up by the riders. When they looked again, hoards of warriors were galloping in their direction. Unknown to the officers, the warriors had finished off Custer and were now directing their attention to the remaining cavalrymen.

With the warriors streaming towards them, the companies began to fall back to the redoubt. Benteen directed the withdrawal. He ordered Captain French and Lieutenant Godfrey to take up positions on each side of Weir's company.[130] According to Benteen, Weir's company withdrew "pell-mell." Next, French's company followed, leaving Godfrey to cover the retreat with only twenty-two men[131] and a few of Weir's soldiers.[132] Godfrey quickly dismounted his men and had the horse-holders take the reins. He then formed a skirmish line. Carbine in hand, he ordered the men to dress on him, and begin firing at the enemy.[133] His company slowly fell back in good order. Fortunate for the retreating men, the warriors could not outflank them because of the lay of the land, and had to press them directly. The men retreated a short distance, stopped to reload, fired and retreated, repeating the procedure until all the companies were able to reach Reno Hill.[134] The entire excursion had taken two hours.[135] One soldier in Weir's company had been wounded and abandoned to a certain death.

Years later, after having read Godfrey's celebrated account of the Little Bighorn Battle, Benteen was angered because Godfrey made no mention of the fact that it was Benteen who had assigned the flanking positions to French and Godfrey.[136] Benteen seems to have begrudged Godfrey his brief moment of glory.

The mule train finally arrived at Reno Hill with the badly needed ammunition and supplies. Shortly thereafter, twelve men and a scout who had been left across the river, took advantage of the lull in the fighting to rejoin Reno. Also arrived were twenty-nine stragglers from Custer wing. Because of the condition of their horses, they had dropped far behind Custer and so avoided Custer's fate. Their numbers must be subtracted from the original complement in Custer's battalion.

Now that two battalions were on Reno Hill, new defensive positions had to be assigned. To accord with standard military protocol, Benteen first sought permission from Major Reno to make the arrangements. He shortened the defense perimeter, after explaining his reasons to his superior officer. The line took the shape of a narrow frying pan with Benteen's battalion occupying the handle pointing south, from which most of the attack was expected, and Reno's battalion comprising the rim of the pan. Sacks, boxes and saddle packs, etc. were used to reinforce the breastworks. The usually placid Benteen was not above yelling at First Lieutenant Mathey, the pack officer, who had allowed some pack mules to stray.[137] Benteen himself helped round them up.[138] The mules and horses were brought to the center meadow alongside the surgeon's station and saddles were kept on them. The twenty-eight-year-old surgeon had forty wounded soldiers in his immediate care and performed his duties in the highest tradition of his profession.

Enemy fire started and soon turned into a deafening roar that continued throughout the day. The men heard "zip" for carbine fire and "zing-g-g" for rifle fire.[139] The warriors charged the army position three or four times, approaching near enough to throw stones.[140] Warriors on a nearby ridge kept up sporadic fire with Sharps rifles, picking off exposed soldiers. Only when one of the sergeants returned fire with a Sharps 2x telescope rifle, fetched from a pack mule, did the sniper fire from Sharpshooter's Ridge slacken.[141]

At 9 p.m. the warrior fire subsided, and the troops were quickly rearranged to close the gaps in the line. With no construction tools on hand, the men used cups and knives to dig rifle pits, and they arranged the dead animals to protect from enemy fire. Standing erect while the other officers cowered behind obstacles, Benteen was continuously exposed to enemy fire. He moved up and down the line from soldier to soldier, comforting and encouraging. "He never sheltered his own person once during the battle, and I do not see how he escaped being killed," wrote one scout.[142] Varnum remembers that he was the only man he ever saw who did not dodge when the bullets were flying. When his men needed ammunition, Benteen himself distributed it.[143] Private Glenn recalls that "his shirttail worked out of his pants and hung down and he went around that way encouraging the men."[144] Benteen did sustain a minor wound to the right thumb. He drove skulkers back to the line.[145] Lieutenant Gibson accompanied him and was ordered to kick any soldier nodding off to sleep.[146] Some soldiers smoked their pipes and others dozed with eyes open.[147] On the one occasion when Benteen tried to snatch a moment of sleep, a bullet struck the heel of his boot. He hurled the heel contemptuously at the enemy and started up his rounds.[148]

Major Reno also walked the perimeter of his battalion, encouraging the men and the officers. One of the troopers recalled: "I cannot understand why he [Reno] was not shot down, as none of the troopers were able to make a move without drawing the fire of the enemy."[149]

Some officers are said to have hidden behind shelter, among them Moylan, who remained behind stacks of hardtack and bacon until the warriors retreated.[150] He was thereafter known to the soldiers as "Hardtack Mick."[151] The information was related by a sergeant who detested the officer. Captain Moylan was later cited for bravery during the Bear Paw Battle in the Nez Perce War. Sixteen men were to lose their lives on the hill, forty wounded; these in addition to the men lost or wounded in the retreat.

At midnight, trumpet sounds were heard. Hope soared, only to be dashed when the regiment realized that the sound came from warriors across the river who had captured the instrument, probably taken from a fallen trumpeter.

Around 2 a.m., two rifle shots heralded a new surge of warrior fire. The warrior attack was renewed with "great determination."[152]

During the night, Reno is said to have suggested to Benteen that they abandon the wounded and ride off, a proposal which Benteen says that he promptly rejected.

Benteen did not reveal the story, apart from dark hints, until after Reno had left the army. It is quite possible that Benteen may have distorted or exaggerated the conversation or reported it out of context, to officers only too willing to hear and believe the worst about a commander, who, as events enfolded, denied them proper recognition. The enlisted men who served at Little Bighorn had Reno's measure and did not believe that Reno would have willingly abandoned the wounded.[153] Benteen later slyly hinted that Godfrey, Moylan and Gibson "did far from well" at the Little Bighorn, implying cowardice, so we see that Benteen had no reluctance in liberally distributing his accusations.[154] Had the three aforementioned officers known what Benteen wrote of them, they might not have been so ready to accept Benteen's charges against Major Reno.

A commanding officer must consider what must be done if the position were overrun. Had they remained across the river, all would have shared Custer's end. No one present at the battle across the river thought differently. "Fight to the last man!" is a gallant maxim and has merit, especially in instances where escape is impossible. But soldiers must be given an opportunity to escape from certain death, if they chose to do so. Not all the crew wants to go down with the ship. On the night of the June 25, the enlisted men at Reno Hill discussed among themselves the possibility of escaping, but dismissed the idea as impossible.[155] Several of Custer's men and officers had tried to escape, if one accepts the testimony of Chief Gall.[156] Men also fled the Custer

Battlefield down Deep Ravine. At what point should Reno release his men and officers, if they want to flee? This is probably what Reno discussed with Benteen, and it is what any honorable commanding officer would consider when facing highly probable defeat.[157] Reno had no certainty that Terry would show up on the twenty-sixth, nor in fact did he. If no one (Heaven forbid!) thought of escape, then why were the saddles kept on the horses picketed in the depression on Reno Hill?

Half the warriors had bows and arrows, often in addition to firearms. Arrows were especially troublesome when lobbed into the depression in which the horses and mules had been picketed. Benteen's own two horses were wounded.[158] Amazingly, there were no known arrow wounds among the surviving soldiers,[159] suggesting that the arrow was not a primary weapon, but was used chiefly after battle for target practice on dead bodies. The other half of the warriors relied chiefly on firearms of which there were forty-five different kinds, ranging from the muzzleloaders to breechloaders. The myth has sprung up that the warriors' success was due to their many repeating weapons. Given the huge numbers of warriors, it is difficult to see why repeaters would have given them so great an advantage, especially with the scarcity and high cost of ammunition.[160]

As for the army carbine, Benteen never ceased to declare, even long after the Sioux War, that the Springfield trap door carbine was accurate, dependable and deadly to five hundred yards.[161] Nor does he dwell on cartridges jamming the breechblock. The army continued to use the Springfield trapdoor breechloader for another sixteen years.

Daybreak saw the renewal of the siege by hundreds of warriors who had infiltrated the area and concealed themselves behind every depression, mound, rock, cavity or natural feature that could be used to advantage. Men and animals dropped in a shower of bullets. Around 9 a.m., the position on Reno Hill was perilous, as the attackers advanced to within a stone's throw of the defenses. Benteen rushed packers and the wounded to the line, to reinforce the H Company position. He drove the skulkers back to the fight.[162] Benteen instructed Lieutenant Gibson to hold the position at all hazard, if Benteen were to fall. Around 9:30 a.m., the warriors made another desperate attack on Benteen's defenses. One warrior approached close enough to touch a soldier with a coup stick. Somehow, the line held, and the enemy was driven back.

Fearing a renewed attack on his sector of the line, Benteen requested that Reno reinforce him with one of Reno's companies. Reno ordered French's company transferred to the panhandle. Although M Company was a close ally of H Company, both stationed at Fort Rice, Benteen had to yell at their sergeant-major before M Company could be persuaded to move. Standing erect, Benteen continued to pace the defense perimeter, providing inspiration to the fearful.

When a sergeant had his hat shot off, Benteen yelled at him: "Damn you, I told you to keep down!"

Little Bighorn

The sergeant replied, "Captain, sorr, it's you yourself should keep down."

"Oh, pshaw, they won't get me," Benteen grinned and continued on.[163]

Benteen had begun to understand that unless the warriors could be displaced from their nearby sheltered positions, they would continue the assault until the line was overrun. Benteen obtained permission to attack the warrior position. He moved up and down the line, explaining to H and M Companies what he wanted done. He was interrupted by a warrior who raced shrieking towards him. Benteen shot him and resumed his instructions.

The warriors called out to the soldiers: "Come on, come on, if you are brave, we are ready for you."[164]

"Get ready, men. Now, Charge!" cried Benteen. Standing up in full view, he led his screaming men down the bluff, with bullets flying at them from all directions. The warriors promptly scattered. One soldier was killed.

"Now get back to your holes!" cried Benteen, and the men raced back to their rifle pits.[165]

Clearing the warriors had opened the way to a small ravine leading down to the river. By now, the canteens were empty and the wounded were clamoring for water. At 10 a.m., with four men from H Company guarding the path to the ravine, a few brave soldiers and a brave Crow scout[166] made their way to the river three hundred yards away to fetch water in pots, kettles and canteens. Benteen watched the soldiers, standing erect for all to see, including the warriors. "If they're going to get you," he murmured fatalistically, "they will—."[167] Several additional trips were made to the riverbank. Without water, their position might soon have collapsed. The men on Beecher Island had withstood nine days of attack, but they had easy access to water.

Benteen's bravery was not lost on the regiment. "Say nothing about what I am about to tell you," wrote Gibson to his wife, "but if it had not been for Benteen, every one of us would have been massacred."[168] "Too much cannot be said in favor of Captain Benteen," wrote one non-commissioned officer whom Benteen had twice court-martialed. "His prompt movements saved Reno from utter annihilation and his gallantry in clearing the ravines of Indians and opening the way for water for the suffering wounded."[169]

The savage fusillade continued into the afternoon and then subsided, enabling the soldiers to further perfect their position. At 2 p.m. the enemy barrage restarted, driving the soldiers back to their rifle pits. Then the firing began to wane. Hours passed, interrupted by an occasional enemy shot.

Across the river smoke appeared. The warriors had set fire to the grass, to hinder pursuit. The regiment watched in amazement as an huge column three miles long and a half mile wide began moving upriver, composed of the warriors, their families and their immense herd of horses. Later it was learned that the chiefs had received word that the "walking soldiers" had reached the Bighorn River.[170]

As night fell, the stench of the dead bodies had become overpowering. The two battalions were moved closer to the river, so that the men could better water the animals. The soldiers lay down for their first good sleep. During the night, the two scouts who had been left behind reappeared in camp, followed shortly thereafter by Lieutenant De Rudio and an enlisted man.

The relief column drew closer. They might have reached the men at Reno Hill on June 26, had the column not become entangled in a shortcut through some badlands. When their scouts learned that Custer had been butchered, they deserted, leaving the column to find its own way.[171] The fate of the Custer wing was confirmed by the Crow scouts, among them a young scout named Curley, who described the massacre by grabbing his scalplock and repeating "Absaroka!" (Soldiers!)." It has been said unfairly that Curley fled the field before the end and fabricated his report, but the fact that he described the dismal outcome confirms that he had witnessed the battle. The Gibbon column steadfastly pushed on and on June 27, made contact with the Reno party.

The following day Benteen led a party to the Custer battleground where he surveyed the bodies, almost all of them naked and mutilated. Custer had a gunshot wound of the left flank and the left temple, neither wound with powder marks.[172] There may have been other injuries as well. On viewing Custer, lying naked except for his socks, Benteen is reported to have said: "there he is, God damn him, he will never fight anymore." He wrote Custer's name on a paper and nailed it to a wooden stake to identify the remains.[173] Some of the bodies had been pierced by many arrows and lances, as if used for target practice. "I served through the Civil War," wrote one sergeant of the mutilations, "and saw many hard sights on the battlefield, but never saw such a sight as I saw there."[174]

Saddles and equipage had all been removed by the warriors, who also took the ammunition in the cartridge belts. Some of the men had been shot with ammunition captured from the fighting across the river.[175] Not all the bodies were accounted for. Later, warriors claimed that some fleeing soldiers were killed as far away as six miles from the battlefield.[176] Others are still buried in a cut (Deep Ravine) leading toward the river.

The dead warriors had been taken back to the village. Chief Gall later estimated that forty-three had been killed on the battlefield, but a number of the wounded warriors had crossed the river and died in the bushes.[177] Crazy Horse's estimate was ninety-six killed, Sitting Bull's was twenty-five,[178] but Sitting Bull was not present during the fight. When the soldiers later inspected the deserted encampment, they found many warrior bodies on scaffolds. In their haste to depart, the warriors had abandoned two hundred wagonloads of supplies and goods.

On June 28, the survivors moved their camp across the Little Bighorn River to the site of the enemy encampment, where there was better grazing. The abandoned tepee poles were used to make shelters. The soldiers stripped the dead warriors of their buckskin shirts and earrings.[179] Benteen was understandably short-tempered from lack of sleep, and Lieutenant De Rudio received the brunt. While at Fort Rice, the lieutenant had borrowed a revolver and holster from Benteen. He lost the holster in the excitement of Reno's retreat and when he returned the revolver without its holster, Benteen railed at him. "Now that is a specimen of the character of Italians," Benteen later wrote of the incident.[180] Such is the paradox of Benteen. He showed extraordinary courtesy and sensitivity to De Rudio, patiently taught him, defended him, lent him money when he was in great need, socialized with him and his wife, did many favors for them; yet is not above insulting the man when it suited his mood.

Transporting the wounded proved to be a daunting task, even with the help of the Gibbon column. How then could the battalions on Reno Hill have rushed to Custer's aid without abandoning the wounded? Transport by hand litter took 150 men six hours just to move the first three miles, with the injured shrieking in agony. A Lieutenant Gustavus Doane of the 2nd Cavalry came to the rescue by making horse litters, using two tepee poles sixteen feet long, covered with horsehide.[181] It took an additional two days to move the wounded to the boat landing on the Bighorn River, fifteen miles away. The wounded were then laid on grass mattresses on the lower deck of the riverboat, the *Far West*. One is amazed to learn that the mortality among the wounded was only nine percent, and there were no known cases of tetanus.[182]

Terry marched Gibbon's column and the remnants of the 7th Cavalry to the Yellowstone River, where the *Far West* awaited them. The wounded were disembarked and in their place the troops were ferried across. The wounded were then reloaded, and the riverboat set off down the Yellowstone to Fort Abraham Lincoln with a full head of steam.

The Yellowstone River is more navigable than the other tributaries of the Missouri. During the summer months, the river is seldom less than four feet deep. Its bed is hard gravel and the bars and channels less likely to shift.[183] Nevertheless, maneuvering a riverboat required frequent backing, hauling and dodging. Fortunately, fuel was plentiful, since the banks of the Yellowstone were more densely timbered than the Missouri.

After fifty-four hours of travel, the *Far West* arrived at Fort Lincoln in the early hours of July 6, to be greeted by the stunned army families as they watched the forty-three wounded being disembarked. Three had died en route. Thirty-two women were left widows, including three Indian wives, who slashed themselves to show their grief.[184] The bereaved families were given a month to evacuate their quarters. Several of the officers had life insurance policies. Custer had left a $4,750 policy; two other officers had policies for twice that amount. Custer had also left behind an unpaid promissory note for $13,000.

The army camped for a week on the northern bank of the Yellowstone. Mail arrived. Benteen received a letter from his brother, Theodore, Jr., in San Francisco who wrote that he had read about the Little Bighorn Battle and hinted that he was short of money. On July 4, in "gratitude to Major Reno and Captain Benteen for saving their lives," 235 survivors signed a petition to the

President requesting that Reno be promoted to lieutenant colonel, Benteen to major, and the other officers "by seniority."[185] Such a petition might have been tolerated during the Civil War, but in the regular army it was considered impertinent. No action was taken on the petition. Many enlisted men suspected that it might have been drawn up at Reno's headquarters and circulated by his chief trumpeter "It was a d—d humbug," said one of the sergeants, "but what's the odds?"[186] It is doubtful that Benteen had a part in engineering the project, since the glowing praise he had been receiving made any efforts at self-aggrandizement unnecessary.

Also in the mail was an early letter from Sheridan to Terry, cautioning Terry not to split his command, since Sheridan had information that at least five thousand warriors were in the vicinity.[187]

After writing letters of commiseration to the bereaved families, Reno drew up the official battle report. In it, Reno commended only one officer by name, Frederick W. Benteen: "During my fight with the Indians, I had the heartiest support from officers and men, but the conspicuous services of Brevet Colonel Frederick W. Benteen, I desire to call attention to especially, for if ever a soldier deserved recognition by his government for distinguished services, he certainly does."

The other officers were outraged that no mention by name was made of their services.[188] At the very least, they felt that they were all entitled to receive one brevet rank for their gallantry,[189] even though by now Congress had suspended the brevet awards. Although

Benteen had not been consulted about the report, he was blamed for it by the other officers.[190] Had Reno spread his praise more liberally, as most field officers do in similar circumstances, he might have fared differently.

In his spare time, Benteen fished. Baseball games were curtailed, since many of the players in Benteen's club had been killed or wounded.[191] Benteen's letters reveal an unceasing hatred of Custer, on whose shoulders he placed sole responsibility for the disaster. In his opinion, Custer should have attacked the village from the south with all twelve companies and held on until relieved by Terry and Gibbon.[192] He was angered to learn that the Sioux had run off with some horses at Fort Rice and hoped that his own mare and colt were safe. He instructed Kate to insure that the stable men graze and feed them properly. Fodder was sometimes in short supply at Fort Rice during the summer, when the depth of the Missouri dropped. If put out to graze, the horses had to be carefully protected from the Lakota warriors.

As the troops wiled away the time, tempers frayed and arguments became frequent. Godfrey noted in his diary that Reno often insulted his staff, so that no one was on speaking terms with him.[193] Crook's adjutant wrote about Reno: "without record, without talent or education or common honesty of purpose, he is a low vulgar-minded, ill-bred ignoramus."[194] Weir nearly came to blows with Benteen, when the former complained about not being mentioned in Reno's report. On another occasion, when deep in his cups, Benteen sent his sergeant to the other officers, with the message that they were all pack of cowards, except for Captain French. He saw Captain Weir talking with the other officers and called him "a damned liar." When Weir proposed a duel, Benteen produced two revolvers, but Weir declined the offer. After Benteen sobered up, Weir offered his hand, which Benteen accepted.[195] Both Weir and French were drinking excessively and drink would shortly ruin them. Benteen's downfall took longer.

In August, Crook sprang belatedly into action, setting out once again from Fort Fetterman in Wyoming. At War Bonnet Creek near the Red Cloud Agency, his column intercepted a band of Cheyenne who were on the way to join the others; and forced them to return to the reservation. Along with Crook came twenty-five to thirty reporters and "Buffalo Bill" Cody, the flamboyant Wild West entrepreneur, who had let it be known back east that he was out to avenge Custer. He managed to scalp a Cheyenne leader about to ambush a messenger and proudly exhibited the scalp on his return to New York.

Following a stale trail, General Terry led the column to the Rosebud River. The valley had been picked clean for grazing. The Rosebud valley had been a favorite burial place for the Lakota, and many cottonwood burial scaffolds were in evidence.[196] The column marched down the Rosebud to its junction with the Yellowstone River and set up camp. The next day they were reinforced by the 5th Infantry under the command of Colonel Nelson A. Miles. Ten days later, Crook's column arrived, having braved hail, flies, mosquitoes, grasshoppers and sickness. The two columns played baseball, officers against the soldiers.[197] Many reporters contrasted Terry's command with its large wall tents, portable beds, and dining room tent, to the small fly-tent where Crook had his headquarters. Terry had two hundred wagons; Crook, only the pack mules.

Benteen faulted Crook for turning back after his defeat in June at the Rosebud River. Not that Benteen made his feelings known to Crook, but the animosity, later fateful for Benteen, is quite evident even at this early time.

"Buffalo Bill" Cody shared Benteen's mess and listened to the stories. In his autobiography, Cody devoted a chapter to the tale of Lieutenant De Rudio, who was separated during Reno's retreat and, after many thrilling moments, found his way to the Reno Hill. The officers and enlisted men of the 7th Cavalry were also widely interviewed by the press. Benteen fared exceedingly well in the newspaper reports. The captain of the *Far West* wrote to the President urging that Benteen be recognized "for the ability and bravery displayed during the General Custer fight."[198]

Terry and Crook joined forces, the combined column numbering an astonishing seven thousand men. They followed another stale warrior trail to the Tongue River and then to the Powder River, without encountering a single warrior. The weather was cold and wet and the trails, muddy. Terry tried to load provisions onto mules, as Crook had done, but was less successful. Also, unlike Crook, Terry was hampered by stragglers.

After an unsuccessful pursuit, Terry broke off from Crook and disbanded his troops. He sent Gibbon's column back to Fort Ellis and allowed a single battalion of the 7th Cavalry to return to Fort Lincoln. Miles was kept on the Yellowstone to supervise the construction of two new forts, which were to serve as supply depots for winter campaigns. The reporters were disgusted: "Not an Indian has been killed since the Custer disaster and nearly a fifth of the U.S. Army has been out here trying to kill some."[199]

In desperate need of a victory, Crook followed a warrior trail south in incessant rain. As time wore on, the rations became alarmingly reduced. On September 9, his cavalry finally encountered a thirty-seven-lodge Oglala Sioux camp at Slim Buttes, a landmark rock formation on the Sioux Reservation. Crook won a fierce and much-publicized battle, but not before having to repulse a savage counterattack by Crazy Horse and his three hundred warriors. After the battle, the warriors split into smaller bands and vanished.

While camped on the Powder River, the 7th Cavalry battalion celebrated the birthdays of three officers, Benteen and De Rudio among them. Benteen had received notice that he was being sent on recruiting duties for two years, on Reno's recommendation. "The regiment will certainly feel his loss," wrote Godfrey.[200]

One of the journalists from the *Chicago Daily Tribune* interviewed Benteen. His report on September 9[201] demonstrates Benteen's skill in manipulating the press:

"Captain Benteen is a remarkable man and it is one of the devilish mean regulations of the army that such a man as Benteen is left in the lurch.

Although well up in years, he had the careful, honest features of a boy. In resources, he is a Napoleon in courage, a coer de Leon. Yet, the great fatherly patriotic government he serves can do nothing better for him...than an assignment to recruiting service."

The Sioux War continued into the snow months. In November 1876, Crook made his way up the Bozeman Trail from Fort Fetterman and encountered a two-hundred-lodge village of Cheyenne on the Powder River, led by Chief Dull Knife and Little Wolf. He routed the warriors and beat back a counter-attack, but was forced to halt his campaign for lack of supplies.

Throughout the winter, the commands of Miles and Crook relentlessly pursued the tribes. They destroyed their provisions, captured their horses, frightened their game and occasionally engaged them in skirmishes. Most ruinous of all to the warrior was his inability to rest up through the winter.

In January 1877, Miles defeated a force of five hundred Sioux-Cheyenne on Wolf Mountain, Montana. The doleful news persuaded Sitting Bull to move his people into Canada. By the coming of spring, the warriors had lost the will to fight. On May 6th, in desperation, Crazy Horse led nine hundred of his people to the Camp Robinson, Nebraska reservation. The next day the Miniconjou Lakota were defeated by Miles at Muddy Creek, Montana, in the last major action in the Sioux War. The reservation warriors had by now returned to the agencies to collect their annuities, and three thousand roamers joined them. The Lakota were allowed to remain on the Great Sioux Reservation, but the Northern Cheyenne were ordered to the Indian Territory in Oklahoma, to join their brothers, the Southern Cheyenne.

Not all the Lakota surrendered. Some remained at large, fearful of becoming an easy target for government reprisals, but by the autumn of 1877, concerted hostile activity had ceased.

The battalion released by General Terry arrived at Fort Lincoln on September 28, in sore need of refitting. They were greeted with awe by five hundred raw recruits, who had enlisted to "avenge Custer." After a stay of three weeks, the two Fort Rice companies set out for home.

Benteen was not with them. He had departed three weeks earlier on his recruiting assignment, aboard the riverboat *Benton*, which carried several officers and sick soldiers. Benteen stopped at Terry's headquarters in St. Paul and stayed at the Merchant's Hotel, while he made travel arrangements. To a young officer in St. Paul, about to join the regiment, Benteen "was the hero of all America, credited with saving the remnant of the Seventh Cavalry."[202] While in St. Paul, Benteen scurried around, trying to get a free railroad pass for his family. Many regarded the free pass as a recognition of his status in society. No man with money, or official position or influence thought it necessary to pay for riding on a railroad.

He began to have second thoughts about the recruiting duty. In the end, he succeeded in persuading Colonel Sturgis to replace him with Captain Tom Weir. Sturgis agreed to the arrangement but made Benteen proceed to Philadelphia until such time as Weir could relieve him. Benteen traveled by way of Chicago and St. Louis, visiting friends and relatives on the way. He arrived in Philadelphia on October 8, 1876, while the Centennial Exposition was still in progress, the greatest spectacle of its kind ever seen in America, consisting of five huge buildings, built on 300 acres. Benteen spent a few days inspecting the exhibits. Perhaps he saw the telephone, the typewriter, the mimeograph, the Otis elevator or the head and torch of the Statue of Liberty, which were on display. He wrote Kate that he was not impressed with the exhibition. He shopped for the wives back in Fort Rice and Lincoln, and, at his wife's insistence, bought some contraceptive condoms,[203] which reflected Kate's fear of another pregnancy. The arrangements with Weir finally concluded, Benteen returned to H Company at Fort Rice.

In November, 1876, the Lincoln and Rice companies were sent to the Standing Rock and Grand River Agencies on the Great Sioux Reservation, to confiscate firearms, ponies and anything bearing a US stamp. A pile of stolen goods as "as high as a haystack" was found and burned. The army seized two thousand ponies, supposedly to provide funds for the purchase of cows and working oxen for the Lakota. This left the warriors completely dependent on the government allotments. Hundreds of the impounded ponies died before they reached Fort Lincoln. In response to public outcry, Congress later appropriated funds to compensate the Lakota.[204]

While in New York, Captain Thomas Weir was approached by an author, Frederick Whittaker, who was engaged in writing a biography of George A. Custer. Whittaker had served with Custer during the Civil War and was acquainted with Libby Custer. From Weir, Whittaker obtained some statements which were said to be damaging to Reno and Benteen regarding their performance during the Little Bighorn Battle. Weir, however, refused to sign an affidavit and protested to a friend that he was being pressured.[205] Weir also corresponded with Libby Custer, darkly hinting at some deep secrets that he would later disclose. On the basis of Weir's information, Whittaker rushed into print a biography, using Custer's Civil War autobiography and selected newspaper clippings of the Little Bighorn Battle taken from the New York press. In his book, Whittaker accused Reno of cowardice and Benteen of indifference. Weir died before publication, from the indirect effects of alcoholism while on recruiting duty in New York. Whittaker now had a safe source to attribute his allegations.

Whittaker's book appeared in print in December 1876.[206] It was an immediate sensation and served as an unchallenged template for other authors during the next five decades. Whittaker concluded that if Reno had fought as Custer had fought and if Benteen had obeyed Custer's orders, the Battle of the Little Bighorn might have proven Custer's last and greatest victory.

The *Army and Navy Journal* reviewed Whittaker's book on December 22, 1876, and noted that the author's conclusions "were frequently based on ex parte sentiments of a few individuals." On December 27, 1876, Whittaker replied to the criticism. He asserted that Benteen had promised to send him his version of the battle but had reneged on his promise.

Benteen answered from Fort Rice on January 27 in a letter to the *Journal*, published under the caption "How History is Manufactured." He stated that the officers on whom Whittaker had relied, were no more than a "Society for Mutual Admiration," which had Colonel Reno as its chief target. "No first class members were contributing members; none of them can bear the test of light and truth; but still they have succeeded in getting vile slanders into public print."

Colonel Sturgis returned to Fort Lincoln from recruiting duty in St. Louis and relieved Major Reno, who had been the acting post commander. Reno had been drinking heavily, especially since the Little Bighorn Battle. The quantity of spirits he had purchased was impressive. There were several disturbing allegations whispered about of other matters, but no evidence has ever surfaced.[207] Reno was sent to Fort Abercrombie, where he soon became mired in trouble, when he tried to foist his attentions on one of the officer's wives, of dubious reputation, whose husband was away from the fort. When the husband returned, he was persuaded to bring charges against Major Reno.

Reno was court-martialed at St. Paul, Minnesota, in March 1877. Benteen testified on his behalf on a minor point. Reno put up a ridiculous defense. He maintained that by seizing the woman's hand, he was only trying to teach her a Masonic handshake; and by holding her, he was trying to keep her from falling. Reno was found guilty and suspended from duty for two years, without pay.

In springtime of 1877, the companies of the 7th Cavalry assembled at Fort Lincoln, in preparation for field duty. The regiment marched to Fort Buford, Dakota Territory, at the junction of the Yellowstone and Missouri Rivers. Colonel Nelson Miles was now commander of the Yellowstone District. His chief task was to intercept Sitting Bull, should he and his people try to slip back across the border. In May, the regiment was ferried across the Yellowstone and ordered to patrol the northern bank, ever on the lookout for Sioux. Benteen wrote Kate to remind her to register the new foal in the New York trotting Stud Book.[208]

At the end of May, the regiment set up camp at Cedar Creek, Montana, sixty miles east of the Tongue River cantonment (Fort Keogh). From there, small patrols were sent out to keep watch for Sitting Bull.

Meanwhile, alarming reports were being received about a tribe that few had heard of.

NEZ PERCE

The Nez Perce lived tranquilly in a wide expanse in Washington Territory and Oregon. They helped develop the Appaloosa horse, a breed known for its unusual spotted markings.[1] When gold was discovered in the Wallowa Valley in Oregon, an attempt was made to drive the Nez Perce onto the Lapwai Reservation in Washington Territory. A band of young braves went on the warpath, and in the course of their rampage, nineteen settlers were killed. Fearing certain reprisals, the Nez Perce fled eastward to join their relatives, the Crows; or failing that, to join Sitting Bull in Canada. They were pursued by the one-armed General Oliver O. Howard, the "praying general," who did not march his troops on Sunday, if it could be avoided. His orders were to arrest the murderers and to drive the Nez Perce back to their reservation.

Encamped at Cedar Creek, the officers of the 7th Cavalry settled back in idleness. Benteen wrote to his wife, instructing her to get rid of their black servant who was setting a bad example for Freddie. The young man was promptly hired by Mrs. De Rudio. Many of the officers were drinking heavily, among them Captain French, who was beginning to stir fears in Benteen that the drinking might drive him out of the army.[2]

A request was received for a company to accompany Lieutenant Gustavus C. Doane of the 2nd Cavalry to the Crow reservation. Lieutenant De Rudio, now E Company commander, volunteered for the task. Benteen wrote his wife that he feared for Doane, since De Rudio would talk him to death.[3] Later, when the Nez Perce appeared on the scene, Benteen mocked De Rudio for volunteering, since he was certain to come in harm's way. The Doane-De Rudio contingent first visited the Crow reservation to enlist twenty-one scouts and to warn the Crow of the harm that would come to them by aiding the Nez Perce. The Crow had been enjoying comparative prosperity, with the fortunes of the Sioux in decline. Buffalo were plentiful, and the Crow had large herds of ponies. After enlisting the scouts, the Doane-De Rudio company was ordered to take station on the banks of the Yellowstone River, as it flows through the Yellowstone Park.

Meanwhile, the Nez Perce, led by Joseph and other chiefs, were proceeding east, in an epic exodus. They had fought General Howard at the Clearwater River, Idaho, and escaped; raided Howard's camp at Camas Meadows, Idaho, and made off with army horses; crossed the Rockies on the Lolo Trail; repulsed an attack by Colonel Gibbon at Big Hole in western Montana and were now heading towards the

Yellowstone National Park in Wyoming. Howard was under strict orders to pursue, no matter the condition of his troops or his horses.

To block an escape of the Nez Perce into Canada, Colonel Sturgis and six companies were ordered to Judith Gap, a strategic gorge through which the Nez Perce were certain to pass, if Canada were their destination. Upon receipt of the orders, Benteen wrote his wife to reassure her, but urged her to settle bills and some life insurance matters. He doubted that they would find the Nez Perce: "Chases after Indians in so vast a country where we must go with a limited quantity of supplies is but a chance in a thousand to hit the mark you are aiming at."[4]

Sturgis and his command of four hundred men traveled west by way of Pompey's Pillar to the Musselshell River and then to Judith Gap, a march of two hundred miles. Benteen was assigned a battalion of three companies, H Company among them. He availed himself of every opportunity to hunt and fish.[5] On August 21, Sturgis received word from the Doane-De Rudio contingent that the enemy had entered Yellowstone Park and was moving toward one of the two exits. Anxious to prevent the Nez Perce from joining with the Crow, higher command ordered Sturgis to march his men two hundred miles south to the Clark's Fork canyon, where he would be in a position to intercept the enemy at either exit. Here, he waited. Benteen deplored the move, arguing that they would have a better chance of intercepting the Nez Perce at Judith Gap.[6] Sturgis might have spared himself the extra march had he known that the Crow had not only refused to join the Nez Perce, but also denied them aid. Thus, for the Nez Perce the only salvation lay in Canada, "the old women's country."

Benteen wrote to his wife, complimenting her on her care of their flower bed. While the companies waited, Benteen fished for trout with his favorite birch fishing pole, wading out into the frigid stream.[7] Benteen also had brought with him a ten-gauge shotgun, which he used for fowling.[8] He also claimed to have shot eleven mallard ducks alighted on the water with eleven carbine cartridges and named a witness to prove it.[9] In later years, his fondest memories of the Nez Perce campaign were the magnificent fishing and hunting.[10]

On September 10, while the cavalry waited, the Nez Perce deceived Sturgis by throwing up dust along the Stinkwater (Shoshone) River exit, while they slipped away through Clark's Fork canyon. Howard might have alerted Sturgis, had his messengers not been intercepted by the Nez Perce. Nor could the Doane-De Rudio company notify Sturgis, since it had been recalled in an administrative mix-up. From the beginning, Benteen had warned Sturgis about a Nez Perce deception,[11] and now the very thing had come to pass. Realizing that he had become a laughing stock, Sturgis sent word to General Howard that the quarry had escaped.

Upon his return from trout fishing, Benteen heard the news of the breakout. He was relishing the discomfiture of his superior officer, when *Officers' Call!* sounded. The forlorn Sturgis announced that he was going to make an attempt to pursue the Nez Perce, but had little hope that he could catch them. The regiment had run out of supplies, and the horses were in desperate condition after their four-hundred-mile march. Benteen vigorously disagreed. He told Sturgis that they could catch up with the Nez Perce, if they marched forty miles today and fifty miles tomorrow. For food, they could eat horsemeat! Benteen recommended that his battalion be allowed to set off that very night, but Sturgis insisted that the entire unit march together.[12] Benteen's determination had galvanized Sturgis and given him hope.

The next day, September 12, 1877, the regiment force-marched fifty miles. They crossed the Yellowstone at the mouth of Clark's Fork River and rode north. The following morning Sturgis called a halt. The horses were completely spent. The Nez Perce, on the other hand, had five ponies for each warrior. When one pony was exhausted, it was killed for food and a healthy one substituted.

Suddenly the scouts rushed into camp with the news that the Nez Perce were only a few miles ahead, near Canyon Creek, Montana Territory, a confluence of three dry streams, surrounded by canyon walls three hundred feet high. Guarding the canyon leading to the river were a high bluff to the right and further north another high butte to the left, both of which were soon occupied by enemy marksmen. The narrow entrance to the canyon had been blocked with boulders, which required dislodging.

Surveying the formidable position of the warriors, Benteen recommended to Sturgis that he dislodge them with twenty to thirty rounds from their smoothbore, twelve-pound mountain howitzer.[13] The howitzer was a small field piece that could fire shell or canister. The barrel was carried on the first mule, the carriage on the next, and the ammunition on the following two mules.

Dismissing Benteen's suggestion, Sturgis ordered Major Lewis Merrill to seize the heights to the right. Merrill's battalion charged on horseback in a vain attempt to overrun the sturdy warrior position but was quickly halted by enemy fire and forced to dismount. Benteen was then ordered to travel down the valley and cut off the enemy horses grazing along the riverbanks. As his battalion galloped on the plain, it came under savage attack from the Nez Perce marksmen, perched high up on the bluffs to the left. Almost comically, Benteen carried in his hand his birch fishing pole, as if it were a lance. Fortunately, he had remembered to remove the fishing line before leading the charge.[14] Chief Joseph is said to have later recalled the gallant officer on a brown horse whom his sharpshooters had tried to bring down.[15]

With the aid of the Crow scouts, the battalion cut out several hundred horses before the Nez Perce could round up the herd. Benteen then turned his battalion towards the bluffs on the left and began charging up the heights. Major Merrill was unavailable to support him, since he was still engaged in his initial assignment. Benteen's battalion had almost reached the Nez Perce line, when it too was turned back by rifle fire. The battalion dismounted and advanced on foot, aided by a few shots from the howitzer. Not until dusk did

Benteen's battalion reach the summit, but by then the enemy had withdrawn.[16] Sturgis had no recourse but to rest the horses, while the Nez Perce slipped out of the canyon during the night. Three men were killed and eleven badly wounded, including one officer. An attempt was made to pursue the enemy, but the Nez Perce had made good their escape. All was not lost, however. The four hundred ponies captured by Benteen's battalion and the Crow scouts, were an important factor in Chief Joseph's later decision to surrender.

In retrospect, Benteen faulted the timidity of Sturgis, but his criticism seems somewhat excessive. Sturgis had made a gallant attempt, and his failure did not reflect on him or on the regiment. Nevertheless, Benteen's unyielding attitude caused him trouble with Colonel Sturgis. And there was more trouble to come. When asked to submit a battle report for his battalion, Benteen wrote a curt four paragraphs, but at the insistence of Colonel Sturgis, he amended it to include the names of several officers and enlisted men.[17]

The regiment arrived at the Musselshell River, where they awaited General Howard and the desperately needed supplies. Still in pursuit of the Nez Perce, Howard reached Sturgis and his six companies on September 22, but after reviewing the condition of their crippled horses, he allowed Sturgis to abandon the chase.

While these events were transpiring north of the Yellowstone National Park, General Nelson Miles had been camped at an cantonment (later Fort Keogh,

Montana Territory) on the Tongue-Yellowstone Rivers, leisurely watching for Sitting Bull. When word of the outcome of the Canyon Creek battle reached him, he quickly gathered a mobile force which included infantry mounted on warrior ponies and three companies of 7th Cavalry, which happened to be in the vicinity. After ferrying them over the Yellowstone River, he marched them northwest for one hundred miles to the Missouri River. A riverboat, conveniently anchored nearby, enabled him to cross the Missouri without delay. The column proceeded northwest for another one hundred miles until they came to Bear Paw, Montana. Here, the Nez Perce had halted to rest and hunt buffalo. The stop was forty miles from the border of Canada, where the Nez Perce hoped to join Sitting Bull and his four thousand followers.

Miles ordered a frontal attack on the encampment, at the same time sending his scouts to seize the pony herd. Once again, the warriors occupied the steep heights surrounding the camp, which made every army assault costly. During the first day, two officers and sixteen soldiers were killed. Realizing that further assault would be prohibitively expensive, Miles resorted to a siege. Miles had with him the new 1.56 inch Hotchkiss steel rifled breech gun, whose 2.62 pound shell had twice the range of the twelve-pound howitzer. Unfortunately, the small shell did not contain an air-burst fuse, which was needed to dislodge the warriors, deeply entrenched and behind thick log breastworks. A twelve-pound howitzer finally arrived, and by using a small charge and by digging a ditch behind the trail of the gun carriage, the artillerists could sufficiently elevate the barrel to send off a few rounds.

The battle continued for five days. The warriors especially aimed at chevrons and officer's uniforms. A total of 126 in Miles's command were killed, 140 wounded. Some of the woundings were inflicted with explosive bullets, which the warriors had obtained from an Englishman's ranch they had raided.[18] Of the 115 officers and men in the 7th Cavalry battalion, fifty-three were wounded or killed! Only one officer in the three companies escaped injury. The 7th Cavalry would never be the same again. Captain Miles Moylan and Captain Edward Godfrey were both wounded and later both were awarded Medals of Honor.

Chief Joseph was finally compelled to surrender after loosing 151 killed and eighty-eight wounded, but half the surviving Nez Perce had managed to slip away to Canada.

The captives were sent for seven long years to barren lands in Kansas and the Oklahoma Territory and then to the Colville Reservation in Washington. Chief Joseph was allowed one brief visit in 1900 to see his beloved Wallowa Valley. Even during his flight, he had become for many a national hero, and for the rest of his life, men were proud to shake his hand.

After the battle, the 7th Cavalry remained in the Montana Territory rounding up Nez Perce and Cheyenne prisoners, while awaiting orders to return to Fort Lincoln. The word never came, but Colonel Sturgis and Major Merrill managed to wangle orders to return home, leaving Benteen in command. Benteen finally obtained permission from General Terry[19] to move his men to Fort Buford, at the junction of the Yellowstone and Missouri Rivers, where a battalion with married officers was allowed to escort Cheyenne prisoners to Bismarck, on their way to the Oklahoma Territory. Benteen was not among the fortunate. In his letters home, he wrote that he was not bitter about remaining, but about seeing the field officers scurry back to a comfortable fort. While at Fort Buford, he was compelled to hand over his exhausted charger, "Dick," to the quartermaster. The horse had served him faithfully for five years.[20]

Benteen exchanged many letters with his wife, some on very intimate subjects. He promised to reduce his drinking, but stoutly denied that he drank excessively.[21] Until now, he had been a binge drinker, overindulging two to three times a year, during which time the loyal men of his company would nurse him until he was fit to go home. He discussed with his wife the possibility of resigning from the army, but decided to hold out until 1891 when his thirty years' service would qualify him for a pension. However, he reserved final judgment until he went on recruiting duty and could survey the civilian prospects.[22]

Orders to return to the Dakota Territory came in December, too late to ensure an arrival before Christmas. He marched his contingent in deep snow to Lincoln. Along the way, ten horses froze to death. He then took H and M companies to Rice, arriving January 2, 1878. The winter passed uneventfully. Many officers went on leave. Godfrey, now a captain and cited in the

Bear Paw battle report, remained at Fort Rice with D Company. Word reached the garrison that Fort Rice was being replaced by Fort Yates in the Standing Rock Reservation. In May, the battalion was officially relocated to Fort Lincoln. Benteen left behind two infants buried in the post cemetery. Fort Rice was formally abandoned the following year.

During the summer of 1878, while the regiment peacefully patrolled the Black Hills, H Company was guarding the Northern Cheyenne prisoners at Fort Lincoln. Orders were received at summer's end to conduct the captives to Bear Butte (Fort Meade), on the first part of their journey to the Indian Territory.

Work had been begun on a fort in the Black Hills, at the junction of several roads leading to the mining country. Built on an eight-square-mile reserve with the help of a sizable labor force from the mining camps, Fort Meade was ready for partial occupancy by the end of 1878. Nearby was the elevation known as Bear Butte, where the Cheyenne fasted in days gone by, while they imbibed the magic of the Black Hills. Fourteen miles from the fort was the wild frontier town of Deadwood. Colonel Sturgis took some of his companies off patrol and assigned them to assist with the fort's construction. Soldiers with special builder's skills were paid an extra thirty-five cents a day; for heavy labor, they received twenty-five cents.[23] H Company arrived at Fort Meade in August and turned over the Northern Cheyenne to a new escort.

Abruptly, the 7th Cavalry was summoned to the Pine Ridge Sioux Agency, 125 miles to the southeast of Fort

Meade, to intercept another band of Northern Cheyenne who were fleeing north from the hated Indian Territory in an astonishing 1,500 mile exodus, as tragic as that of the Nez Perce. Half the tribe were apprehended and conducted to Camp Robinson, Nebraska; the other half escaped to the Montana Territory, where they were allowed to remain. Later, after many pitiful travails, the families from Camp Robinson joined them.

Stagecoaches traveled from the railroad stations in Bismarck, Dakota Territory and Pierre, Dakota Territory, across the Great Sioux reservation to Fort Meade, Deadwood and the other Black Hills towns. The journey might take as long as seven days.[24] On one such trip, Captain French, who had been drinking heavily, abandoned the escort and ran off with a laundress, leaving behind Mrs. De Rudio and some other passengers. A court martial resulted, but the trial was repeatedly delayed by French's delirium tremens. He was found guilty of dereliction of duty and sentenced to suspension for one year at half pay. In 1880 he was removed from the active duty roster and died two years later at the age of thirty-nine.

Major Reno was the next to undergo judicial process, but in his case, a court of inquiry rather than a court martial. Frederick Whittaker, the author, had been publicly accusing Reno of cowardice and responsibility for the Custer debacle, by disregarding his orders to attack the Sioux-Northern Cheyenne encampment.[25] Whittaker contacted a Congressional delegate from the Wyoming Territory and requested that the delegate approach the House Committee on Military Affairs to institute an inquiry into Reno's conduct. Irritated by these charges, Reno preempted the investigation by himself requesting a court of inquiry, which was within his rights as an officer. Perhaps he was bored with living on suspended duty or tired of the insinuations. Some cynics say that Reno waited until Weir had died and the statute of limitations had expired.[26]

The court of inquiry was convened at the Palmer House in Chicago, January 13, 1879, and continued for almost a month. Although still under suspension, Reno was allowed to wear his uniform. Before and during the proceedings, Reno held open house in his hotel room, with plentiful whiskey and cigars, attended by all the officers, except Godfrey.[27] The officers discussed the situation among themselves, and, despite their anger at Reno, a consensus was soon reached to support him and stifle their criticisms, "for the good of the regiment." The officers carefully rehearsed the testimony to be given the next day.[28] Reno, his counsel and Benteen were inseparable, according to the imaginative Whittaker, "and the hotel loungers said that they frequently slept 3 in a bed, though this we cannot vouch for."[29]

Twenty-three sworn witnesses were heard, including officers of the 7th Cavalry, scouts, teamsters, packers, two non-coms and the trumpeter. Two packers and Fred Girard, the interpreter, testified that Reno had been drunk during the engagement. One packer testified that Reno had been drunk when he struck him and threatened to shoot him.[30] The remaining witnesses supported Reno. Two officers, with no great affection for Reno, steadfastly maintained for the next fifty years that Reno had not been intoxicated.[31] Godfrey took a long moment before answering whether Reno acted in a courageous manner.[32] The white-haired, ruddy-faced Benteen denigrated the testimony of the packers by declaring that they had stolen from him and had sheltered skulkers. He told the court that at one time he had discharged Girard, only to have him reinstated by Custer. Benteen was not given an opportunity to offer an opinion of Custer's actions. Neither of Reno's most vocal accusers could testify, since Weir was dead and French himself was undergoing a court martial.

Reno enumerated Custer's errors to the court: an exhausting march; an attack in late day, instead of early morning; and the division of the regiment into three battalions (four, with the pack train), none within supporting distance of one another. Reno further criticized the breech block of the Springfield carbine. He stated that it did not fit snugly to the head of the cartridge, nor did it completely close, due to the lateral motion of its hinge. The court duly noted his observations.

In the end, the court of inquiry found no cause for further action, concluding in effect that the Little Bighorn disaster was not attributable to Reno, and that Custer alone was responsible. No fault was assigned to Benteen. Whittaker publicly withdrew his charge of cowardice against Benteen and held him blameless for the Little Bighorn disaster.[33] His attacks on Reno continued unabated.

Benteen wrote Kate that he was tired of Chicago. People gawked at his uniform. He disliked performing errands for the wives and rebelled against corset shopping for Kate, especially since he did not know her size. He bought a 175-piece white china set, which could easily be matched if a plate were to break. He complained to Kate that he had no facility for bargaining,[34] which seems at odds with his reputation as a cunning horse trader.

It appears that 1879 was the year for courts-martial. No sooner had Benteen returned, when he was ordered to appear in Fort Vancouver, Washington Territory, at the trial of an officer who had maligned a lieutenant colonel during the Nez Perce campaign. This was an unexpected diversion for Benteen. He traveled to San Francisco by train on the ten-year-old Union Pacific Railroad and from there by ship to Vancouver Barracks, Washington. Along the way, he met many friends and acquaintances. The court martial lasted from April 24-28 and was settled when the libeler issued a formal apology.

Following the trial, Benteen left by steamship for San Francisco for a visit which he said he did not enjoy. He complained to Kate that people tried to cheat him: bootblacks tried to short-change him, and baggage handlers charged at least fifty cents. "So the d——d town & country goes, all trying to swindle each other."[35] He did buy Kate an ivory-backed hairbrush (sixteen dollars), four Chinese fans and some shell jewelry. It is not known whether he stayed at the old Occidental Hotel, long a favorite with the army officers.[36] Since he planned to send Freddie to an eastern boarding school, he had to be frugal. On the way home, he stopped at Sacramento for a brief visit with his younger brother, Theodore Benteen Jr., an architect, who lived with his wife and three children in very modest circumstances. He spent a day with the family and was favorably impressed with Theo's wife and children.[37]

He returned to Fort Abraham Lincoln on May 18, 1879. By this time, work on Fort Meade was progressing nicely under the supervision of Major Reno, who had since returned to duty. The 7th Cavalry was ordered to move into their new quarters at Fort Meade, and so on June 25, Benteen departed from Lincoln in advance of Colonel Sturgis, who arrived a week later to take over the command from Reno.

Reno, poor fellow, was by now deep in his cups. To make matters worse, he, a forty-four-year-old widower, was in love with Colonel Sturgis' twenty-one-year-old daughter. Evenings, he brawled with the junior officers in the post trader's building. A court martial was ordered and, while it was being convened, Reno, still under arrest, stole out of his quarters and peeped through a window into the parlor of Sturgis' quarters at the daughter. Her screams brought the colonel running, and other charges followed. Benteen had great sympathy for Reno and believed that Sturgis had overblown the affair: "Sturgis treated Reno like a dog. Reno was a far better soldier than Sturgis and that isn't much praise."[38]

At the trial, Reno conducted his own defense. He gallantly declined to cross-examine the daughter, so that her testimony was particularly damaging. Benteen testified in Reno's behalf that Reno was deeply in love with the daughter, as an explanation of sorts for Reno's conduct. He further testified that Reno had tried to send Mrs. Sturgis a note of apology, which he had first shown to Benteen. Colonel Sturgis was furious with Benteen's testimony.

Sturgis might have been under an emotional strain since his son, James (Jack), fresh out of West Point, had died at the Little Bighorn and his daughter's fiancé had recently committed suicide. Even so, he might have shown more compassion. During the Civil War, just before the Union Troops departed Memphis to meet defeat at the hands of Nathan Bedford Forrest at the battle of Brice's Crossroads in Mississippi on June 10, 1864, Sturgis had been drinking heavily and was seen putting his arm around the waist of a girl passerby.[39] To make matters worse, he suffered defeat at the hands of Forrest, who had only half the number of the Union troops. Sturgis spent the rest of the war "awaiting orders."

Reno was found guilty of the window peeping and drunkenness and sentenced to be cashiered from the service. The court recommended leniency. The sentence eventually reached President Rutherford B. Hayes. According to Benteen, the President's wife, Lucy Hayes ("Lemonade Lucy"), was irritated by Reno's ungallantry to the ladies and made her displeasure known to her husband.[40] At one time it was thought that during the Civil War Marcus Reno[41] had become embroiled in a verbal battle with Colonel Rutherford Hayes, then commanding officer of the 23rd Ohio, about some hay which the regiment had appropriated for bedding. It has since been shown that it was Major General Jesse L. Reno,[42] who had the altercation.

In any event, President Rutherford Hayes confirmed the sentence. Later, Reno's sentence was shown to be illegal, since it had not first been submitted to General Terry before moving up the chain of command for review. The details of the irregularity were made known to the Secretary of War, Robert Lincoln, who ruled that, even admitting the facts, there was no place in the army for Reno, since his commission had been given to someone else and that the President had no power to make another appointment. Year after year, bills were dropped into the Congressional hopper in an effort to reinstate Reno, but public opinion, driven by the Libby Custer cachet and the Whittaker biography, made any bill unpopular.[43]

Reno left Fort Meade in disgrace, with only Benteen to wish him well. He moved to Washington, D.C., and unsuccessfully sought reinstatement. His financial condition deteriorated, and he died in 1889 from an agonizing tongue cancer. Reno was buried in an unmarked pauper's grave. A year later, Benteen had not heard of his death. In 1967 charges against him were dismissed by a review board and his body disinterred and reburied at the cemetery at Little Bighorn Battlefield, where he lies today, without special distinction. To add to his ill fortune, the hill which his men successfully defended, has been officially renamed the Reno-Benteen Hill. Benteen had a strong sense of military propriety, and it seems highly unlikely (to the author) that he would have agreed to a name change, especially since its main objective was to denigrate his superior officer. Others may dispute this assessment.

Life at Fort Meade was vastly more comfortable than it had been at Fort Rice, especially during the last year. Gibson was promoted and given French's company; Varnum replaced Gibson in H Company. Benteen went on a two-week scout in May 17, 1880. Other patrols were sent to the Great Sioux Reservation and to the Powder River country, often with junior officers in charge. The unceded lands finally had been surrendered to the government, not by treaty but by an "agreement," signed by compliant reservation chiefs. This did not require approval by the Senate. A sharp watch was kept for the return of Sitting Bull and his people from Canada. In 1881, Benteen was sent for two months of field duty to the headwaters of the Little Missouri River, ever on the lookout for hostile Sioux.

Benteen received word in May 1881 of a two-year assignment in New York, consisting of eight months with a small arms board, followed by fifteen months of recruiting duty. Since he was traveling on orders, Benteen was issued a warrant but was required to pay half-fare for his family. He tried to obtain railroad passes for his wife and son by writing to E. F. Winslow and J. H. Wilson, his old Civil War commanders, who were now high officials in railroad companies.

Change of station meant complete removal of household furnishings. Furniture was put up for sale, and horses sold or auctioned. Baggage allowance included no more than a few trunks and some household items. Anything in excess had to be shipped by freight at the officer's own expense. Officers found it cheaper to give away excess baggage than to pay for its transport over a long distance.[44] One wonders about the fate of the 175-piece china set.

Before journeying East, Kate first visited her family in St. Louis. She doubtless wrote to her sister in New York, Mrs. Anita Norman Dice, who, for her own reasons, had changed her name to Diaz, following her conversion to Catholicism. After surrendering the temporary command of H Company to Lieutenant Varnum, Benteen departed for New York with his family on June 28, 1881. They arrived after a week's journey, and Benteen reported for duty at the Army Building on Houston and Green Streets to a small arms board headed by Colonel R. I. Dodge, 21st Infantry.[45] Weekdays were spent at work and weekends at the beaches. Libby Custer was living in New York at the time, in a modest apartment on Third Avenue and 18th Street,[46] not far from the army building, where she eked out a livelihood as a writer of newspaper articles. She saw Godfrey, who was then an instructor at West Point, New York, but it is unlikely that she received Benteen or acknowledged the letter of sympathy that Kate had sent her after the Little Bighorn Battle.

In August, Benteen received a testimonial from fourteen soldiers of H Company, seven of them sergeants, whose term of enlistment had recently expired, conveying to him their warmest regards.[47] The letter further attests to the high esteem in which Benteen was held by H Company. Since he had already left the regiment, he cannot be accused of promoting the letter.

Benteen left New York in October 1881 for four months of temporary duty at the National Arsenal at Springfield, Massachusetts. He inspected and tested various .45 caliber rifles and carbines. Although many cavalrymen preferred the Winchester repeating carbine, which they purchased at their own expense, the army steadfastly favored the Springfield for its accuracy and firepower. Moreover, it had twice the range of the Winchester.[48]

Among the weapons tested and rejected was the Lee bolt-action, the forerunner of the Lee-Enfield later adopted by the British Army. Nitrocellulose (smokeless) powder was about to be introduced, which would generate a tremendous increase in chamber pressure, requiring a tighter closure of the breech block. Such a closure could best be provided by a turnbolt action. The Krag-Jorgensen turnbolt carbine was marketed that very year, but had not yet been offered up for military consideration. The Springfield would continue to see service until 1892, when it was replaced by the Krag-Jorgensen.[49]

Benteen finished his service with the arms board in February 1882, and began cavalry recruiting duty in New York, a five and one-half day job. There were many events in New York that might have engaged the interest of the Benteen family. The Brooklyn Bridge had just opened; the city was being electrified by Thomas Edison; a huge three-ton elephant named Jumbo was being exhibited by the Barnum and Bailey Circus at Madison Square Garden and the Metropolitan Opera gave its inaugural performance.

Benteen was plagued by a succession of family troubles. His brother, Theo, had died in a fall from a scaffolding, leaving a wife and three children. Benteen gave financial aid to the family and helped the son, William Henry, through college and medical training. Fortunately, the widow found employment in 1883 as librarian in the Sacramento library. Benteen's sister, "En," Henrietta Fairbanks,[50] asked Benteen to care for her daughter, but Benteen declined. He explained that Freddie had contracted osteomyelitis in a lower extremity, requiring two operations and much medical care, the cost of which had to be borne by Benteen. Most insistent of all was Kate's older sister, Anita Diaz. She also asked for financial help and even followed the family to a beach hotel where they were spending the weekend. Benteen had to have the owner send her away.[51]

The Benteens participated in the army social events. They attended the Grand Ball at the Seventh Regiment Armory on January 11, 1883,[52] an elegant contrast to the dreary "hops" in the Dakotas. Doubtless, Benteen saw his old Civil War commander, E. F. Winslow, who lived in New York and was now President of the New York, Ontario and Western Railway. Captain Godfrey and his family visited the Benteens. Godfrey was then an instructor in cavalry tactics at West Point and destined for a long and honorable career, retiring as brigadier general.

During a fishing trip to Point Pleasant, New Jersey,[53] Benteen confided to Godfrey unequivocally that Reno had proposed that they abandon the wounded in a breakout from Reno Hill,[54] but that Benteen had vigorously objected. Benteen came to believe that this revelation, offered eight years after the event and four years after Reno's dismissal, caused Godfrey to turn against Reno, but it is clear that from the very beginning Godfrey had little regard for Reno and was solidly in the Custer camp. Perhaps it had been Custer who had intervened with the Benzine Board to safeguard Godfrey's commission, and to whom Godfrey would be forever grateful. Godfrey steadfastly attributed the Custer massacre to Reno's rout and found no fault with Custer's actions.[55]

Benteen and Freddie in New York, 1882. [Benteen Photo Collection, Hargrett Rare Book and Manuscript Library, University of Georgia]

FINAL YEARS

Word came in July 1883 of Benteen's promotion to major and his assignment to the 9th Cavalry, a black regiment. At the same time, H Company passed into the hands of the newly promoted Captain Charles De Rudio, Benteen's erstwhile subordinate. Two years older than Benteen, De Rudio soldiered on with the 7th Cavalry through illness and infirmity, until his mandatory retirement in 1896 at the age of sixty-four.

The established custom called for an officer attaining field rank (major) to be transferred out of his regiment. Benteen doubtless believed that his service at Little Bighorn entitled him to a preferential assignment. If he were a graduate of the Military Academy or had a college education, he might have been considered for a tour of duty at West Point; but having made enemies in high places, beginning with Colonel Sturgis, he could hardly be surprised to have been denied a coveted appointment.

Benteen did his best to avoid transfer to the 9th Cavalry. He knew, from his service with the USCT and his years in the peacetime army, that the black regiments and their officers got the worst of everything—stations, rations, supplies, quarters, assignments and horses. He applied to General Sheridan, now the General of the Army, for an appointment as assistant inspector of ordnance, having heard that Congress was about to create five such appointments.[1] "Were I not rapidly approaching fifty years of age," he wrote to Sheridan, "I should not desire to leave the cavalry arm of the service, but winter's cold and summering suns have made one old before his time."[2] Congress did not establish the new positions.

Benteen next applied for a delay in reporting to his regiment, explaining that he first wanted to complete a nine-month course in "veterinary science" at a veterinary college. Considerable correspondence ensued before it was finally decided that Benteen would not be granted a delay but could apply for a four-month leave, with two two-month renewable extensions.[3] Benteen could not have been contemplating a career as a veterinary surgeon, since after 1879 only graduates of approved veterinary colleges were accepted for army service. The course in which he was enrolled was probably designed for the layman, possibly dealing with stable management.

Upon the completion of his studies, Benteen joined his new regiment in Fort Riley, where first he had begun his regular army service sixteen years before. A photograph taken in New York showed him to be overweight, slightly stooped and prematurely aged, not the ideal figure of a cavalry officer. No matter to the army, a cavalryman's place is in the saddle. Benteen's predicament was not unique. Slow promotion had resulted in an aging field officer corps. As the *Army and Navy Journal* noted, only one-fourth of the field officers could endure the hardship of an active campaign.[4]

The 9th Cavalry, to which Benteen reported in July 1883, had been formed in Louisiana after the Civil War. The recruits were former slaves, very few of whom had served in black regiments during the war. Many of their white officers were less than enthusiastic about their new assignment, despite the fact that black soldiers deserted less, reenlisted more and gave their officers less trouble than did the white soldiers. In return for their loyal services, the soldiers were given sour beef and spoiled canned peas and deprived of molasses, canned tomatoes, dried peaches or dried apples.[5] Many of their mounts were rejects, so that their few healthy horses were often ridden into the ground.[6] Custer had been offered a lieutenant colonelcy in the 9th Cavalry when it was first being formed, and he had refused the offer. Benteen claimed that he had been offered a majority in the 10th Cavalry, also a black regiment, when he first entered the regular army and that he too had refused the assignment.[7] There is no proof of this claim. Although in the early days social condescension had been attached to service with the "Buffalo Soldiers," by the 1880's, this had greatly diminished, and many officers were to have served with distinction in black regiments, including John "Black-Jack" Pershing, Commanding General of the American Expeditionary Force in 1917, who was early assigned to the 10th Cavalry.

It has been said that Benteen tried to avoid duty with a black regiment because he was a southern racist, born to slave-owning gentry. Benteen, his father and grandfather were in no way "gentry." All three generations worked with their hands. If Charley did own a slave, she was there not to generate income, but to assist his frail, sickly wife.

On Benteen's behalf, it might be noted that he chose service with the USCT during the Civil War and insisted that he was so listed in the Army Register.[8] How many of his fellow officers made an effort to befriend the Indian chiefs, to enjoy warm social relations with them, and to invite them into their homes? When writing to his wife about the death of the black plainsman, Isaiah Dorman, at the Little Bighorn, Benteen writes: "I believe I told you that Isaiah was horribly mutilated."[9] But it must be conceded that when angered by what he considered misconduct, he did not scruple to refer to the black offender in derogatory terms.[10] In a letter from San Francisco, he refers to "nigger Minstrels," but elsewhere has considerable respect for the "Negro opera Bouffe—all Opera being Negroes."[11] At another time, "Nigs are no good as mechanics."[12] Nevertheless, these infrequent abrasions should not be taken as proof that Benteen was less than fair and considerate to the black soldiers in his command, nor, in the context of his times, should his remarks be considered other than as intemperate.

The 9th Cavalry first served in the high plains of Texas, protecting against the incursions of Kickapoos, Comanches, Cheyennes and Kiowas. In the winter of 1875-76, it was transferred to the Arizona Territory, where it spent eight hard years fighting the Apache. Following the service in the southwest, the regiment was posted to the southern plains and distributed to Fort Riley, Fort Supply and Fort Reno, the last two in the Indian Territory. For the next four years, its principle task was to prevent the homesteaders ("boomers") from squatting on Indian lands. The regiment well understood that any fatalities inflicted on the white settlers would meet with national indignation.[13]

The commanding officer was Colonel Edward Hatch, who had helped form the regiment. He had risen in the Civil War to become a brigadier general, participating in the battles of Franklin and Nashville and in Grierson's Raid.

Interest in the Indian Territory was first stimulated by the railroads, which lobbied Congress for land grants within the thirteen million acres of public domain in the Oklahoma District and in the Cherokee Outlet of the Oklahoma panhandle.[14] The land-hungry public also discerned opportunity in these last great unsettled areas. Two civilians, David L. Payne and his successor, W. L. Couch, tirelessly tried to settle squatters in the Indian Territory, only to have them ejected by the army.

Soon after Benteen's arrival at Fort Riley in July 1883, Colonel Hatch led a detachment from Fort Riley, to evict Couch and his followers. Benteen remained behind at Fort Riley as post commander, claiming to have difficulty sitting in the saddle for prolonged periods. "Were I a Czar," he later wrote, "I would have no regimental officer in the cavalry beyond the age of 45 years."[15] He began using a buggy with a spring seat, a buckboard, to get around.

Benteen's letters show that his promotion to field officer rank had brought with it an improvement in the furnishings of his quarters. He wrote to Kate that he wanted a roll of carpet, nice easy chairs, cane-seated black walnut chairs, two sets of furniture for the upstairs, three double mattresses—and possibly a sideboard.[16] All these luxuries were hitherto beyond his reach. In fact, Benteen seemed quite content with his new garrison duties in Fort Riley. There is no mention of any reluctance to serve with black troops.

On May 16, 1884, Benteen was assigned to Fort Sill, Indian Territory, where he would remain for one year as post commander. It was the same fort that the 7th Cavalry had helped establish back in 1868. Fort Sill was located on the Comanche and Kiowa reservation, and at the time quartered two black cavalry and four black infantry regiments. The nearest railroad station was Henrietta, Texas, sixty-seven miles away.

The buildings at Fort Sill had crumbling gables and unreliable foundations, all of which required extensive repair, once it had been decided that the fort would be retained as a permanent post.[17] Although the drinking water was excellent, malaria was rife. On his arrival, Benteen carefully examined the accounts of the previous post commander for possible financial irregularities. The captain was eventually dismissed from the army for misappropriation of government funds and other fiscal offenses.

While at Fort Sill, Benteen renewed his friendship with Stumbling Bear, the Kiowa chief, whom he had first met during his earlier service in Kansas. The chief immediately recognized Benteen and took him in his arms, calling him by his Indian name "Ole-Tankel" (Greyhair). Benteen got to know the other chiefs and seemed to have a warm regard for the Indian people. He invited the chiefs to the mess, and Stumbling Bear became a frequent visitor to the Benteen's home and a friend of Benteen's son Freddie, to whom the chief had given a set of bows and arrows fifteen years before. Fred had become a fine horseman and an avid hunter. His father gave him a Spencer repeating (!) shotgun.[18] Benteen made an effort to learn the Kiowa language and even tried to compile a crude dictionary. He condemned the agents who were cheating the Kiowa.[19]

Word was received of the death of his mother-in-law, Elizabeth Norman, on March 3, 1884, at age of seventy. She had been living with her twenty-one year old granddaughter, Violet, in Benteen's home in St. Louis. Benteen had been paying the taxes and the upkeep of the property, although Mrs. Norman had a son living in the city. Violet's mother, Anita Diaz, had not only abandoned her daughter, but had proven to be "a first class fraud," having been jailed (and acquitted) in New York for impersonating a well-known actress, to avoid having to pay a hotel bill.[20] Benteen promptly took the granddaughter into his home. She proved a wonderful asset to the household and a boon companion to Kate and Freddie. Like most officer families, they envisioned finding her a suitable officer husband.

The 9th Cavalry was called out in June 1884 to evict a large party of 1,500 boomers, who had illegally tried to settle. The squatters were surrounded and made to understand that the army meant business. The Buffalo Soldiers took pity on these hungry hopefuls and shared with them their beans and hardtack.[21] In December, Colonel Hatch and the 9th Cavalry were again called out against Couch and three hundred boomers. The interlopers were surrounded and starved into submission; but they vowed to return.

In February 1885, Benteen was removed from garrison duty and ordered into the field to guard the Kansas-Oklahoma border with a squadron (formerly called a battalion) of cavalry. Benteen was furious with his assignment. Patrolling the plains in the cold months was not a pleasant prospect. He reported for duty in bellicose mood to Arkansas City, Kansas, on March 4, 1885, and was informed by Colonel Hatch that he had been selected by higher authority. Benteen later acquired a copy of a letter written by Hatch to Crook proposing Benteen's assignment. Benteen wrote about Hatch on the back of the letter: "A more thorough lying scoundrel than even George A. Custer, if such were possible."[22]

Benteen set up his headquarters at Chilloco, Indian Territory[23] and sent out patrols along the Kansas-Oklahoma border. The squatters were, for the moment, excluded from tribal land but continued to give trouble until 1889, when the United States threw open for settlement two million acres in the Oklahoma District. Within two weeks, ten thousand tent dwellers had elected W. L. Couch mayor of Oklahoma City. Other tracts would be offered for settlement in 1892 and 1893.

Shortly after he went on patrol, Benteen received word of the death of his father on March 9, 1885, in Atlanta.[24] Benteen took emergency leave to settle the affairs. In former years, leave would not have been granted to an officer in the field. Reno could not obtain leave in 1874 to bury his wife. At the time of Benteen's departure for Atlanta, Kate and Violet were in St. Louis, and his son was in college in Chicago. Benteen arranged for Freddie to take over the management of the farm.[25]

While in Georgia, Benteen learned that his regiment was being deployed to the Wyoming Territory. He notified Kate and hastened back to Fort Sill to begin making the hectic arrangements for departure.

The Benteens set out by wagon from Fort Sill to the train station in Henrietta, Texas, accompanied by three other families and twenty-five enlisted men. The wagons were heavily padded with straw and had canvas strung on top. Women preferred the wagon to other transportation, since passengers traveling by stagecoach or ambulance were pitched from their seats every five minutes, often bumping heads with the people sitting across from them.[26]

A savage storm struck the convoy, swelling the rivers and making them unfordable. The Red River suddenly became a mile wide. The trip turned into a nightmare.

As the party waited for the rains to subside, it ran out of food. The men had to hunt for turkey, duck and wild pig, which the women prepared as best they could. Instead of a journey of five days, the sixty-seven mile trip took three weeks, in the course of which Benteen's Ninth Edition of the Encyclopedia Britannica got a soaking.[27] From Henrietta, the weary party traveled by train to Fort Riley, where the Benteens met their son. Freddie was given further instructions about the farm.

Benteen was ordered to march a squadron of three troops (as battalion and companies were now called) from Fort Riley, Kansas, to Fort McKinney, Wyoming, a journey of seven hundred miles. McKinney had been built in 1876 as a supply base on the Powder River, for the troops engaged in herding the Sioux onto the reservations.

The trip took six weeks, and Benteen arrived on August 1, exhausted and ill. The post surgeon pronounced a diagnosis of "cholera morbus"[28] and confined him to bed. For his back pain, Benteen had the choice of spiritus frumenti or tincture of opium. The following month Kate and Violet arrived and set his house in order.

Benteen's difficulties with Colonel Hatch grew worse. In fairness to the colonel, Hatch needed a major, not a garrison clerk. A field rank required service in the field. If Benteen could not perform his duties, propriety demanded that he resign, and a competent replacement would be found. There were no permanent garrison assignments in the 9th Cavalry, least of all for a junior major.

Officers' Quarters, Fort Sill, Indian Territory, 1884. Major Benteen, Cathy and Violet are standing outside. [Benteen Photo Collection, Hargrett Rare Book and Manuscript Library, University of Georgia]

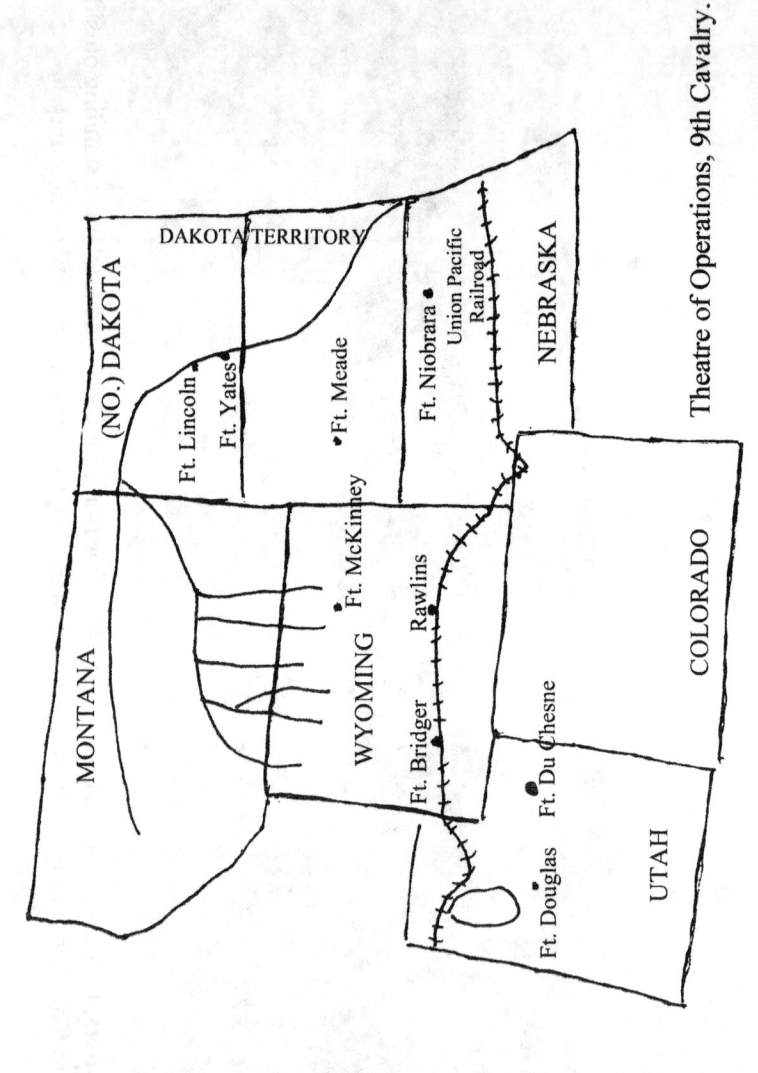

Theatre of Operations, 9th Cavalry.

The forty-nine-year-old Benteen again considered resigning. His presence was badly needed on his farm. Unfortunately, the length of service needed for retirement had been increased in 1882 from thirty to forty years, but mandatory retirement still remained at the age of sixty-four. By now, Benteen had only twenty years of army service. Retirement for forty years of service would come in 1901; mandatory retirement, in 1899.[29]

Another recourse would be to retire on disability. But a medical retirement was difficult to obtain. Congress had authorized no more than four hundred places on the disability list, so that the applicant might have a long wait before a vacancy appeared. Meanwhile, he would have to soldier on, saddling his regiment with his services until his application was approved. Of the three-quarters of the field officers who had limited capacity to serve in the field, doubtless many would have desired a disability retirement; and some may have been more deserving than Benteen.

At Fort McKinney, Benteen was assigned the duty as range officer, but ill health continued to trouble him. Unknown to Benteen, Colonel Hatch had him carried for three months on the sick list, an obvious reflection on his performance.

Benteen tried to arrange an exchange of regiments with Major Lewis Merrill of the 7th Cavalry. Perhaps he thought that his disabilities would disappear if he were transferred to his old regiment, or, more likely, that he would be assigned less arduous duties. His efforts seemed at first successful, and notice of the change even appeared in the *New York Times* on December 30, 1883, but the War Department eventually disallowed the arrangement, since Major Merrill was a senior major and, if transferred to the 9th Cavalry, would become a junior major, interrupting the sequence of promotion.[30] Colonel Sturgis also may have had a hand in disallowing the transfer, since his approval was required.

Meanwhile, Anita Diaz was causing trouble. She had erroneously concluded, probably from the premature notice in the *New York Times*, that Benteen was coming east. She wrote to the magazine board, inquiring about the date. The army was displeased to learn that Benteen contemplated leaving his station without authorization.[31] When Benteen was told about the Diaz letter, he became furious. He made Anita's husband write to the War Department to correct the misunderstanding.[32]

While at Fort McKinney, Benteen received a letter from Edward Godfrey, who was then stationed in Fort Yates, Dakota Territory. Godfrey informed him that Libby Custer wanted Godfrey to write an account of the Little Bighorn Battle. He asked if he should mention Reno's conversation about abandoning the wounded. In other words, would Benteen support him if Godfrey were to report the alleged conversation? Reno, meanwhile, had been living in poverty and disgrace in Washington since his discharge from the army. Benteen replied to Godfrey: "Don't you think that Reno has been sufficiently damned before the country that it can well be afforded to leave out in the article the proposition from him to saddle up and leave the field of the Little Bighorn in the first night of fight."[33] As will be seen later, Godfrey did not directly mention the conversation in his article, but made a sly allusion to it.

In June 1886, Benteen was sent on temporary duty to Fort Custer for the Tenth Anniversary of the Battle of Little Bighorn. The battleground had undergone great changes since Benteen had last been there. Custer's remains had been disinterred in 1877 and sent to the Military Academy at West Point, where they were reburied with appropriate pomp; and an imposing bronze statue was erected to his memory. Benteen was philosophic about the hagiolatry. "If it makes better soldiers and men of them [the cadets]," he wrote, "why the necessity of knocking the paste eye out of their idol?"[34] At the Little Bighorn, a wood marker had commemorated the deaths of the officers and men until 1881, when it was replaced by a modest granite obelisk, standing with its base thirteen and one half feet high. Captain Edward Godfrey had visited the site in 1884.

Benteen took with him to the tenth reunion his nineteen-year-old son, Freddie. Also among those present were Godfrey, who helped arrange the ceremonies, several other 7th Cavalry officers, two enlisted men, the surviving physician, Curley and another Crow scout and Chief Gall. In addition, there were the soldiers and officers from the nearby forts, and the journalists. The gathering toured the battle sites on horseback, with Godfrey and Chief Gall on hand to give running accounts of the battle, each from his own perspective. The party camped on the battleground, and the corks flew.

Upon his return to Fort McKinney, Benteen learned that he was due for yet another change of station. The troops of the 9th Cavalry were being deployed to Fort Niobrara, Nebraska; Fort Robinson, Nebraska, and to the Utah Territory. Benteen was assigned to the Utah Territory, the worst of the lot.

The Ute warriors on the Uintah Reservation east of Salt Lake City had been showing signs of unrest. The Utes had previously dwelled in northwestern Colorado in a large reserve coveted by the miners. After an inept Indian agent summoned the army to settle a misunderstanding, a battle ensued between the Utes and a troop of cavalry. In the course of the fighting, twelve soldiers and the Ute agent had been killed, and three women raped and taken into captivity. Secretary of the Interior Carl Schultz personally intervened to secure the release of the women and to prevent further bloodshed.

As punishment, the Utes were driven from their lush lands onto the Uintah Reserve in Utah. Now, they were thoroughly dissatisfied with their condition, their shortages of food and supplies; and their Indian agents. An army wife conveyed her uncharitable distain for the Ute, whom she described as short and stocky, with "blankets worn over dirty old shirts."[35]

Meanwhile, the turmoil on the Uintah Reservation required immediate attention. On August 2, 1886, Benteen was ordered to move two troops of the 9th Cavalry, together with the officer families and household possessions, to the Utah Territory. The troops marched 250 miles in two weeks from Fort McKinney through Wyoming to the rail station at Rock Creek, thirty-five miles northwest of Laramie, where a train awaited them. Without being given an opportunity to rest, the detachment was hurriedly loaded on "three small, dingy and filthy emigrants cars"[36] and carried two hundred miles to the Carter Station at Fort Bridger, Wyoming Territory.

General George Crook was determined to end the Ute unrest by a show of force. To begin with, he planned the construction of a new post on the Uintah Reservation. Crook had three infantry companies in hand and was anxiously awaiting Benteen and his two troops.

General Crook was an impatient man with prickly sensibilities. He had done a skillful job subduing the Chiricahua Apaches in Arizona, apart from his failure to capture Geronimo. In a fit of pique at the criticism leveled at him, he asked to be relieved of his command; whereupon Brigadier General Nelson Miles finished the task and took most of the credit. Crook also nursed grievances about the reproaches he had received for his role in the Sioux War; and was especially sensitive about his failure to join up with Custer.

When Benteen and his seventy-five cavalrymen arrived at the rail station in Fort Bridger, he learned that Crook had gone ahead with the infantry. Benteen was ordered to overtake him and bring along a Hotchkiss gun. The 130-mile march to the Uintah Reservation was pure torture for Benteen. His back ached, his body ached, his eyes smarted and his enlarged prostate compelled him to stop every fifteen minutes. Crook, riding ahead in an ambulance, kept sending messages to hurry along. Benteen sent one troop ahead at a brisk pace to satisfy Crook, and he rode with the second troop and the wagon train. With only a few wagons to carry their supplies, rations were short. The troops finally arrived at their destination six miles from the junction of the Du Chesne and Uintah Rivers, where the Buffalo Soldiers and their Hotchkiss gun were enthusiastically welcomed by the white infantry companies, who had been under threat of Ute attack. Crook indicated the location where he wanted the fort built and then left.

The site was along the banks of a warm river, with no fish to delight the sportsman. The ground was covered with sagebrush, shad scale and prickly pear, with the Uintah Mountains twenty miles distant and the nearest town thirty-two miles away. The wind blew alkali dust, which choked the men and the horses. Fine sand sifted through the tents into the food. During the day, the temperature reached ninety-six degrees; at night, ice formed in the tents and water buckets.

On August 23, 1886, Benteen took formal command of Fort Du Chesne, then a collection of tents. He was to remain here for four eventful months. Benteen had a protective trench dug around the camp and established a picket line. The men lived in tents, banked with soil or adobe bricks to preserve heat and warmed by a coal-burning stove whose stack protruded from the top of the tent. Bathing was done in the river. Kate Benteen and her niece were with him in camp, along with another officer wife and several laundress wives. The officers' tents were grouped around a large Sibley tent, which was used as a parlor-dining room. Before long, all the tents had wooden floors and carpets.[37]

Benteen's first task was to calm the unrest on the reservation. Besides their displeasure with the barren terrain, the three thousand Utes were further incensed by the presence of the 9th Cavalry. They had encountered the Buffalo Soldiers in 1869 at the battle of Milk Creek, Colorado, following which the tribe had been driven from their verdant hunting lands to their present bleak reserve.

Benteen spent several days offering assurances to the chiefs and finally succeeded in calming tensions. The command was especially anxious to discourage bands of warriors from returning to Colorado on marauding expeditions. Construction of the fort was next begun. Timber was collected from nearby Fort Thornburg, which had been recently abandoned after the white squatters had refused to vacate the land.[38] In any event, the weather-worn wood was suitable only for stables and outbuildings. Obtaining other construction materials proved equally difficult. Not only were building supplies slow to arrive, but when they did, they came in inappropriate order. The first shipment was lampposts. Food, forage and other supplies were also late, adding to the frustrations. Personal effects sat in the rail station in Fort Bridger. Benteen begged the command to expedite delivery, to no avail. Mules arrived unshod, so that the blacksmith had to fashion shoes from the iron in bunk straps or wagon wheels. There were no nails. The officers' tents leaked. The quartermaster sent wood for their coal-burning stoves, and cottonwood at that. Mail remained undelivered. Their sawmill blew up, killing one man and injuring another. According to Benteen, the trader, who had been given the contract to build the post, sat on his hands and did nothing. The post came to be called Fort Damn Shame.

There is no evidence of racial disharmony while Benteen was in command at Du Chesne, nor was this claimed at his court martial, except for the testimony of the local doctor, who pointedly stated that Benteen abused everybody.[39] One visitor to the fort noted that the black and white soldiers ate together, fraternized and played in the same band. The soldiers especially enjoyed playing baseball together, although boxing matches were contentious. Within a few years, two black graduates of West Point were to serve at Du Chesne.[40]

Benteen continued to be plagued by Anita Diaz. She had left the New York area and was living rent-free in Benteen's home in St. Louis. Unbelievably, she complained to the army that Benteen owed her three hundred dollars for her portrait, which she claimed he had in his possession. Benteen had Kate's brother, Leslie Norman, write a statement, attesting that Mrs. Diaz had no claim to the painting, which had been given to Violet by her grandmother.[41] Benteen's accompanying letter to the Adjutant General shows him to be near the end of his patience.[42]

It took a month for their belongings to arrived from Fort Bridger. On September 26, 1886, the night the baggage arrived, Benteen had been entertaining a new officer and his wife in the company of his niece, Violet, when he left the tent and urinated against the side. This caused great consternation within the tent. Then, seemingly without justification, Benteen changed his officers' assignments. The officers were furious. On October 10, while drinking excessively at the post trader's store, Benteen was particularly abusive to civilians who had come to trade, calling one of them a "Mormon-son-of-a-bitch." He then proceeded to drink himself into a stupor. On November 11, Benteen got into an unprovoked argument with some local men, again insulting them with the same epithets he had used before. When the sheriff arrived, Benteen hurled similar abuse at him and threatened him with a weapon. A fistfight was narrowly averted. Clearly, Benteen was falling apart.

It is not known where Benteen acquired his dislike for the Mormons. "Some think I came here to fight Indians," he declared, "but I came here to fight Mormons."[43] There was longstanding hostility directed against Brigham Young and the Mormons for their role in the Mountain Meadows Massacre of 1857, in which 120 overland emigrants had been murdered. Most disturbing to the officers was the widespread impression that the American flag did not fly over the buildings in Salt Lake City. Polygamy was also the subject of lively discussions among the "gentiles," although it was infrequently practiced and punishable by law. In the nearby Ashley Valley, for example, there were only thirteen polygamists in a population of two thousand, seven-eights of whom were Mormons.[44] Whatever Benteen's reasons, there is some merit in Huetter's observation that "had the predominant religion in the area been Methodist or Catholic, it is likely Benteen would have taken his wrath out on them."[45]

Benteen had come to believe that the post trader, a Mormon, had obtained the building contract through a rigged bid, but he lacked proof. The trader lagged far behind in the construction and winter was drawing near. This fueled Benteen's anger, since after four months, the post was still in tents. Some of Benteen's officers did not share Benteen's low opinion of the post trader. In late October 1886, one officer wrote to his wife, who was not living at the fort, "it [the camp] is not to me so 'awfully dreadfully' bad as it has been pictured."[46] Further, he stated that the trader, "a rustling energetic fellow, has already up quite a collection of board buildings and is getting in a large stock of goods. He will bring his family here in a few weeks, swelling the number of ladies to six."[47] Benteen's family, of course, had been there for two months, living in leaking tents.

Complaints against Benteen mounted, and eventually reached General Crook, possibly by way of the army paymaster. Crook had been involved previously in fiscal scandal and was anxious to avoid a repetition. He sent an inspector general to investigate. The inspector arrived in November 1886 and is supposed to have conducted a two-day inquiry before making his presence known to Benteen. How this could have been done in a small fort without word reaching the commanding officer is difficult to understand, unless, perhaps, the commanding officer was incapacitated. According to a letter of suspicious provenance, the inspector-general did not interview any soldiers or officers. In any event, his report was devastating. After noting that foundations had been laid, buildings framed and tens of thousands of adobe bricks had been manufactured, he concluded:

"Perhaps the principle cause of the delay has been the conduct of Major FW Benteen, 9th Cavalry, the officer in command. I am informed that he is frequently unfitted for duty through the excessive use of intoxicating liquors; and this for periods of two or three days at a time."

On December 18, 1886, Colonel Hatch relieved Benteen of command. The regimental commander drew up a list of particulars including the events of September 25, October 10, and November 11. The report was submitted to General Crook, who, although no great admirer of the accused, discretely offered him a six-month leave of absence, to allow the affair to subside. The matter might have ended, had the offer been accepted.

An article appeared on January 3, 1887, in the *Kansas City Times*, allegedly written by an unmarried enlisted man who had just left the army. In it, the writer condemns the army command, especially General Crook, for the disgraceful state of affairs in Fort Du Chesne; and depicts Benteen as the long-suffering victim. There is a lingering suspicion that, despite his denials,[48] Benteen himself may have written the letter, as he did after the Washita battle, and sent it to a friend in Leavenworth, Kansas, knowing that it would be published. If so, Benteen miscalculated—worse, he shot himself in the foot.

The letter was the last straw. On January 7, 1887, four days after the publication of the letter, Crook ordered a court-martial. The offer of six months leave was withdrawn, and Benteen was placed under arrest for drunkenness and conduct unbecoming an officer. Inspector-General Absalom Baird, whom Sheridan had sent to inquire independently into the matter,[49] did not choose to intervene. Colonel Hatch was detailed to assemble the evidence. On February 7, 1888, a court martial was convened at Fort Du Chesne. Although the Judge Advocate (prosecutor) was a trained lawyer and a graduate of the Harvard Law School,[50] Benteen chose for his defense counsel his adjutant, rather than seek the services of a professional attorney. Another grave mistake.

The trial began with Benteen challenging the members of the court as a body. Next, he unsuccessfully challenged several majors on the court who had brevets junior to his, on the premise that no judge can hold a rank inferior to that of the accused officer. He did succeed in having one member replaced for possible bias.[51] He then pleaded not guilty to all charges.

Eleven witnesses were called by the Judge Advocate to testify about the three specified events, and Benteen himself participated in the lively cross-examination. Benteen then summoned three civilian witnesses to impeach the testimony of the civilians who testified against him. In his own behalf, he called his niece, Violet Norman, who saw no signs of drunkenness.

Lieutenant Eugene F. Ladd, who was destined to marry Violet the following year, also vouched for his sobriety.[52]

Benteen attributed the urination episode to the residuum of spinal meningitis, which he asserted was the cause of the deaths of his four children. This explanation is at best creative. The tubercle bacillus had been reported five years earlier by Robert Koch of Germany and was the subject of popular discussion. Benteen submitted a forty-page statement of his spotless Civil War record and concluded with a denunciation of the post trader-contractor, "notwithstanding whose friends they may be." He attributed to him all his difficulties, hinting of collusion and dark conspiracy between the post trader and Crook's quartermaster.

On February 25, 1887, the Court Martial found Benteen guilty of six specifications of drunkenness and ordered him dismissed from the army; but unanimously recommended that the President show him mercy.[53]

While the sentence was being reviewed, Benteen visited Fort Douglas near Salt Lake City, so that he would not be present at Fort Du Chesne during the change of command. He was assigned accommodations in the field officer's quarters outside the fort. The officers at Fort Douglas were friendly,[54] among them Lieutenant Richard W. Young of the 4th Artillery, the son of Brigham Young.

Crook endorsed the findings of the court. Anticipating that Benteen's sentence might later be mitigated, he suggested that "he [Benteen] receive some discipline for his insubordination and disrespectful language, and his unsoldierlike conduct as shown in these proceedings, indicating as they do that he is sadly in need of such discipline."[55]

General Sheridan, now General of the Army, recommended remission of the sentence for previous service and in recognition of his "long and honorable service."[56] Benteen wrote five letters to influential people asking them to plead his case with the President. Grover Cleveland had not had military service. Although unmarried at the time, he did not serve during the Civil War, and instead furnished a substitute. Since becoming President, Cleveland did his best to oppose the avalanche of applications for Civil War pensions. In any event, on April 20, 1887, the President reduced Benteen's sentence to suspension in rank and duty and half-pay for one year.[57] The reader might wish to compare this with Reno's sentence for peeping through a window!

Upon receiving word of the final outcome, Benteen returned to Du Chesne, where he joined Kate and their niece, both of whom had remained at the fort, engaged in planning for Vi's marriage to Lieutenant Ladd. Benteen spent the summer exploring the region, while awaiting permission to leave the Department of the Platte. He wrote to the Adjutant General requesting a year's furlough to attend classes at a veterinary college;[58] but this was denied. For an officer under sentence to make this request was quite audacious. Permission was finally granted to leave the department,[59] and on September 16, the family left for Georgia.

Benteen and family at Fort Du Chesne, 1886. [Benteen Photo Collection, Hargrett Rare Book and Manuscript Library, University of Georgia]

Benteen (standing) at Fort Douglas, 1887, while awaiting review of his court martial. [Benteen Photo Collection, Hargrett Rare Book and Manuscript Library, University of Georgia]

Benteen took up residence on his farm outside of Atlanta. Since Charley's death, the farm had suffered some ten thousand dollars' worth of neglect, according to Benteen,[60] but the property itself had greatly appreciated in value, since the city was fast expanding. He gave thought to his son's future. Freddie Benteen had indicated that he wanted an army career and Kate concurred, but Benteen did his best to discourage him. He did not believe that his son was suited to the army and, instead, offered to set him up in the hardware business.

Even before his sentence expired, Benteen applied to the Adjutant General for permission to appear before a retirement board. He had made himself an insufferable nuisance by his conduct at Fort Du Chesne, so that he might have hoped that the army would expedite his request. He returned to duty April 17, 1888, after first submitting to a medical examination given by the medical officer for the Department of the Platte in Omaha. The exam lasted three days and included inspection of eye, rectum, urine and, as Benteen put it, "all the pranks he [the medical officer] knew of."[61] Benteen's symptoms were noted and were determined to be service-related. He made no mention of the bullet in his left thigh, since it was not sustained in line of duty. Noting that "there have been no continuous attentive observations," the medical department recommended that Benteen be observed for at least one month before being allowed to appear before a retiring board. He was deemed unfit for mounted duty, but meanwhile could perform garrison assignments.[62] The report was submitted to the retirement board, which was the final arbiter. Benteen was returned to duty, pending process of his application.

When informed that Colonel Hatch would be at his new post, Benteen succeeded in having himself transferred to Fort Niobrara, Nebraska, declaring that "rather than stay with the crowd Hatch...kept around him, I would have resigned outright."[63]

Benteen arrived at Fort Niobrara, Nebraska, on April 26, 1888, without Kate. He telegraphed for a wagon to transport him the four miles from the railroad station to the fort,[64] made necessary, perhaps, by the baggage which accompanied him. Fort Niobrara had been established to oversee the Rosebud Agency on the Great Sioux Reservation. It had a complement of two troops of 9th Cavalry and six infantry companies. Fortunate for Benteen, the post commander was away at the time, inasmuch as it was he who had presided over Benteen's court martial. Benteen was well received by the other officers and assigned only nominal duties. He was lodged in the bachelor officers' quarters.[65]

While at Fort Niobrara, Benteen applied for six months' leave for health reasons, to visit a "celebrated electrical cave" in Taliaferro County, Georgia.[66] He also asked the post doctor to recommend the southern climate for relief of his symptoms.[67] Both letters appear to have been brazen attempts to get the Adjutant General to advance the date for his appearance before the retirement board, but there may be another explanation which is not immediately apparent.

Final Years 261

After a spell of inclement weather, Benteen again became ill. The medical officer saw him on several occasions and marked him fit for duty.[68] Benteen saw in this an attempt to force him to resign, which made him all the more determined to hold out for the retirement board. Benteen wrote that he regretted that he could not attend Vi's wedding, but hoped that she would begin to feel less dependent on him. Now more than ever, he wanted to see his son in the hardware business.[69]

Fortunate for him, Benteen did not have long to wait. On June 3, 1888, after no more than a month of medical observation, Benteen received the order to appear before the retirement board. The panel would consist of two physicians and several infantry and cavalry officers, presided over by General Wesley Merritt. Benteen arrived in Fort Leavenworth and promptly underwent further examinations. His medical records were scoured for reports of previous illness,[70] and the information collated with the recent examinations. The retirement board concluded that Major Benteen was incapacitated for active duty "because of defective vision, frequent micturition caused by either spinal lesion or inflammation of the prostate gland or neuralgia." Benteen was taken off the active duty roster at the age of fifty-four and retired for disability on July 7, 1888, with a pension of $2,625 a year.[71] He boarded a train and went home.

* * *

Benteen spent the first four years of his retirement on his farm, which by this time had grown to 170 acres and was fast becoming a very valuable holding. He then moved to an Atlanta townhouse on 39 Pavilion Street, near Grant Park, but occasionally returned to his farm to spend the night.[72] At times, he managed to "go off with the boys and keep the bowl o'erflowing."[73] It is not known whether he visited the "celebrated electrical cave" in Taliaferro County, about one hundred miles from Atlanta, to hasten his recovery.

In 1890, the House of Representatives resumed the practice of issuing brevets, which had been suspended for two decades. Benteen applied for a brigadier general's brevet and submitted the required endorsements. He requested in particular that Reno's recommendation be sent back to him, since Reno wanted it returned. Apparently, Benteen did not know that Reno had died in Washington the year before. In due time, Benteen was awarded a brevet of brigadier general for gallantry at Little Bighorn and Canyon Creek. Although he had waited for this a quarter of a century, Benteen was indignant because Lieutenant Colonel Lewis Merrill had also received the same brevet. Merrill was the officer who had led the first charge at Canyon Creek and who later had agreed to exchange regiments with Benteen.[74] Merrill had generated scorn (and envy?) in the regiment when in 1872, while serving in South Carolina, he accepted a grant of $20,000 from the state legislature to suppress Klan activities. Benteen lost no time in purchasing the brigadier general's accouterments and in having his picture taken in uniform. He complained that only one officer from the 7th Cavalry wrote to congratulate him.

He began correspondence in 1891 with a former soldier in the 7th Cavalry, named Theodore W. Goldin, who served in G Company at the Little Bighorn and the Canyon Creek battles. His parents later had him released from the army because he was under age. After finishing college, Goldin had a varied career as lawyer, politician and colonel in the Wisconsin National Guard.

Goldin indicated to Benteen that he intended to write an account of his service in the 7th Cavalry. He had already written an article for the Janesville, Wisconsin, newspaper on July 8, 1886, when he first began his law practice.[75] In it, Goldin lavishly praised Custer. Goldin also claimed that he had carried a message from Custer to Reno.[76] The message incident is doubted by many historians. For one thing, G Company had been assigned to Reno's command. Goldin maintained, however, that he, like trumpeter Martin, had been assigned for the day to Custer headquarters. Also, Goldin makes no mention of seeing Lieutenants Cooke and Keogh, who had been detailed to accompany Reno to the Little Bighorn River.

Benteen, who had himself written two unpublished articles about the Battle of Little Bighorn, was immediately interested in a book or article about to be written by a former enlisted man in the 7th Cavalry, who was also a college graduate and a lawyer; especially if Benteen himself could supply the information. Benteen encouraged him: "And I know of no one so capable of doing it as yourself, so give it to us. Spare no one! Not even the dead, as they, through their living friends, have assailed everyone who could not think with them, from the President U. S. Grant down."[77]

Benteen's interest in a literary project escalated after January 1892, when Godfrey at long last published his classic account of the Little Bighorn Battle in the *Century* magazine, in which he reinforced Custer's reputation and modestly lauded his own role. With regard to the Reno abandonment story, Godfrey cryptically wrote: "The question of moving was discussed, but the conditions coupled to the proposition caused it to be indignantly rejected." Interestingly, Godfrey quoted Moylan in the article as questioning Custer's judgment in dividing the regiment. Libby Custer must have been furious when she read this, for in Godfrey's later version of the battle, which Libby Custer helped edit, Moylan's opinion was omitted.[78]

After Godfrey's article appeared in the *Century*, Benteen's letters to Goldin become increasingly waspish. Goldin visited Benteen in Atlanta on two occasions. He states that the two sat on the porch of Benteen's home "puffing on our Missouri corn cob pipes, now and then sipping an undeniable mint julep prepared by the old colored butler, who had been in the family since childhood."[79] Goldin published a two-part article in 1894 in the *Army Magazine*,[80] and only upon request did he send Benteen a copy. The article was hardly the exposé that Benteen was expecting, but was more a vehicle for self-promotion. In it, Goldin assigned himself a role in fetching water for the thirsty men on

Reno Hill. Twenty-three enlisted men at the Little Bighorn had received the Medal of Honor in 1878, but Goldin was not among them. He persisted in his claim, and with the assistance of the Assistant Secretary of War, a fellow Wisconsin resident, he received the medal in 1895, with Benteen's endorsement.[81] Goldin also sought an appointment as superintendent of the Little Bighorn National Monument. Godfrey contacted Libby Custer and advised her not to support him.[82]

Benteen made little comment on Goldin's article, but it could not have been to Benteen's liking, hardly justifying the effort he had expended in his lengthy correspondence. His letters to Goldin came to an end in 1896.

Benteen also wrote to D. F. Barry, a noted frontier photographer, who was attempting to become established in New York. Benteen sent him the names of acquaintances living in the city, especially that of General Edward Winslow who was a respected business executive. Barry was also a friend of Libby Custer, who had since prospered, following the success of her three books and public lectures. Benteen, too, wrote a series of essays, each describing a part of his military service on the plains, inspired perhaps by Custer's successful magazine articles. Benteen's stories were not published in his lifetime, which must have been a deep disappointment, since he had expended much effort in their preparation. Curiously, Benteen had a close friend in the publishing business who should have been able to find a market for another firsthand account of army *Life on the Plains*.

In a long letter to Godfrey, written on August 14, 1893, Benteen boasted of his financial assets and explained why he did not remain in the army: "I struck it fat in buying lots of land in this town in 1865—I couldn't afford to remain longer in the army away from it. There is no telling how many—don't laugh when I say millions of dollars—Fred [his son] will have to look out for it in the not so very far-away..."[83]

Benteen offered another reason for leaving the 9th Cavalry: "it was not proper to remain with race of troops I could take no interest in—and this on account of their low-down, rascally character...."[84] Of course, this oft-quoted remark is somewhat gratuitous. Benteen did not "leave" the 9th Cavalry (the first time) because of his lack of interest in the Buffalo Soldier but was suspended for drunkenness. To his credit, none of the black soldiers complained about him, nor, as mentioned above, did Benteen complain about them during his service with the 9th Cavalry.

The Benteens were not socially prominent, but they numbered among their friends Joel Chandler Harris (Bre'r Rabbit), the governor of Georgia, the mayor of Atlanta, John S. Chandler (Coca Cola), and many other celebrated citizens. Closest of all, perhaps, was Joseph Nash, a publisher and lifelong friend going back to Petersburg days, who had accompanied Benteen on the march to Fort Harker during the Washita campaign. Benteen declared to the newspapers that he "much preferred feeding his chickens to posing as a central figure in a social function."[85] The old Atlanta families, with long memories of the 138th USCT and the distress purchase of Benteen's land, continued to regard him as a carpetbagger. Although his finances were quite satisfactory, he viewed his life with melodramatic remorse: "I've been a loser in a way all my life by rubbing against the angles—or hair—of folks, instead of going with their whims; but I couldn't go otherwise—'twould be against the grain of myself."[86]

The health of their son, Fred, continued to give the Benteens much concern. After loosing four children while "touring around the continent,"[87] they were understandably worried about even the smallest illness. In 1894 Fred had an injury from a mowing machine, which took several months to heal. The following year, Fred was injured while driving a milk wagon, when the wagon collided with a carriage driven by a woman. Benteen paid the woman one hundred dollars, to spare his son the bother of returning from college in Chicago to face a law suit.[88] Fred became an excellent horseman and twice won Georgia State cavalry tilting championships.[89]

Benteen also corresponded with Francis Gibson, his former lieutenant, who had left the army to take up a position as supervisor of stables with the Sanitation Department of New York. Benteen continued to show an interest in the 7th Cavalry and exchanged letters with its current adjutant. Even after he left the regiment, Benteen sometimes drew beneath his signature the crossed cavalry sabers with the number 7 superimposed.[90]

As time passed, Benteen's recollections became more congenial: "Those were pretty rollicking gay days and I don't regret a day I spent in the saddle." Horses and poetry continued to interest him. In his copy of Custer's *Life on the Plains*, he wrote: "General Custer did me many wrongs, but I never bore him any malice, but on every occasion offered rendered him valuable service and supported him far better than the boot-licks who thronged around him."[91]

In March 1896, the sixty-one-year-old Brevet. General Frederick Benteen doffed his hat and took the salute, as an infantry battalion marched in his honor past his home. Not long after, he was invited to attend a magic lantern talk about the Little Bighorn Battle, given by an infantry officer on leave, with whom Benteen had conversed prior to the lecture. Despite the gratifying remarks made about him, Benteen was quite perturbed at the lecturer's criticism of Reno and Custer.[92]

He met newspaper reporters on occasion, but never discussed with them the Little Bighorn Battle. In private, his view of Custer never changed. He continued to berate Custer. "The newspapers killed Custer," he is reported to have said, "they puffed him up and boosted him, and sang his praises to the skies until it ruined him"[93]

His rancor also extended to Nelson Miles, a vigorous Custer supporter; Crook, and to a host of others. He ridiculed an article about De Rudio which appeared on September 27, 1897, in *Harper's Weekly*, remarking that the account differed from the story De Rudio had related after the battle.[94] Edward Godfrey's description of the Little Bighorn Battle never ceased to outrage Benteen. He belittled Godfrey for taking exclusive credit for guarding the retreat from Weir Point, when it was Benteen who had assigned him to the strategic site. "Godfrey can't remember the fact," he complained.[95] Godfrey, who so unremittingly condemned Reno, himself came under intense public criticism for his role as D Troop commander in the Wounded Knee disaster of 1890, where the army killed or wounded three hundred Miniconjou Sioux, many of them women and children, with devastating fire from its Hotchkiss guns. Godfrey's later advancement to brigadier general engendered a storm of public protest, prompting President Theodore Roosevelt to delay the promotion.

Benteen experienced a recurrent bout of malaria and following four days of fever, he suffered a stroke. He died on June 17, 1898, at the age of sixty-three. The official diagnosis was "cerebral apoplexy."[96] The funeral was held three days later at St. Philip's Church. It had military pallbearers and was attended by the Governor of Georgia, the Mayor of Atlanta and many prominent people. Benteen was buried at the Westview Cemetery in Atlanta. Four years later, the body was moved to the Arlington Cemetery in Virginia, where it now rests in glory in the company of the many who have faithfully served their country.

Kate received a widow's pension of twenty dollars per month, based on her husband's service as a captain, at the time when, according to the retirement board, he developed his disabilities. It is said that officers from the 7th Cavalry were always welcome at her home, but no such visit is known. On February 15, 1904, she petitioned the Pension Committee of the House of

Representatives for an increase in her pension to fifty dollars per month. A bill was introduced in her behalf by Hon. Campbell Slemo of Virginia. Kate died in 1906, eight years after the death of her husband, and is buried beside him.

Libby Custer made similar application for an increase in pension.[97] She occasionally received visitors from the 7th Cavalry at her home in New York[98] and to the end continued to vigorously defend the reputation of her late husband,[99] responding to as many as eight hundred letters in six months.[100] She died in 1933, leaving an estate of $113,000, earned from books, lectures and shrewd real estate investments. A year after her death the first book critical of George Armstrong Custer appeared in print.

Despite his father's misgivings,[101] Frederick Wilson Benteen ("Freddie") was commissioned in the army by President McKinley, although overage for the rank of second lieutenant. He served with the 2nd U.S. Infantry in Cuba during the Spanish-American War; with the 22nd Infantry in the Philippines; with General Pershing on the Mexican border and in France during WWI, where he was wounded. He retired with the rank of lieutenant colonel, after twenty-nine years of service. He had three daughters and three grandchildren. One of his granddaughters married the brother of Margaret Mitchell, who used the name Benteen in her celebrated novel, *Gone with the Wind*. Another granddaughter, Maria Louisa Benteen Steves, lived to an old age and was the source of many "family traditions," although she had never seen her grandfather.

There are several place names of "Benteen" in Atlanta and elsewhere. A mountain and a county have been named after him, but it is unlikely that many associate the name with a quiet, white-haired officer, who stood erect for hours as bullets flew about him, while he fearlessly passed along the line, steadying his terrified men.

Theodore Goldin, Benteen's confidant (of sorts). [Benteen Photo Collection, Hargrett Rare Book and Manuscript Library, University of Georgia]

NOTES

Source abbreviations used in the notes:

HMC NYPL Hagner Manuscript Collection, New York Public Library

HC UG Hargrett Library, Rare Book and Manuscript Department Frederick William Benteen Papers, University of Georgia, Athens, Georgia

WHMC UM Western Historical Manuscript Collection, University of Missouri, Columbia, Missouri

NA National Archives Records of the Adjutant General's Office: Appointment, Commission and Personnel file. Letters received. Pension File: Frederick W. Benteen [Catherine Benteen]

NOTES TO INTRODUCTION

[1] John M. Carroll, *Camp Talk*, x.

[2] Clipping, *Atlanta Constitution*, July 23, 1898. HC UG.

[3] Sherry H. Olson, *Baltimore*, 102.

[4] *Ibid.*, 71.

[5] Works Progress Administration (WPA), *Maryland: A Guide*, 198.

[6] John Tasker Howard, *Stephen Foster, America's Troubadour*, 145.

[7] *Ibid.*, 304.

[8] Olson, *Baltimore*, 103.

[9] *Ibid.*, 115.

[10] *Ibid.*, 100.

[11] (WPA), *Maryland: A Guide*, 212.

[12] (WPA) *Virginia: A Guide*, 276.

[13] Scott and Wyatt, *Petersburg's Story*, 80.

[14] *Ibid.*, 77.

[15] Scott and Wyatt, *Petersburg's Story*, 76, 157.

[16] *Ibid.*, 73.

[17] Benteen Collection Box 1, HC UG.

[18] Scott and Wyatt, *Petersburg's Story*, 121.

[19] W. E. Woodward, *Meet General Grant*, 143.

[20] Scott and Wyatt, *Petersburg's Story*, 261.

[21] Suzanne Lebsock, *The Free Women of Petersburg*, 201.

[22] Arthur Kyle Davis, "Three Centuries of an Old Virginia Town," *Magazine of History with Notes and Queries*, April 1914, 21.

[23] Scott and Wyatt, *Petersburg's Story*, 119.

[24] *Petersburg Republican*, Oct. 4, 1846.

[25] Charles S. Sydnor, *The Development of Southern Sectionalism*, 59.

[26] Clement Eaton, *The Growth of Southern Civilization*, 8.

[27] Suzanne Winckler, *The Smithsonian Guide to Historic America: The Plains*, 10.

[28] Cator Print # 184, Cator Collection, Enoch Pratt Free Library, Baltimore, MD.

[29] Willard B. Hall to Abraham Lincoln, Nov. 23, 1864 in Benteen ACP NA.

[30] Eaton, *Southern Civilization*, 114.

[31] Edgar W. Knight, *A Documentary History of Education in the South before 1860*, 149.

[32] Lebsock, *Free Women,* 91.

[33] Stephen B. Oates, *The Fires of Jubilee*, 91.

[34] Lebsock, *Free Women,* 92.

[35] Allen Nevins, *Ordeal of the Union*, Vol. 2, 218-9.

[36] *Petersburg Republican*, March 17, 1849.

[37] Reference GA 37, Corporation Plaintiffs, 1824-1911 New York Chancery.

[38] Ralph Henry Gabriel, *Pagent of America: Lure of the Frontier*, 99.

[39] Winckler, *The Plains,* 47.

[40] May 18, 1850, Marriage of Henrietta Benteen to James L. Doyle.

[41] John McElroy, *The Struggle for Missouri*, 9.

[42] *Ibid.,* 11.

[43] *Ibid.,* 18.

[44] Benteen to Lane, Dec. 4, 1864, Benteen ACP B 1729 NA.

[45] Born Philadelphia, March 5, 1836.

[46] Henry Norman to Catherine Norman, Jan. 20, 1855, HC UG.

[47] Born September 14, 1806.

[48] Born May 13, 1813.

[49] *New York Times,* Jan. 1, 1905.

[50] Benteen to Henrietta, Aug. 24, 1882, HC UG.

[51] Nevins, *Ordeal of the Union*, 504-5.

[52] Steven Rowan, *Germans for a Free Missouri*, 4.

[53] *Ibid.,* 6.

54 *St. Louis Democrat*, May 5, 1859.

55 Rowan, *Germans for a Free Missouri*, 13.

56 Woodward, *Meet General Grant*, 170.

57 Geoffrey Perret, *Lincoln's War*, 76.

NOTES TO CIVIL WAR

1 Jay Monaghan, *Civil War on the Western Border 1854-1860*, 129.

2 Perret, *Lincoln's War*, 80.

3 Carroll, *Court Martial of Benteen*, 87.

4 Monaghan, *Civil War on the Western Border 1854-1860*, 131.

5 *War of the Rebellion* Series I, Vol. III, Chapter X, 5.

6 *Ibid.*, Series I, Vol. III, Chapter X, 9.

7 Perret, *Lincoln's War*, 90.

8 *War of the Rebellion*, Series I, Vol. III, Chapter X, 67.

9 Monaghan, *Civil War on the Western Border 1854-1860*, 181.

10 Paul C. Nagel, *Missouri: A History*, 129.

11 Carroll, *Court Martial of Benteen*, 87.

12 Monaghan, *Civil War on the Western Border 1854-1860*, 150.

13 Davis, "Three Centuries of an Old Virginia Town," 393.

14 *Ibid.*, 395.

15 *Ibid.*, 401.

16 Russ A. Pritchard, Jr., *Civil War Weapons and Equipment*, 43.

[17] Jack Coggins, *Arms and Equipment of the Civil War*, 54.
[18] *Ibid.*, 55.
[19] Paddy Griffith, *Battle Tactics of the Civil War*, 176.
[20] Coggins, *Arms and Equipment of the Civil War*, 49.
[21] Davis, "Three Centuries of an Old Virginia Town," 398.
[22] Griffith, *Battle Tactics,* 180.
[23] *War of the Rebellion*, Series I, Vol. III, Chapter X, 240.
[24] "Baseball Playing in Kansas," HC UG.
[25] *War of the Rebellion,* Series I, Vol. III, Chapter XVIII, 33.
[26] Alison Mills, *My Story*, 4.
[27] L. Vanloan Naisawald, *Cannon Blasts*, x.
[28] *War of the Rebellion*, Series I, Vol. VIII, Chapter XVIII, 59.
[29] *Ibid.*, Series I, Vol. VIII, Chapter XVIII, p 170, 651.
[30] Benteen to Goldin, Feb. 22, 1896 in Carroll, *Benteen-Goldin*, 278.
[31] *War of the Rebellion,* Series I, Vol. VIII, Chapter XVIII, p 200, 202.
[32] Benteen to Goldin, Jan. 11, 1896, in Carroll, *Benteen-Goldin*, 237.
[33] Benteen to Major General S. R. Curtis, April 22, 1862, Benteen ACP NA.
[34] *War of the Rebellion*, Series I, Vol. XIII, Chapter XXV, 122.
[35] *Ibid.*, Series I, Vol. XIII, Chapter XXV, 242-3.
[36] Graham's Interview with Major Frederick Wilson Benteen. W. A. Graham, *The Custer Myth*, 158.
[37] Karol Asay, *Gray Head and Long Hair*, 4.

[38] W. A. Graham, *The Custer Myth*, 158.

[39] *War of the Rebellion*, Vol. XXVII, Chapter XXIX, 238.

[40] *Ibid*, Series I, Vol. XXIII, Chapter XXV, Part I, 255.

[41] Elisha Jennings to Mary Elbers, April 23, 1863. "Letters of Elisha Middleton Jennings," 4, WHMC, UM.

[42] *War of the Rebellion*, Series I, Vol. XXIII, Chapter XXXV, Part I, 257.

[43] *Ibid.*, 258.

[44] *Ibid.*, 350.

[45] Jennings to Mary Elbers, July 21, 1863 in Jennings, "Letters," 15, WHMC, UM.

[46] Jennings to Mary Elbers, July 9, 1863, 9 in *Ibid*.

[47] *War of the Rebellion*, Series, I, Vol. XXIV, Chapter XXXVI, Part I, 665.

[48] Jennings Diary, July 9, 1863 in Jennings, "Letters," WHMC UM.

[49] "Extract of Original Report of Battle at Iuka, Miss." in Benteen ACP NA.

[50] Jennings to Mary Elbers, July 9, 1863 in Jennings, "Letters," 11, WHMC UM.

[51] George A. Custer, *My Life on the Plains*, 11, n.5, 6.

[52] Jennings to Mary Elbers, August 11, 186323 in Jennings, "Letters," WHMC UM.

[53] Len Eagleburger, *The Fighting 10th*, 87.

[54] *War of the Rebellion*, Series I, Vol. XXX, Chapter XLII, Part II, 811.

[55] *Ibid.*, Series I, Vol. XXX, Chapter XLII, Part II, 811.

[56] Benteen ACP 1863 B 1561 NA.

[57] *War of the Rebellion*, Series I, Vol. XXXII, Chapter XLIV, Part I, 249.

[58] *Ibid.*, Series I, Vol. XXXII, Chapter XXXIX, Part II, p 248-251.

[59] *Ibid.*, Series I, Vol. XXX, Chapter XLII, Part II, 812.

[60] Carroll, *Court Martial of Benteen*, 89.

[61] *Ibid.*, 90.

[62] Benteen to W. H. Morgan, July 30, 1864, Benteen ACP B 17228 NA.

[63] Carroll, *Custer in Periodicals*, 185.

[64] Perret, *Lincoln's War*, 401.

[65] *War of the Rebellion*, Series I, Vol. XLI, Chapter LIII, 331.

[66] Davis, "Three Centuries of an Old Virginia Town," 404.

[67] Shelby Foote, *The Civil War*, Vol. 3, 583.

[68] *Ibid.*, Vol. 3, 574.

[69] *War of the Rebellion*, Series I, Vol. XLI, Chapter LIII, 332-336.

[70] Eagleburger, *The Fighting 10th*, 130.

[71] Carroll, *Court Martial of Benteen*, 90.

[72] General Orders # 11 in Benteen ACP B1728 [ACP 1864 f/w 5142].

[73] *War of the Rebellion*, Series I, Vol. XLI, Chapter LIII, Part 4, 333.

[74] *Ibid.*, Series I, Vol. XLI, Chapter LIII, Part 4, 333.

[75] Curtis to Gov.Willard Hall, Nov. 8, 1864 in Benteen ACP NA; also in Carroll *Court Martial of Benteen*, 91.

76 Gov. Hall to President Lincoln, Nov. 23, 1864, in Benteen ACP NA; also in Carroll, *Court Martial of Benteen,* 92.

77 Letter, Dec. 23, 1864, Benteen Papers HMC NYPL.

78 Griffith, *Battle Tactics,* 183.

79 *War of the Rebellion,* Series I, Vol. XLIX, Chapter LXI, Part I, p 479; 469-483.

80 Clipping, *Atlanta Constitution,* June 25, 1898, HC UG.

81 *Ibid.,* Series I, Vol. LXIX, Chapter LXI, Part I, 473.

82 Charles F. Hinricks, *Diary & Company Books,* April 2, 1865, AH 50 WHMC UM.

83 *Ibid.,* April 2, 1865.

84 *Ibid.,* April 3, 1865.

85 *Ibid.,* April 11, 1865.

86 David Willams, *A People's History of the Civil War,* 315.

87 *War of the Rebellion,* Series I, Vol. XLIX, Chapter LXI, Part I, 479.

88 Hinricks, *Diary.* April 16, 1865, WHMC UM.

89 *War of the Rebellion,* Series I, Part I, Vol. XLIX, Chapter LXI, 477.

90 Hinricks, *Diary,* April 28, 1865, AH 50 WHMC UM.

91 Benteen to Wilson, April 23, 1865, 549 Benteen ACP 1864 NA.

92 Hinricks, *Diary,* May 8, 1865 AH 50 WHMC UM.

93 "Volunteer Organizations," Benteen ACP 1125 NA.

94 Benteen to E. M. Stanton, Sept. 16, 1865 in Benteen ACP B 1124 NA.

95 Benteen B 1428 ACP 1864 [f/w 5142 ACP 1876] NA.

[96] Oct. 12, 1865 on reverse of AGO Oct. 15, 1865 ACP Benteen B 1125 NA.

[97] Clipping, letter addressed to A. R. Watson, editor, Nov. 29, 1865, HM UG.

[98] Benteen Collection HM UG.

[99] Clipping, *The Weekly Atlanta Intelligencer*, May 9, 1865, in HM UG.

[100] Asay, *Gray Head and Long Hair*, v.

[101] Newspaper clipping, no date, Benteen Collection, HMC UG.

[102] Benteen to Mrs., July 24, 1876, in Carroll, *Camp Talk*, 44.

[103] Benteen to Major General Frank Blair, Jr., Sept. 13, 1866 in Benteen ACP B 1836.

NOTES TO THE SOUTHERN PLAINS

[1] Robert M. Utley, *Frontier Regular*, 37, n 10.

[2] Johnson and Taunton, *Benteen's Ordeal and Custer's Field*, 9.

[3] Benteen 5142 ACP 1876 NA.

[4] W. Thompson to Adjutant General, Dec. 21, 1866 ACP B 1836.

[5] L. Hunter to Adjutant General, Dec. 21, 1866 ACP Benteen B 1836.

[6] Ray Allan Billington, *Westward Expansion*, 653.

[7] Jocelyn, *Mostly Alkali*, 97.

[8] Elizabeth Custer, *Tenting*, 233.

[9] William A. Dobak, *Fort Riley and its Neighbors*, 29.

[10] *Ibid.*, 35.

[11] Elizabeth B. Custer, *Tenting,* 233.

[12] Sandy Barnard (ed.), *Ten Years with Custer*, 18.

[13] Jocelyn, *Mostly Alkali*, 105.

[14] Katherine Gibson Fougera, *With Custer's Cavalry*, 125.

[15] Elizabeth Custer, *Tenting,* 262.

[16] *Ibid.*, 264.

[17] Benteen to Goldin, Feb. 12, 1896, in Carroll, *Benteen-Goldin*, 253.

[18] Elizabeth Custer, *Tenting*, 266.

[19] Benteen to Goldin, Feb. 12, 1896, in Carroll, *Benteen-Goldin*, 247.

[20] Benteen to Goldin, Feb. 12, 1896, in *Ibid.*, 248.

[21] Louise Barnett, *Touched by Fire*, 197.

[22] Benteen to Goldin, Feb. 12, 1896, in Carroll, *Benteen-Goldin*, 248.

[23] Hugh L. Scott, *Some Memories of a Soldier*, 454.

[24] Benteen to Tom Noell, July 9, 1867, in Benteen ACP.

[25] Benteen ACP 76 B. 5142 NA.

[26] Elizabeth Custer, *Tenting*, 315.

[27] Benteen Papers, No. 770 1:10, HMC UG.

[28] Benteen "In Old Fort Hays, Kansas: A Champion Buffalo Hunt," Benteen Papers, HMC UG.

[29] Blaine Burkey, *Custer, Come at Once!*, Hays, Kansas: Society of Friends of Historic Fort Hays, 1991, 17.

[30] *Ibid.*, 16.

[31] *Ibid.*, 9.

Notes

[32] Burkey, *Custer, Come at Once!*, 15.
[33] Ibid., 8.
[34] Benteen to Goldin, Feb. 12, 1896 in Carroll, *Benteen-Goldin*, 249.
[35] Don Rickey, Jr., *Forty Miles a Day on Beans and Hay*, Norman and London: University of Oklahoma Press, 1963, 200.
[36] Barnard, *Ten Years with Custer*, 34.
[37] Burkey, *Custer, Come at Once!*, 11.
[38] Benteen Papers, "A Champion Buffalo Hunt," HMC, UG.
[39] Burkey, *Custer, Come at Once!*, 14.
[40] Ibid., 9.
[41] Rickey, *Forty Miles a Day on Beans and Hay*, 103.
[42] Barnard, *Ten Years with Custer*, 48.
[43] Ibid., 34.
[44] Burkey, *Custer, Come at Once!*, 23.
[45] Ibid., 51.
[46] Ibid., 25.
[47] Elizabeth Custer, *Tenting*, 340.
[48] Ibid., 381.
[49] H. Wayne Morgan and Ann H. Morgan, *Oklahoma*, 283.
[50] Thom Hatch, *The Custer Companion*, 40.
[51] Barnard, *Ten Years with Custer*, 38.
[52] Paul A. Hutton, *The Custer Reader*, 126.
[53] Hatch, *The Custer Companion*, 64.
[54] Benteen Papers, "A Champion Buffalo Hunt,"4 HC, UG.

[55] Billington, *Westward Expansion*, 660.

[56] Burkey, *Custer, Come at Once!*, 38.

[57] Barnard, *Ten Years with Custer*, 47.

[58] Rickey, *Forty Miles a Day on Beans and Hay*, 103.

[59] Benteen to Goldin, Feb. 17, 1896 in Carroll *Benteen-Goldin*, 264.

[60] Benteen to Goldin, Feb. 22, 1896 in Carroll *Benteen-Goldin*, 277.

[61] Barnard, *Ten Years with Custer*, 53.

[62] *Ibid.*, 55.

[63] Elizabeth Barr, *Kansas*, 32.

[64] Benteen Papers, "Cavalry Scraps," 9, HC UG.

[65] Barr, *Kansas*, 30.

[66] Benteen Papers, "Baseball Playing in Kansas in 1868," 4, HC UG.

[67] Benteen Papers, "Baseball Playing in Kansas in 1868," 5, UG HC.

[68] Benteen Papers, "Cavalry Scraps," 16, HC UG.

[69] Benteen Papers, "Baseball Playing in Kansas," HC UG.

[70] Benteen Papers, "Cavalry Scraps,"17, HMC UG.

[71] Frances Roe, *Army Letters from an Officer's Wife*, 1871-1888, 12.

[72] Frank Gilbert Roe, *The Indian and His Horse*, 263.

[73] Frances Roe, *Army Letters from an Officer's Wife, 1871-1888*, 75.

[74] Frank Roe, *The Indian and His Horse*, 253.

[75] Burkey, *Custer, Come at Once!*, 42.

Notes

[76] *Ibid.*, 262.

[77] Fougera, *With Custer's Cavalry*, 120.

[78] Benteen to Goldin, Feb. 17, 1896, in Carroll, *Benteen-Goldin*, 267.

[79] Benteen to Goldin, Feb. 17, 1896, in *Ibid.*, 262.

[80] *Ibid.*, 264.

[81] Rickey, *Forty Miles a Day on Beans and Hay*, 103.

[82] Stan Hoig, *The Battle of the Washita*, 76.

[83] Benteen to Goldin, Feb. 17, 1896, in Carroll, *Benteen-Goldin*, 264.

[84] Barnard, *Ten Years with Custer*, 69.

[85] Paul Hutton, *Phil Sheridan and His Army*, 63.

[86] Barnard, *Ten Years with Custer*, 71.

[87] *Ibid.*, 72.

[88] Benteen to Goldin, Feb. 17, 1896, in Carroll, *Benteen-Goldin*, 264.

[89] Transcript, Ben Clark, *New York Sun,* May 17, 1894, 4, HMC NYPL.

[90] Hoig, *Washita*, 125.

[91] Transcript, Ben Clark, 5, HMC NYPL.

[92] Barnard, *Ten Years with Custer*, 74.

[93] Transcript, Ben Clark, 6, HMC NYPL.

[94] George A. Custer, *My Life on the Plains*, [1872-6] 241.

[95] Barnard, *Ten Years with Custer*, 85.

[96] Transcript, Ben Clark, 14, HMC NYPL.

[97] Hoig, *Washita*, 135.

[98] Transcript, Ben Clark, 10, HMC NYPL.

[99] Barnard, *Ten Years with Custer*, 79.

[100] Hoig, *Washita*, 130.

[101] Transcript, Ben Clark, 11, HMC NYPL.

[102] Benteen Papers, "Turkey Hunting in the Indian War," HC, UG.

[103] Hoig, *Washita*, 155.

[104] Hatch, *The Custer Companion*, 92.

[105] Barnard, *Ten Years with Custer*, 80 n.5.

[106] Benteen to Goldin, Feb. 17, 1896, in Carroll, *Benteen-Goldin*, 268.

[107] Transcript, Ben Clark, 13, HMC NYPL.

[108] Graham, *Custer Myth*, 212.

[109] Elizabeth Custer, *Following the Guidon*, 46.

[110] Benteen to Goldin, Feb. 14, 1996, in Carroll, *Benteen-Goldin*, 258.

[111] Benteen to Goldin, Feb. 17, 1996, in Carroll, *Benteen-Goldin*, 262.

[112] *Ibid.*, 267.

[113] Benteen to Goldin, Feb. 22. 1896, in Carroll, *Benteen-Goldin*, 280.

[114] *Ibid.*, 280.

[115] Benteen Papers, "From Medicine Bluff Creek Indian Territory to Sweetwater Creek, Texas" HC, UG.

[116] Benteen Papers, "Hunting the Southern Cheyenne," 6, HC UG.

[117] Benteen Papers, "Hunting the Southern Cheyenne," HC UG.
[118] Custer to Libby, March 24, 1868, in Elizabeth Custer, *Guidon*, 56.
[119] Benteen to Goldin, Feb. 12, 1896, in Carroll, *Benteen-Goldin*, 254.
[120] Frazier Hunt and Robert Hunt, *I Fought with Custer*, 126.
[121] Benteen to Goldin, Feb. 17, 1896, in Carroll, *Benteen-Goldin*, 267.
[122] *Ibid.*, 268.
[123] *Ibid.*, 243.
[124] Benteen Papers, "Among the Mesquite in Colorado," HC UG.
[125] Elizabeth Custer, *Guidon*, 77-81.
[126] *Ibid.*, 124.
[127] *Ibid.*, *Guidon*, 252.
[128] *Ibid.*, 256.
[129] *Ibid.*, p 251, 324.
[130] Elizabeth Custer, *Boots and Saddles*, 222.
[131] Brian Pohanka, *A Summer on the Plains from the Diary of Anne Gibson Roberts*, 30.
[132] *Ibid.*, 28.
[133] *Ibid.*, 153.
[134] Barnard, *Ten Years with Custer*, 107-9.
[135] Burkey, *Custer, Come at Once!*, 60.
[136] Pohanka, *Summer on the Plains*, 8.
[137] Elizabeth Custer, *Tenting*, 235.

[138] Pohanka, *Summer on the Plains*, 28.

[139] Elizabeth Custer, *Guidon*, 244.

[140] Benteen to Mrs. B., March 12, 1871, in Carroll, *Camp Talk*, 4.

[141] Clipping, *Atlanta Constitution*, Nov. 18, 1894, in Benteen Papers HC UG.

[142] J. C. Ladenheim, *Alien Horseman*, Bowie, MD: Heritage Books, 2003.

[143] Benteen to Goldin, Jan. 16, 1892, in Carroll, *Benteen-Goldin*, 209.

[144] Transcript, Benteen to Barry, March 29, 1998, Newberry Library Collection, Chicago; also Benteen to Goldin, Feb. 14, 1896, in Carroll, *Benteen-Goldin*, 159.

[145] Burkey, *Custer, Come at Once!*, 78.

[146] Elizabeth Custer, *Tenting*, 67.

[147] Regular Army Record f/w 5142 Benteen ACP 1876 NA.

[148] Burkey, *Custer, Come at Once!*, 98.

[149] Benteen Papers, "Among the Mesquite in Colorado," HC UG.

[150] Benteen to Goldin, Feb. 17, 1896, in Carroll, *Benteen-Goldin*, 160.

[151] Hatch, *The Custer Companion*, 239.

[152] Louise Barnett, *Touched by Fire*, 263.

[153] Benteen to Mrs. B., March 12, 1871 in Carroll *Camp Talk*, 3.

[154] Benteen to Goldin, Feb. 17, 1896, in Carroll, *Benteen-Goldin*, 265.

[155] Elizabeth Custer, *Boots and Saddles*, 11.

[156] Mark A. Tabbert, *American Free Masons*, 112.
[157] Benteen to Kate, July 4, 1876, in Carroll, *Camp Talk*, 25.
[158] Utley, *Frontier Regulars*, 140.
[159] Hunt and Hunt, *I Fought with Custer*, 4.
[160] Hatch, *The Custer Companion*, 157.
[161] Barnett, *Touched by Fire*, 263.

NOTES TO THE NORTHERN PLAINS

[1] Dee Brown, *Best of Dee Brown's West*, 189.
[2] Benteen to Goldin, Feb. 12, 1896, in Carroll, *Benteen-Goldin*, 256.
[3] Elizabeth Custer, *Boot and Saddles*, 14.
[4] Fougera, *With Custer's Cavalry*, 213.
[5] Billington, *Westward Expansion*, 713.
[6] Larned letter, April 25, 1873 in Hutton, *The Custer Reader*, 184.
[7] Larned letter, April 30, 1873, in *Ibid.*, 187.
[8] Elizabeth Custer, *Boots and Saddles*, 37.
[9] Ernest Garlington in *New York Herald*, Aug. 7, 1876, quoted in James Willert, *March of the Column: A Chronicle of the 1876 War*, 214.
[10] Larned letter, April 12, 1873, in Hutton, *The Custer Reader*, 182.
[11] Larned letter, Aug. 11, 1873 in *Ibid.*, 188.
[12] Custer to Libby, July 19, 1873, in Elizabeth Custer, *Boots and Saddles*, 277.
[13] Custer to Libby, Sept. 6, 1873, in *Ibid.*, 292.

[14] Benteen to Goldin, Jan. 19, 1890, in Carroll, *Benteen-Goldin*, 270.

[15] Benteen to Goldin, Feb. 12, 1896, in Carroll, *Benteen-Goldin*, 256.

[16] Barnard, *Ten Years with Custer*, 197.

[17] Elizabeth Custer, *Tenting,* 248.

[18] Transcript, John Ryan in the *Billings Gazette*, June 25, 1923, Bismarck, ND Public Library.

[19] Barnard, *Ten Years with Custer*, 252.

[20] Ibid.

[21] Larned letters, Aug. 19, 1873, in Hutton, *The Custer Reader,* 197.

[22] Rickey, *Forty Miles a Day on Beans and Hay*, 276.

[23] Benteen Papers, "From the Missouri River to the Yellowstone," HC UG.

[24] Custer to Libby, Sept. 6, 1873, in Elizabeth Custer, *Boots and Saddles*, 291.

[25] Benteen Papers, "From the Missouri River to the Yellowstone," HC UG.

[26] Roe, *Letters from an Army Wife*, 183.

[27] Barnard, *Ten Years with Custer*, 206.

[28] Fougera, *With Custer's Cavalry*, 168.

[29] *Ibid.*, 162.

[30] Roe, *Letters from an Army Wife*, 66.

[31] Elizabeth Custer, *Boots and Saddles*, 112.

[32] Barnard, *Ten Years with Custer*, 218.

[33] Willert, *March of the Column*, 180.

[34] Barnard, *Ten Years with Custer*, 184.
[35] Roe, *Letters from an Army Wife*, 289.
[36] *Ibid.*, 98.
[37] *Ibid.*, 64.
[38] Fougera, *With Custer's Cavalry*, 246.
[39] Elizabeth Custer, *Boots and Saddles*, 99.
[40] *Ibid.*, 139.
[41] Fougera, *With Custer's Cavalry*, 63.
[42] Transcript, "Narrative, Deputy US Marshall Ben Ash, South Dakota" HMC NYPL.
[43] Robert Lee, *Fort Meade and the Black Hills*, 2.
[44] *Ibid.*, 5.
[45] Benteen to Barry, Oct.15, 1895, in C. K. Mills, *Harvest*, 217.
[46] Fougera, *With Custer's Cavalry*, 106, 119.
[47] Kenneth M. Hammer, *The Springfield Carbine in the Western Frontier*, 4.
[48] Barnard, *Ten Years with Custer*, 180.
[49] *Ibid.*, 223.
[50] *Ibid.*, 234.
[51] *New York Tribune*, Aug. 20, 1874, in Herbert Krause and Gary Olson, *Prelude to Glory*, 217.
[52] Harry H. Anderson, "The Benteen Baseball Club," *Magazine of Western History*, Vol. 20 (1970), 82-85.
[53] Benteen to Goldin, Feb. 22, 1896, in Carroll, *Benteen-Goldin*, 280.
[54] Benteen to Goldin, Feb. 22, 1896, in Graham, *Myth*, 208.

55 Roe, *Letters from an Army Wife*, 154.

56 Benteen to Goldin, Feb. 22, 1896, in Carroll, *Benteen-Goldin*, 280.

57 Fougera, *With Custer's Cavalry*, 96.

58 Benteen Papers, "From New Oreleans Louisiana to the Black Hills," HC UG.

59 Ibid.

60 Barnard, *Ten Years with Custer*, 251.

61 Benteen Papers, "From New Orleans Louisiana to the Black Hills," HC UG.

62 Barnard, *Ten Years with Custer*, 236.

63 Fougera, *With Custer's Cavalry*, 254.

NOTES TO LITTLE BIGHORN

1 John S. Gray, "Veterinary Service on Custer's Last Campaign," *Kansas Historical Quarterly*, Autumn 1977, 3. Online Service:
http://www.kancoll.org/khq/1977/77_3_gray.htm

2 Shirley A. Leckie, *Elizabeth Bacon Custer and the Making of a Myth*, 163.

3 Hatch, *The Custer Companion*, 136.

4 Hunt and Hunt, *I Fought with Custer*, 126.

5 Barnett, *Touched by Fire*, 129.

6 Edgerly's Reply to Colonel Hughes, 4, HMC NYPL.

7 Ron Nichols, "Command Decision—1876 Style," *Greasy Grass*, May 2005, 5.

8 Adolph Roenigk, *Pioneer History of Kansas*, 290.

[9] Benteen to Goldin, Feb. 22, 1896, in Carroll, *Benteen-Goldin*, 282.

[10] Roy Johnson, "Jacob Horner of the 7th Cavalry," *North Dakota History*, Vol. 16, 1949, 81.

[11] Oren G. Libby, *The Arikara Narrative of Custer's Campaign and the Battle of Little Bighorn*, 46, 50.

[12] Barnard, *Ten Years with Custer*, 285.

[13] Terry to Miss J. R. Terry, May 17, 1876. In Alfred Howe Terry, *The Terry Letters* (ed. James Willert), 1.

[14] Transcript of Narrative of Ben Ash, Deputy Marshall, HMC NYPL.

[15] Terry to Betsy, May 18, 1876, in Willert, *Terry Letters*, 3.

[16] Terry to E. H. Terry, May 28, 1876, in Willert, *Terry Letters*, 7.

[17] General Godfrey Narrative, Graham, *Myth*, 127.

[18] Libby, *The Arikara Narrative*, 66.

[19] *Ibid.*, 72.

[20] Terry to Fanny, May 30, 1876, in Willert, *Terry Letters*, 8.

[21] Terry to Fanny, May 30, 1876, in *Ibid.*, 8.

[22] Johnson, "Jacob Horner," 82.

[23] Barnard, *Ten Years with Custer*, 287.

[24] John Ryan in *Billings Gazette*, June 25, 1923, Special Collections, Bismarck Public Library.

[25] Libby, *The Arikara Narrative*, 66.

[26] Graham, *Myth*, 235.

[27] Memoranda of Captain Carter in *Ibid.*, 302.

[28] Robert M. Utley, *Custer and the Great Controversy*, 73.

29. Narrative of General W. S. Edgerly, 2, HMC, NYPL.
30. Terry to My Dearest Girls, June 2, 1976, in Willert, *Terry Letters*, 13.
31. Dennis Lynch, Oct. 1908, Feb. 8, 1909 in Kenneth Hammer (ed.), *Custer in 76*, 139.
32. Daniel A. Knipe's Account in *Ibid.*, 88.
33. Libby, *The Arikara Narrative*, 72.
34. "Men Who Fought With Custer" (Jacob Adam), George R. McCormack, *National Republic,* 15, Box 2, HMC, NYPL.
35. Rickey, *Forty Miles a Day on Beans and Hay*, 265.
36. Benteen to Mrs. B., June 13, 1876, in Carroll, *Camp Talk*, 14.
37. Libby, *The Arikara Narrative*, 79.
38. Barnard, *Ten Years with Custer*, 288.
39. Godfrey's Narrative in Graham, *Myth*, 128.
40. Willert, *March of the Column*, 186.
41. Benteen's Second Narrative of Little Bighorn in Carroll, *Benteen-Goldin*, 162.
42. Benteen Papers, Second Narrative of Little Bighorn, 16, HC UG.
43. Benteen Papers, First Narrative (c. 1890), 5, HC UG.
44. Willert, *March of the Column*, 314.
45. Barnard, *Ten Years with Custer*, 271.
46. Interview with Sitting Bull, *New York Herald*, Nov. 16, 1877 in Graham, *Myth*, 67.
47. Libby, *The Arikara Narrative*, 78.

[48] Benteen Papers, First Narrative of Little Bighorn, 21, HC UG.

[49] Benteen Papers, Second Narrative of Little Bighorn, 10, HC UG.

[50] Narrative of John F. Donoughus in HMC NYPL.

[51] Ibid.

[52] John Ryan, *Billings Gazette,* June 25, 1923, in Custer Collection, Bismarck Public Library.

[53] Associates of Graduates of the U.S. Military Academy, *Annual Report*, June 11, 1936 in Box II, HMC NYPL.

[54] Libby, *The Arikara Narrative*, 91.

[55] First Narrative of Little Bighorn in Carroll, *Benten-Goldin*, 180.

[56] Narrative of Donoughus, HMC NYPL.

[57] Benteen's First Narrative in Carroll, *Benteen-Goldin*, 166.

[58] Statement of Girard in Graham, *Myth*, 251.

[59] Statement of Martin in Graham, *Myth*, 289.

[60] Benteen's Second Narrative of the Little Bighorn in Carroll *Benteen-Goldin*, 180.

[61] *Ibid.*, 181.

[62] Vic was a mare, according to the horse's groom, John Burkman.

[63] Narrative of Donoughus in HMC NYPL.

[64] Godfrey fragment, 27 in HMC NYPL.

[65] Benteen Second Narrative, 15 HC UG; Carroll, *Benteen-Goldin*, 182.

[66] Transcript, T. M.Couhlan, "Battle of the Little Big Horn," *The Cavalry Journal*, Jan-Feb.1934, in HMC NYPL.

[67] Hunt and Hunt, *I Fought with Custer*, 76.

[68] Benteen Papers, Second Narrative of the Little Bighorn, 15 HC UG. The manuscript which is in Benteen's handwriting in the HC UG differs from the account in Carroll, *Benteen-Goldin*, 182. HC UG: "To say the country "terrain" goes now—was "rough," is but putting it mildly..." Carroll: "To say the country "Terrain" goes now—was "rough," that would be more truly descriptive." This suggests that there was more than one manuscript or an imperfect transcription.

[69] Second Little Bighorn Narrative, 17 HC UG; also in Carroll *Benteen-Goldin*, 183.

[70] First Little Bighorn Narrative, 33; Carroll *Benteen-Goldin*, 168.

[71] Second Little Bighorn Narrative, Carroll, *Benteen-Goldin*, 184.

[72] Benteen to Wallace, Report, July 7, 1876, in Box I, Benteen Papers HC UG.

[73] Benteen to Mrs. B., July 4, 1876, in Carroll, *Camp Talk*, 24.

[74] Benteen to Wallace, Report, July 4, 1876, 6. HC UG.

[75] Benteen Papers, Second Little Bighorn Narrative, 20 HC UG; Carroll *Benteen-Goldin*, 184.

[76] Benteen's First Narrative in Carrol, *Benteen-Goldin*, p, 170.

[77] Benteen Papers, First Narrative, 21, HC UG; Carroll *Benteen-Goldin*, 169.

[78] Godfrey Narrative in Graham, *Myth*, 141.

[79] "Benteen's Own Story" in E. A. Brininstool, *Troopers with Custer*, 79.

[80] Transcript of Donoughus Narrative in HMC NYPL.

Notes

81 W. A. Graham, *The Reno Court of Inquiry*, 120, 212.
82 Interview with Girard, April 3, 1901, in Hammer, *Custer in 76*, 23.
83 Hunt and Hunt, *I Fought with Custer*, 86.
84 Graham, *Myth*, 296.
85 *Ibid.*, 290.
86 Hairy Moccasin in Graham, *Myth*, 24.
87 Interview with Tall Bull, July 22, 1910, in Hammer, *Custer in 76*, 212.
88 Narrative of Mrs. Spotted Horn Bull in *Ibid.*, 84.
89 Foolish Elk Sept. 22, 1908, in Hammer, *Custer in 76*, 199.
90 Frank Gilbert Roe, *The Indian and his Horse*, 230.
91 General Godfrey's Comments on Chief Gall in Graham, *Myth*, 95.
92 Crow King's Story in *Ibid.*, 77.
93 Morgan and Morgan, *Oklahoma*, 298.
94 General Luther Hare, "Godfrey Defense Movement," 1, HMC NYPL.
95 Edgerly Narrative, 12, HMC NYPL.
96 Transcript, French to Mrs. Cooke, June 16, 1880, in HMC NYPL.
97 "Benteen's Own Story" in Brininstool, *Troopers with Custer*, 85.
98 Willert, *March of the Column*, 13.
99 *Ibid.*, 15.
100 Graham, *Myth*, 85.
101 McCormack, "Men Who Fought With Custer," 15.

[102] Godfrey's Narrative in *Ibid.*, 139.

[103] Narrative of W. J. Ghent, undated, in HMC NYPL.

[104] Narrative of Red Bear in Graham, *Myth*, 41.

[105] Donoughus in HMC NYPL.

[106] Barnard, *Ten Years with Custer*, 291.

[107] Donoughus in HMC NYPL.

[108] Goldin to Dustin, Dec. 14, 1931, in Carroll, *Benteen-Goldin*, 74.

[109] Ghent, "Arikaras in the Little Bighorn Battle," HMC NYPL.

[110] Chief Gall's Report in Graham, *Myth*, 90.

[111] Libby, *The Arikara Narrative*, 118, 154.

[112] Ghent, "Arikara in the Little Bighorn Battle," NMC NYPL.

[113] Jerome A. Greene (ed.), Battles and Skirmishes of the Great Sioux War, 48.

[114] Transcript, Ryan in *Billings Gazette*, June 25, 1923 in Custer Collection, Bismarck Public Library.

[115] Testimony of William C. Slaper, in Brininstool, *Troopers with Custer*, 51.

[116] Transcript of Donoughus in HMC NYPL.

[117] "Another Version of the Story of Red Horse," in Graham *Myth*, 61.

[118] Narrative of Young Hawk in *Ibid.*, 37.

[119] Ghent, "Narrative of the Arikara in the Little Bighorn," 2, HMC NYPL.

[120] Dustin to Goldin, May 25, 1934, in Carroll, *Benteen-Goldin*, 127.

[121] Kenneth Hammer, "Wounded Casualties in the Little Big Horn River Fight," *LBH Newsletter*, Oct. 2005.

[122] "With Colonel Varnum" in Brininstool, *Troopers with Custer*, 93.

[123] Benteen to Goldin, Jan 31, 1896, in Carroll, *Benteen-Goldin*, 242.

[124] Rickey, Forty Miles a Day on Beans and Hay, 291.

[125] Dustin to Goldin, Feb. 17, 1934 in *Ibid.*, 107.

[126] W. H. Ghent to Harvey Olson, March 5, 1936, HMC NYPL.

[127] Benteen to Goldin, March 1, 1892, in Carroll, *Benteen-Goldin*, 215.

[128] Brininstool, *Troopers with Custer*, 189.

[129] Narrative of W. S. Edgerly, 9, in HMC NYPL.

[130] First Narrative of Little Bighorn, 47, HC UG; Graham, *Myth*, 171.

[131] Graham, *Myth*, 318.

[132] Goldin's Narrative in Carroll, *Custer in Periodicals*, 318.

[133] *New York Times*, July 11, 1884.

[134] Donoughus Transcript in HMC NYPL.

[135] Edgerly's Narrative in HMC NYPL.

[136] Benteen to Goldin Feb. 24, 1892, in Carroll, *Benteen-Goldin*, 216.

[137] Benteen to Mrs. B., July 10, 1876, in Carroll, *Camp Talk*, 32.

[138] Benteen to Goldin, Jan. 16, 1892, in Carroll, *Benteen-Goldin*, 210.

[139] Varnum to Graham, no date, in Graham, *Myth*, 347.

[140] Herendeen's Statement in William O. Taylor, *With Custer on the Little Bighorn*, 166.

[141] Barnard, *Ten Years with Custer*, 300.

[142] Herendeen's Statement in Taylor, 166.

[143] Robert Vaughn, *Then and Now, or Thirty-six Years in the Rockies*, 322.

[144] Interview, Private Glen, Jan. 22, 1914, in Hammer, *Custer in 76*, 130.

[145] Taylor, *With Custer on the Little Bighorn*, 166.

[146] Benteen to Goldin, Jan. 16, 1892 in Carroll *Benteen-Goldin*, 20.

[147] Edgerly Narrative, 11, in HMC NYPL.

[148] Benteen Papers, First Narrative of Little Bighorn, 57, HC UG; Carroll, *Benteen-Goldin*, 173.

[149] Account of William C. Slaper in Brininstool, *Troopers with Custer*, 60.

[150] Taylor, *With Custer on the Little Bighorn*, 54.

[151] Transcript, T. W. Goldin, "Interesting Facts written by a trooper of the 7th Cavalry," Janesville, Wisconsin, July 8, 1888, 29, in HMC NYPL.

[152] Donoughus Transcript in HMC NYPL.

[153] Goldin to Johnson, Dec. 27, 1932, in Carroll, *Benteen-Goldin*, 39.

[154] Benteen to Goldin, Jan. 6, 1892, in Carroll, *Benteen-Goldin*, 206.

[155] Transcript, Goldin to Ghent, Jan. 6, 1932, HMC NYPL.

[156] Gall's Story, Aug. 18, 1886, in Graham, *Myth*, 92.

[157] Dustin to Goldin, Nov. 17, 1932, in Carroll, *Benteen-Goldin*, 92.

[158] Benteen to Mrs. B., July 4, 1876, in Carroll, *Camp Talk*, 24.

[159] Walker, "Military Medicine at Little Bighorn," 194.

[160] Scott, *Some Memories of a Soldier*, 72.

[161] Benteen's Papers, "Duck Shooting," HC UG.

[162] Taylor, *With Custer on the Little Bighorn*, 166.

[163] Goldin to Johnson, April 5, 1933 in Carroll *Benteen-Goldin*, 43; also Frederic F. Van de Water, *Glory Hunter*, Lincoln & London: University Nebraska [1934], 1988, 353.

[164] Libby, 105.

[165] Transcript, Edgerly Narrative, 11, in HMC NYPL.

[166] Transcript, G. R. McCormack, "Men who Fought with Custer," HMC NYPL.

[167] Sgt. James Richardson in *Portland (Maine) Sunday Times*, June 27, 1909.

[168] Gibson to Mrs. G., July 4, 1874, in Fougera, *With Custer's Cavalry*, 272.

[169] Narrative of John Ryan in Graham, *Myth*, 247.

[170] Red Horse's Story in *Ibid.*, 60.

[171] Ghent to Olson, March 5, 1936, HMC NYPL.

[172] Transcript, *Yankton Daily Press and Dakotaian*, May 31, 1877; Godfrey to Mrs. G., July 2, 1876, in HMC NYPL.

[173] Willert, *March of the Column*, 5.

[174] Barnard, *Ten Years with Custer*, 303-5.

[175] *Ibid.*, 302, 306.

[176] Willert, *March of the Column*, 192.

[177] Chief Gall in Graham, *Myth*, 88.

[178] Transcript, "Sitting Bull's Own Narrative of the Custer Fight," *Canadian Historical Review*, University of Toronto Press, June 1935. 175 HMC NYPL.

[179] Narrative of Young Hawk in Graham, *Myth*, 37.

[180] Benteen to Barry, April 1, 1898, in Little Bighorn Battle National Monument, Crow Agency, Special Collections.

[181] Willert, *March of the Column*, 12, 36.

[182] Walker, "Military Medicine at Little Bighorn," 194.

[183] *Ibid.*, 408.

[184] Transcript, *Bismarck Tribune*, Aug. 6, 1938, "Widow of Custer's Indian Scouts," HMC NYPL.

[185] Willert, *March of the Column*, 68.

[186] Taylor, *With Custer on the Little Bighorn*, 119.

[187] Varnum to Parents, July 4, 1876, in Graham, *Myth*, 343.

[188] Benteen to Goldin, March 19, 1892, in Carroll, *Benteen-Goldin*, 209.

[189] James J. O'Kelly, in *New York Herald*, August 7, 1876, in Willert, *March of the Column*, 40.

[190] Benteen to Goldin March 19, 1892, in Carroll, *Benteen-Goldin*, 219.

[191] Hatch, *The Custer Companion*, 115.

[192] Benteen to Mrs. B., July 10, 1876, in Carroll, *Camp Talk*, 30.

[193] Willert, *March of the Column*, 375.

[194] *Ibid.*, 424.

[195] Benteen to Goldin, March 19, 1892, in Graham, *Myth*, 196.
[196] Willert, *March of the Column*, 324.
[197] *Ibid.*, 257.
[198] Marsh to Executive Mansion, Benteen 5142 ACP 1876.
[199] Cuthbert Mills, *New York Times*, Sept. 14, 1876, 3.
[200] Willert, *March of the Column*, 451.
[201] *Ibid.*, 397.
[202] Scott, *Some Memories of a Soldier*, 27.
[203] Benteen to Mrs. B., Oct. 10, 1876 in Carroll *Camp Talk*, 52.
[204] Roy Johnson, "Jacob Horner," 86.
[205] Robert Price, *Philadelphia Times*, March 13, 1879, in Graham, *Myth*, 330.
[206] Frederick Whittaker, *A Complete Life of Gen. George A. Custer*, 2 Vols. Bowie, Maryland: Heritage Books, [1876] 1993.
[207] W. A. Graham, *Reno Court of Inquiry*, xxv.
[208] Benteen to Mrs. B., May 17, 1877, in Carroll, *Camp Talk*, 64.

NOTES TO NEZ PERCE

[1] Roe, *The Indian and the Horse*, 255.
[2] Benteen to Mrs. B., June 9, 1877, in Carroll, *Camp Talk*, 67.
[3] Benteen to Mrs. B., Aug. 4, 1877, in *Ibid.*, 83.
[4] Benteen to Mrs. B., Aug. 11, 1877, in *Ibid.*, 85.
[5] Benteen to Goldin, Feb. 29, 1896, in Carroll, *Benteen-Goldin*, 274.

[6] Benteen to Goldin, Nov. 17, 1897, in Graham, *Myth*, 91.
[7] Benteen to Mrs. B., Sept. 2, 1877, in Carroll, *Camp Talk*, 89.
[8] Benteen Papers, "Among the Mesquite in Colorado," HC UG.
[9] Benteen to Goldin, Feb. 20, 1896, in Carroll, *Benteen-Goldin*, 274.
[10] Benteen to Goldin, Oct. 19, 1894, in Carroll, *Benteen-Goldin*, 230.
[11] Benteen to Goldin, Nov. 17, 1891, in *Ibid.*, 202.
[12] Benteen to Goldin, Nov. 17, 1891, *Ibid.*, 203.
[13] Benteen to Goldin, Jan. 11, 1896, in *Ibid.*, 234.
[14] Benteen to Goldin, Nov. 17, 1891, in *Ibid.*, 204.
[15] Jerome A. Greene, *Nez Perce Summer*, Chapter 13, n. 146. [http://www.nps.gov/nepe/greene/chap13d.htm].
[16] Terry's "Annual Report, Department of the Dakota," Benteen ACP.
[17] Benteen to Goldin, Nov. 17, 1891, in Carroll, *Benteen-Goldin*, 204.
[18] Jerome A. Greene, *Nez Perce Summer*, Chapter 13, n. 146. [http://www.nps.gov/nepe/greene/chap13d.htm].
[19] Benteen to Goldin, March 23, 1896, in Carroll, *Benteen-Goldin*, 292.
[20] Benteen Papers, "Hunting the Southern Cheyenne," HC UG.
[21] Benteen to Mrs. B., Dec. 11, 1877, in Carroll, *Camp Talk*, 116.
[22] Benteen to Mrs. B., Nov. 18, 1877, in *Ibid.*, 105.
[23] Rickey, *Forty Miles a Day on Beans and Hay*, 95.

24 Scott, *Some Memories of a Soldier*, 111.
25 *New York Times,* June 16, 1876.
26 Transcript, Carter Memoranda, Aug. 23, 1938, HMC, NYPL.
27 Transcript, W. J. Ghent to Brininstool, Feb. 17, 1930, in HMC NYPL.
28 Transcript, Carter Memoranda, Aug. 23, 1938, HMC NYPL.
29 *New York Sun*, Feb. 26, 1879, in Graham, *Myth*, 328.
30 *New York Times*, Feb. 6, 1879.
31 Varnum to Graham, July 15, 1925; Edgerly to Graham, July 15, 1925, in Graham, *Myth*, 323.
32 *New York Times*, Feb. 6, 1879.
33 *New York Times*, Jan. 24, 1879.
34 Benteen to Mrs. B., Jan. 31, 1879, in Carroll, *Camp Talk*, 120.
35 Benteen to Mrs. B., May 3, 1879, in *Ibid.*, 128.
36 Jocelyn, *Mostly Alkali,* 298.
37 Benteen to Mrs. B., May 5, 1879, in Carroll, *Camp Talk*, 129.
38 Benteen to Goldin, Feb. 20, 1996, in Carroll, *Benteen-Goldin*, 274.
39 Lee, *Fort Meade and the Black Hills*, 69.
40 Benteen to Goldin, Feb. 22, 1986 in Carroll *Benteen-Goldin*, 277.
41 Hans Trefousse, *Rutherford B. Hayes*, 28.
42 Ari Hoogenboom, *Rutherford B. Hayes,* 141.

[43] John Upton Terrill and George Walton, *Faint the Trumpet Sounds*, 301.

[44] Roe, *Letters from an Army Wife*, 150.

[45] *New York Times*, March 23, 1881.

[46] Shirley Leckie, *Elizabeth Bacon Custer*, 236.

[47] Soldiers' Testimonials, Aug. 1881, HMC NYPL.

[48] Rickey, *Forty Miles a Day on Beans and Hay*, 218.

[49] Hatch, *The Custer Companion*, 195.

[50] Henrietta Elizabeth Benteen Doyle married Franklin Tinkham Fairbanks, Aug. 17, 1878.

[51] Benteen to "En," August 24, 1882, HC UG.

[52] *New York Times*, Jan. 12, 1883.

[53] Godfrey to Shoemaker, March 2, 1926, in Graham, *Myth*, 333.

[54] Transcript, Godfrey to John G. Neihardt, Jan. 6, 1924, HMC, NYPL.

[55] W. S. Godfrey, *The West: Custer's Last Battle*, 71.

NOTES TO FINAL YEARS

[1] Service Report, Feb. 4, 1882, 740, ACP 1882 NA.

[2] Graham, *Myth*, 377.

[3] Adjutant General to Benteen, Feb. 20, 1883, in 347, ACP 1883 NA.

[4] Utley, *Frontier Regulars*, 21.

[5] William H. Leckie, *The Buffalo Soldiers*, 99.

[6] *Ibid.*, 71, 88.

[7] Benteen to Goldin, Oct. 20, 1891, in Carroll, *Benteen-Goldin*, 196.

[8] Benteen to Adjutant General March 14, 1867, in Benteen ACP NA.

[9] Benteen to Mrs. B., July 10, 1876, in Carroll, *Camp Talk*, 3.

[10] Benteen to Mrs. B., July 3, 1877, in *Ibid.*, 80.

[11] Benteen to Mrs. B., May 2, 1879, in *Ibid.*, 126.

[12] Benteen to Mrs. B., Sept. 28, 1883, in *Ibid.*, 139.

[13] William H. Leckie, *The Buffalo Soldiers*, 247.

[14] Billington, *Westward Expansion*, 717.

[15] Benteen to Goldin, March 23, 1896, in Carroll, *Benteen-Goldin*, 295.

[16] Benteen to Mrs. B., Sept. 28, 1883, in Carroll, *Camp Talk*, 138.

[17] Scott, *Some Memories of a Soldier*, 141.

[18] Benteen Papers, "Turkey Hunting in the Indian War," HC, UG.

[19] Elizabeth Custer, *Guidon*, 288.

[20] Benteen to General Green, Nov. 10, 1886, 5700, ACP Benteen NA.

[21] William H. Leckie, *The Buffalo Soldiers*, 249.

[22] Carroll, *Cavalry Scraps*, 43.

[23] *New York Times*, March 23, 1885, 5.

[24] Benteen Papers, "Picnicking," 1, HC UG.

[25] Carroll, *Cavalry Scraps*, xi.

[26] Roe, *Letters from an Army Wife*, 161, 207.

[27] Benteen Papers, "Picnicking," HC UG.

[28] Benteen 5142 ACP 1876 NA.
[29] Utley, *Frontier Regulars*, 40 n. 48.
[30] Memorandum, Adjutant General Kelton, Dec. 29, 1885, 7229 ACP 1885 [f/o 5142 ACP 1876].
[31] Adjutant General to A. E. Diaz, Nov. 7, 1885, 6566 ACP 1885 [f/w 5142 ACP 1876].
[32] Diaz to Adjutant General, Nov. 9, 1885, Benteen ACP NA.
[33] Benteen to Godfrey, Jan. 3, 1886, in Hunt and Hunt, *I Fought with Custer*, 203.
[34] Benteen to Price, March 6, 1979, in Graham, *Myths*, 325.
[35] Roe, *Letters from an Army Wife*, 13.
[36] *Kansas City Times*, Jan. 3, 1887, in Mills, *Harvest*, 353.
[37] Jocelyn, *Mostly Alkali*, 313.
[38] *Ibid.*, 242.
[39] Carroll, *Court Martial of Benteen*, 79.
[40] Robert Foster, *Wild West*, Feb. 2000, 34.
[41] Norman to Benteen, Dec. 28, 1886, in Benteen ACP NA.
[42] Benteen to O. D. Green, Nov. 18, 1886, ACP Benteen NA.
[43] http://historytogo.utah.gov/hmbuffsold.html
[44] Jocelyn, *Mostly Alkali*, 311.
[45] Robert Huetter, *A History of Fort Duchesne, Utah*. Master's Thesis. Brigham Young University, April 1990, 95.
[46] Jocelyn, *Mostly Alkali*, 311.
[47] *Ibid.*, 314.
[48] Carroll, *Court Martial of Benteen*, vi.
[49] *New York Times*, Jan. 13, 1887, 3.

50 Johnson and Taunton, *Benteen's Ordeal and Custer's Field*, 27.
51 Carroll, *Court Martial of Benteen*, 3.
52 *Ibid.*, 85.
53 *New York Times*, March 19, 1887, 1.
54 Benteen to Mrs. B., May 11, 1887, in Carroll, *Camp Talk*, 141.
55 Mills, *Harvest*, 364.
56 *Ibid.*
57 Special Orders No. 50, 2211 ACP 1887 NA.
58 Benteen to Adjutant General, May 1, 1887, f/w 5143 ACP 1876.
59 4th Endorsement, May 14, 1887, 2125 ACP NA.
60 Benteen to Goldin, Oct. 20, 1891, in Carroll, *Benteen-Goldin*, 196.
61 Benteen to Mrs. B., Apr. 21, 1888, in Carroll, *Camp Talk*, 143.
62 Adjutant General's Office, June 8, 1888, 1244 ACP 1888 NA.
63 Benteen to Godfrey Transcript, Aug. 14, 1893, HMC NYPL.
64 Benteen to Mrs. B., April 27, 1888, in Carroll, *Camp Talk*, 144.
65 Benteen to Mrs. B, April 28, 1888, in *Ibid.*, 146.
66 Benteen to Adjutant General, May 29, 1888, in 3095 Benteen ACP NA.
67 Affidavit of Timothy Wilcox, May 29, 1888, in Benteen ACP NA.

[68] Benteen to Mrs. B., May 5, 1888, in Carroll, *Camp Talk*, 151.
[69] *Ibid.*, 151.
[70] Benteen 5142 ACP NA.
[71] Johnson and Taunton, *Benteen's Ordeal and Custer's Field*, 49.
[72] Benteen to Goldin, Nov. 17, 1891, in Carroll, *Benteen-Goldin*, 205.
[73] Transcript, Benteen to Godfrey, Aug. 14, 1893, HMC NYPL.
[74] Benteen to Goldin, Apr. 3, 1892, in Carroll, *Benteen-Goldin*, 222.
[75] Transcript, "Interesting Facts Written by a Trooper of the 7th Cavalry," Janesville, July 8, 1888, in HMC NYPL.
[76] Goldin to Cole, Jan. 15, 1933, in Carroll, *Benteen-Goldin*, 60.
[77] Benteen to Goldin, March 1, 1892, in *Ibid.*, 217.
[78] Shirley Leckie, *Elizabeth Bacon Custer*, 292.
[79] Goldin to Cole, Dec. 31, 1932, in Carroll, *Benteen-Goldin*, 34.
[80] Carroll, *Periodicals*, 98-118.
[81] Benteen to Goldin, Feb. 22, 1896, in Carroll, *Benteen-Goldin*, 284.
[82] Transcript, W. J. Ghent, "T. W. Goldin and his ride to Reno," Nov. 10, 1932, in HMC NYPL.
[83] Transcript, Benteen to Godfrey, Aug. 14, 1893, in HMC NYPL.

Notes 311

[84] Benteen to Goldin, Oct 20, 1891, in Carroll, *Benteen-Goldin*, 196.

[85] Clipping, *Atlanta Constitution,* June 24, 1898, in HC UG.

[86] Benteen to Goldin, Nov. 17, 1891, in Carroll, *Benteen-Goldin*, 206.

[87] Benteen to Goldin, Jan. 16, 1892, in Carroll, *Benteen-Goldin*, 210.

[88] Benteen to Barry, Apr. 1, 1898, Little Bighorn National Monument, Special Collections, White Swan Library.

[89] Benteen to Goldin, Jan. 16, 1892, in Carroll, *Benteen-Goldin*, 210.

[90] Newspaper clippings, July 23, 1898, HC UG.

[91] Barnett, 319.

[92] Benteen to Goldin, April 25, 1896, in Carroll, *Benteen-Goldin*, 300.

[93] Clipping, *Atlanta Journal*, May 24, 1897, HC UG.

[94] Benteen to Barry, March 29, 1898, in Newberry Library, Chicago, Special Collections.

[95] Benteen to Goldin, March 1, 1892, in Carroll, *Benteen-Goldin*, 216.

[96] June 1, 1898, Bureau of Pensions, Benteen ACP NA.

[97] Elizabeth Custer, *Guidon*, xxvi.

[98] *Portland (Maine) Sunday Times*, June 27, 1909.

[99] Graham to Carter, March 29, 1923, in Graham, *Myth*, 312.

[100] Transcript, Elizabeth Custer to W. M. Shelling, July 5, 1919, Custer Collection, Bismarck Public Library.

[101] Transcript, Benteen to Godfrey, Aug. 14, 1893, Box I, HC UG.

BIBLIOGRAPHY

Published Works

Asay, Karol. *Gray Head and Long Hair.* Mattituck, NY and Paris, Texas: privately printed, 1983.

Associates of Graduates of the U.S. Military Academy. *Annual Report.* June 11, 1936. (Box II, HMC, NYPL).

Barnard, Sandy. *Ten Years with Custer.* Terre Haute, IN: AST Press, 2001

Barnett, Louise. *Touched by Fire.* New York: Holt, 1996.

Barr, Elizabeth. *Kansas.* Salina, Kansas: Centennial Committee, [1908] 1961.

Bernstein, Peter L. *Wedding of the Waters: The Erie Canal and the Making of a Great Nation.* New York and London: Norton, 2005.

Billington, Ray Allan. *Westward Expansion.* New York: Macmillan, 1949.

Brininstool, E. A. *Troopers with Custer.* Lincoln and London: University of Nebraska, 1989.

Brown, Dee. *Best of Dee Brown's West.* Sante Fe, NM: Clear Light, 1999.

Burkey, Blaine. *Custer, Come at Once.* Hays, Kansas: Society of Friends of Historic Fort Hays, 1991.

Carroll, John M. *Camp Talk.* Mattituck, NY, and Bryan, Texas: privately printed, 1983.

———. *The Benteen-Goldin Letters on Custer and His Last Battle.* Lincoln and London: University of Nebraska, 1991.

———. *Custer in Periodicals.* Fort Collins, CO: Old Army Press, 1975.

———. *The Court Martial of Frederick W. Benteen.* Bryan, Texas: privately printed, 1981.

———. (ed.) *Cavalry Scraps.* Bryan, Texas: Guidon Press, 1971.

———. *Benteen's Footnotes to Wild Life.* Bryan, Texas: privately printed, 1981.

Catton, Bruce. *The Army of the Potomac: Mr. Lincoln's Army.* Garden City, NY: Doubleday, 1962.

Coggins, Jack. *Arms and Equipment of the Civil War.* Mineola, NY: Dover, 1990.

Corbusier, Fanny Dunbar (ed. Patricia Y. Stallard). *Recollections of Her Army Life, (1869-1908).* Norman: University of Oklahoma, 2003.

Couhlan, T. M. "Battle of the Little Big Horn." *The Cavalry Journal.* Jan-Feb. 1934

Custer, Elizabeth B. *Boots and Saddles.* Williamstown, MA: Corner House, 1974.

———. *Following the Guidon.* Norman and London: University of Oklahoma Press, 1976.

———. *Tenting on the Plains.* Williamstown, MA: Corner House, 1973; and Norman: University of Oklahoma, 1973.

Custer, George A. *My Life on the Plains.* New York: Citadel Press, [1876] 1962; Norman: University of Oklahoma, 1976.

Dabney, Virginius. *The New Dominion.* Garden City, NY: Doubleday, 1971.

Davis, Arthur Kyle. "Three Centuries of an Old Virginia Town." *Magazine of History with Notes and Queries.* April, 1914.

Davis, William C. *The Civil War.* New York: Southmark, 1996.

Dobak, William A. *Fort Riley and its Neighbors.* Norman: University of Oklahoma, 1998.

Eagleburger, Len. *The Fighting 10th.* Bloomington, IN: 1st Books, 2004.

Eaton, Clement. *The Growth of Southern Civilization.* New York: Harper, 1961.

Foote, Shelby. *The Civil War.* New York: Random House, 1974.

Fougera, Katherine Gibson. *With Custer's Cavalry.* Lincoln and London: University of Nebraska Press, [1882], 1940.

Bibliography

Gabriel, Ralph Henry. *Pageant of America: Lure of the Frontier.* New Haven: Yale University Press, 1929.
Garlington, Ernest. In the *New York Herald*, August 7, 1876.
Godfrey, W. S. *The West: Custer's Last Battle.* Freeport, NY: Maverick Publ. 1966.
Graham, W.A. "Come on! Be Quick! Bring Packs!" *Cavalry Journal*, July 1923.
———. *The Custer Myth,* Harrisburg, PA: Stackpole, 1953.
———. *The Reno Court of Inquiry*, Mechanicsburg, PA: Stackpole, 1954.
Gray, John. "Veterinary Service on Custer's Last Campaign." *Kansas Historical Quarterly*, Autumn 1977, 249.
Greene, Jerome A. *Battles and Skirmishes of the Great Sioux War.* Norman and London: University of Oklahoma, 1993.
———. *The Nez Perce Summer.* Helena, MT: Montana Historical Society, 2000.
Griffith, Paddy. *Battle Tactics of the Civil War.* New Haven, Yale University Press, 1987.
Hammer, Kenneth M. *The Springfield Carbine in the Western Frontier.* Bozeman MT: Little Buffalo Press, 2002.
Hammer, Kenneth (ed.) *Custer in 76.* Norman and London: University of Oklahoma, 1976.
Hatch, Thom. *The Custer Companion.* Mechanicsburg, PA: Stackpole, 2002.
Hoig, Stan. *The Battle of the Washita.* Garden City, NY: Doubleday, 1976.
Hoogenboom, Ari. *Rutherford B. Hayes.* Lawrence, Kansas: University of Press Kansas, 1995.
Howard, John Tasker. *Stephen Foster, American's Troubadour.* New York: Thomas Crowell Co., 1953.
Hunt, Frazier and Robert. *I Fought with Custer.* Lincoln and London: University of Nebraska, 1947.
Hutton, Paul A. *The Custer Reader.* Lincoln and London: University of Nebraska, 1992.
———. *Phil Sheridan and His Army.* Lincoln and London: University of Nebraska, 1985.

Jocelyn, Stephen Perry. *Mostly Alkali*. Caldwell, Idaho: Caxton Printers, 1953.
Johnson, Barry and Taunton, Francis. *Benteen's Ordeal and Custer's Field*. London: Johnson-Taunton, 1983.
Johnson, Roy P. "Jacob Horner and the 7th Cavalry," *North Dakota History*, Vol. 16, 1949.
Knight, Edgar W. *A Documentary History of Education in the South before 1860*. Chapel Hill: University of North Carolina, 1953.
Koury, Michael. *The Field Diary of General Alfred H. Terry*. Fort Collins, CO: Old Army Press, 1978.
Krause, Herbert and Gary Olson. *Prelude to Glory*. Sioux Falls, SD: Brevet, 1974.
Ladenheim, Jules C. *Alien Horseman*. Bowie, MD: Heritage Books, 2003.
Lebsock, Suzanne. *The Free Women of Petersburg*. New York, London: Norton, 1984.
Leckie, William, H. *The Buffalo Soldiers* Norman: University of Oklahoma Press, 1967.
Leckie, Shirley A. *Elizabeth Bacon Custer and the Making of a Myth* Norman and London: University of Oklahoma, 1993.
Lee, Robert. *Fort Meade and the Black Hills*. Lincoln and London: University of Nebraska, 1991.
Libby, Oren G. *The Arikara Narrative of Custer's Campaign and the Battle of Little Bighorn*. Norman: University of Oklahoma, 1998.
Longacre, Edward G. *The Cavalry at Appomattox*. Mechanicsburg, PA: Stackpole Books, 2003.
McCormack, George R. "Men Who Fought With Custer." (Jacob Adam). *National Republic* (undated), found in Box 2, HMC, NYPL.
McElroy, John. *The Struggle for Missouri*. Washington, D.C.: National Tribune, 1909.
Mills, Alison. *My Story*. Washington, D.C.: Byron S. Adams, 1919.

Bibliography

Mills, Charles K. *Harvest of Barren Regrets*. Glendale, CA: Clark Co., 1985.

Mills, Cuthbert. *New York Times*. September 14, 1876, 3:1.

Monaghan, Jay. *Civil War on the Western Border 1854-1860*. Boston: Little Brown, 1955.

Morgan, H. Wayne and Ann H. *Oklahoma*. New York: W. W. Norton, 1977.

Nagel, Paul C. *Missouri: A History*. Nashville, TN: W. W. Norton, 1977.

Naisawald, L. Vanloan. *Cannon Blasts*. Shippenburg, PA: White Mane, 2004.

Nevins, Allen. *Ordeal of the Union*. Vol. 2. New York and London: Scribners, 1947.

Nichols, R. "Command Decision—1876 Style." *Greasy Grass*, May 2005.

O'Kelly, James J. In *New York Herald*, Aug. 15, 1876.

Oates, Stephen B. *The Fires of Jubilee*. New York, Evanston, San Francisco, London: Harper and Row, 1975.

Olson, Sherry H. *Baltimore*. Baltimore and London: John Hopkins University Press, 1997.

Panzeri, Peter. *Little Big Horn 1876*. Campaign Series 39. Oxford: Osprey, 1995.

Perret, Geoffrey. *Lincoln's War*. New York: Random House, 2004.

Phocion, Howard. In *Chicago Daily Tribune*, September 9, 1876 1:4,5,6.

Pohanka, Brian. *A Summer on the Plains from the Diary of Anne Gibson Roberts*. Mattituck, NY, and Bryan, Texas: Carroll, 1983.

Pritchard, Russ A. Jr. *Civil War Weapons and Equipment*. Guilford, CT: Lyons, 2003.

Rickey, Don Jr. *Forty Miles a Day on Beans and Hay*. Norman and London: University of Oklahoma Press, 1963.

Roe, Frances, M.A. *Army Letters from an Officer's Wife, 1871-1888*, New York and London: D. Appleton, 1909.

Roe, Frank Gilbert. *The Indian and the Horse*. Norman: University of Oklahoma, 1968.

Roenigk, Adolph. *Pioneer History of Kansas*. Chapter 33: "Henry Benien, a Custer's Seventh Cavalry Man and Pioneer Settler."
http://www.kancoll.org/books/roenigk/chpt33.htm

Rowan, Steven. *Germans for a Free Missouri*. Columbia, MO: University of Missouri Press, 1983.

Scott, James G. and Edward A. Wyatt, IV. *Petersburg's Story*. Petersburg, VA: Telonus Optical Co, 1960.

Scott, Hugh L. *Some Memories of a Soldier*. New York: Century Publishing Company, 1928.

Sydnor, Charles S. *The Development of Southern Sectionalism*. Baton Rouge, LA: Louisiana State University Press, 1948.

Taylor, William O. *With Custer on the Little Bighorn*. New York: Viking, 1996.

Terrill, John Upton and George Walton. *Faint the Trumpet Sounds*. New York: McKay, 1966.

Trefousse, Hans L. *Rutherford B. Hayes*, New York: Times Books, Holt, 2002.

Utley, Robert M. *Frontier Regulars*. New York and London: Macmillan, 1973.

———. *Custer and the Great Controversy* Los Angeles: Westermore, 1962.

Van de Water, Frederic F. *Glory Hunter* Lincoln and London: University of Nebraska, [1934], 1988.

Vaughn, Robert. *Then and Now, or Thirty-Six Years in the Rockies*. Minneapolis: Tribune Print, 1900.

Walker, L. J. "Military Medicine at Little Bighorn." *Journal American College of Surgeons*. January 2006, 191-196.

War of the Rebellion. A Compilation of the Union and the Confederate Armies 1861-1865. Washington, D.C.: Government Printing Office, 1880.

Whittaker, Frederick. *A Complete Life of General George A. Custer*. 2 Vols. [1876] Bowie, MD: Heritage Books, 1993.

———. in *New York Sun*, Feb. 26, 1879 in HMC, NYPL.
Willert, James. *March of the Column: A Chronicle of the 1876 War*. El Segundo, CA: Upton and Sons, 1994.
Willert, James (ed.) *The Terry Letters (Alfred Howe Terry)*. La Mirada, CA: James Willert, 1980.
Williams, David. *A People's History of the Civil War*. New York and London: New Press, 2003.
Winckler, Suzanne. *The Smithsonian Guide to Historic America: The Plains*. New York: Stewart, Tamori and Chang, 1998.
Woodward, W. E. *Meet General Grant*. New York: Liveright, 1928.
Works Progress Administration (WPA). Federal Writers' Project. *Maryland. A Guide to the Old Line State*. American Guide Series. New York: Oxford University Press, 1940.
———. Federal Writers' Project. *Virginia. A Guide to the Old Dominion*. American Guide Series. New York: Oxford University Press, 1941.
Zimmer, William F. [Herine and Greebe, eds.] *Frontier Soldier*. Helena, MT: Montana Historical Society Press, 1998.

Articles from Newspapers and Periodicals

Billings Gazette, June 24, 1926. Found in HMC, NYPL.

Bismarck Tribune, Aug. 6, 1938. "Widow of Custer's Indian Scouts" HMC, NYPL.

"Sitting Bull's Own Narrative of the Custer Fight," *Canadian Historical Review,* University Toronto Press, June 1935, found in HMC, NYPL.

Unpublished

Carter, R. G. "Memorandum." Aug. 23, 1938, HMC NYPL.

Edgerly. Reply to Colonel Hughes by Edgerly, page 4; HMC, NYPL.

Godfrey fragment. HMC, NYPL.

Godfrey to John G. Neihardt, Jan 6, 1924, HMC, NYPL.

Goldin, Theodore. "Interesting Facts written by a trooper of the 7th Cavalry," Janesville, July 8, 1888 in Hagner Manuscript Collection, NYPL.

Hinricks, Charles F. *Diary and Supply Books: 1863-5.* A H50, WHMC UM, Columbia, Missouri.

Huetter, Robert. *A History of Fort Duchesne, Utah.* Master's Thesis. Brigham Young University, April 1990.

Jennings, Elisha. "Letters of Elisha Middleton Jennings." WHMC UM, Columbia, Missouri.

Index

----, Ham; Custer's Black Cook 132
----, Mary; Custer's Black Cook 132
"Bob Tail" (Dishonorable Discharge), 81
"Boomers" (Homesteaders), 239 242
"Bushwhackers" (Confederate Irregulars), 25
2nd Cavalry, 197 212
2nd Missouri Cavalry (Merrill's Light Horse), Absorbs 10th Missouri 60
2nd US Infantry, 270
3rd Iowa Cavalry, Joined by Bowen's Battalion 31
4th Artillery, 257
4th Iowa Cavalry, at Battle of the Osage 50
5th Cavalry, Defeats Western Cheyenne at Summit Springs Colorado 109 Moylan 69
5th Infantry, 201
7th Cavalry, 79 92-94 115 117 121 124 128 141 169 197 203 209 218 226 235 240 245 263 267 269 270 Army Rotation 122 Benteen Captain in 66 Benteen the Hero of 205 Black Hills Expedition 138 Custer Restored to Command 152 Custer's Influence 96 Familiar Histories xii First Major Campaign 77 First Victory 91

7th Cavalry (cont.) Formed after the War for Service on the Plains 65 Gear and Equipment on Black Hills Expedition 140 Many Soldiers and Officers Interviewed by the Press 202 Moylan 69 Never the Same after Bear Paw Battle with Nez Perce 219 Officers Were Witnesses at Reno Court of Inquiry 223 Ordered to Drive Nez Perce Back to Reservation 211 Ordered to Hunt down Cheyenne Villagers 78 Sharpshooters 97 Some Officers at Tenth Anniversary of Little Bighorn Battle 247 Summoned to Pine Ridge Sioux Agency 221 Training 96 Winter Clothing Issued 96
8th Cavalry, Formed after the War for Service on the Plains 65
9th Cavalry, Black Regiment; 65 235 239 242 244 246 248 251 260 266 Benteen Tried to Avoid Transfer 236 History 237
9th Missouri Cavalry, Formation 35
10th Cavalry, Black Regiment; 65 93 237 238 Benteen May Have Been Offered a Major's Commission, 66

10th Missouri Cavalry, after the War 61 at Ebenezer Church, Alabama, Battle 54 Benteen Exchanged Horses 88 Benton Reverts to Regimental Commander 53 Consolidated with Winslow's Brigade 41 Ended Its Service outside of Atlanta 59 Formation 35 in Battle at Iuka Mississippi 40 Incorporated into Grierson's Cavalry Corps 45 Incorporated with 2nd Missouri Cavalry (Merrill's Light Horse) 60 Meets Resistance at Chattahoochee River 57 Secures Important Hilltop at Kansas City Battle 49 Skirmish near Bolton Mississippi 43 Soldiers Mustered out as Enlistments Were about to Expire 46 with Winslow's Brigade 42
19th Kansas Volunteer Cavalry, 108
21st Infantry, 230
22nd Infantry, 270 on Yellowstone Expedition 131
23rd Ohio, 228
24th New York Cavalry, 87
39th Regular Virginia Militia, Charged with Ensuring Law and Order among Blacks 6
138th USCT (United States Colored Troops), 266 Benteen Given Command 60 Discipline and Reputation 61 to Be Disbanded 61
"A Tents," Description 112

Alabama, 143
Alexander II, Czar of Russia 115 126
Alexandria, Virginia 2
Alexei, Grand Duke 115 126
Alton, Union Prison 34
American Expeditionary Forces, 238
Ammunition, Extra Taken on Little Bighorn Campaign 159
Anaconda Plan, Southern Blockade Proposed by Winfield Scott 15
Anderson, "Bloody Bill" 26
Animals, Sent by Custer to Bronx Zoo 131
Antelope, Hunted by Benteen 134
Apache, 239 Chiricahua 249
Aparejos (Packsaddles), 149
Appaloosa Horse, 211
Appomattox River, 3
Appomattox Court House, Surrender 57 58
Arapaho, 67 92 105 at Fort Larned 88 in Washita Valley 100 Offered Reservation Area in Western Indian Territory 86 Pursued by 7th Cavalry 106
Arikara Scouts, 162 164 165 172 181 184 185 Appearance Described 158 Hunted Meat for Custer's Expedition 154 Not Familiar with Little Bighorn Region 158 Refused to Cross Little Bighorn River 179

Index

Arikara Scouts (cont.)
Remained with Reno 182
with Custer's Little Bighorn Expedition 153
Arizona Territory, 239
Arkansas River, 77 78 86 94
Arkansas City, Kansas 242
Arkansas, Secured for the Union 31 32
Army of the Mississippi, Approaches Vicksburg 36
Army of the Tennessee, Approaches Vicksburg 36
Artillery Charge, Employed by Napoleon 24
Ash, Ben; U S Marshall 154
Ashley Valley, Utah 253
Associated Press, Benteen's Cousin a Co-Founder 153
Atlanta, Georgia 66 122 262 271 Benteen's Farm 259 Mayor 266 269
Audubon Club (Detroit, Michigan), 120
Bacon, Elizabeth; Marries Custer 70
Badlands, 132 134 155
Baird, Absalom; Inspector-General 256
Baltimore, Maryland 1
Band, Regimental, 153 155
Bank of Maryland, Collapse 3
Barnum and Bailey Circus, 232
Barnum, P T 115
Barry, D F 265
Baseball, 91 125 252 Benteen's Athletics 141 Many of Benteen's Players Wounded or Killed at Little Bighorn 200

Baseball (cont.)
Played by Fred Benteen 25
Popular in St Louis in the 1850s 12
Battle of the Osage, (Mine Creek, Kansas) 50
Bear Butte, Fort Meade 221
Bear Paw Battle, Heavy Casualties on Both Sides 219 Many Nez Perce Escape to Canada 219 Nez Perce War 189
Bear Paw, Montana 218
Beecher Island, 93 194
Belknap, William; Secretary of War Charged with Selling Post Trader Concessions 151
Bell, John; Presidential Candidate 13
Bells, on Indian Ponies at Night 98
Benet Cup Primer, 140
Benteen Base Ball Club, 144 Formally Organized in Nashville 125
Benteen, Beulah Kane 7
Benteen, Caroline Davis 2 Poor Health 3
Benteen, Caroline Elizabeth; Birth 39
Benteen, Catherine (Kate) Louisa Norman 46 48 62 117 123 125 135 144 200 206 209 225 230 232 240 242- 244 250-252 258-260 269 Arrives at Fort Harker 87 Bears First Child 39 Death 270 Married to Fred 26 Depressed after Death of Baby Catherine 104

Benteen, Catherine (Kate)
Louisa Norman (cont.)
Entertained Visitors at New
Fort Hays 115 Fed up with
Army Life 122 Pregnant 37
Benteen, Catherine Norman;
Infant Daughter of Fred and
Kate 104
Benteen, Charley 3 10 11 259
Angered at Fred's Decision
to Join Union Army 20
Comes to Live on Fred's
Farm after the War 63
Confederate Prisoner 33 34
Death 243 Freemason 124
House Painter and Paint
Purveyor 4 Moves to St
Louis 8 Not in 1860 St Louis
Directory 12 Not Present at
Fred's Wedding 26 Owned
Slaves 3 238 Southern
Sympathizer 12 17
Benteen, Fanny; Birth 125
Death 136
Benteen, Frederick Damish 2 7
Benteen, Frederick William xi 1
2 11 48 65 69 71-73 80 87-
91 93-95 106 108 110 117
122-124 126 128 129 132
134 135 137 142 143 145
152 160-167 170-176 186
187 189-193 196-198 200
203 205-209 211-213 215
216 219 225 226 228 229
233 235 238 242 243 245
247-249 251 252 257-260
262-268 and 10th Missouri
Rush the Breastworks at
Selma 55 56 and Family
Move to New York 230 231

Benteen, Frederick William
(cont.)
and Regiment Seize
Important Bridge near
Jackson, Mississippi 43
Applies for Brig Gen Brevet
but Is Rejected 60 61 Argues
with Custer 158 Arrives at
Fort Riley 68 Artistically
Talented 5 at Battle of the
Osage 50 at Fort Hays 112 at
Pea Ridge Mountain Battle
29 at Reno Court of Inquiry
223 224 at Sugar Creek
Battle 28 Attacked on His
Farm 62 63 Attitude toward
Blacks 238 239 Avid
Outdoorsman 103 Bad
Attitude towards Sturgis 217
Becomes Acting Regimental
Commander of 10th
Missouri 41 Becomes
Second in Command of 10th
Missouri Cavalry 36 Binge
Drinking 220 Birth 3 Blames
Custer for Elliott's Death
103 Brawls with Reno 118
Captain in 7th Cavalry 66
Character xi xii Cited by
Winslow as Gallant and
Valuable 42 Civil War Battle
Perspective xii Claimed to
Have Shot Black Kettle 101
Comes to Reno's Aid 184
Commands Brigade at
Kansas City Battle 49
Complaints against 254
Considers Rejoining the
Army after the War 63

Index 325

Benteen, Frederick William (cont.)
Continued to Court Catherine Norman 12 Correspondence with Goldin 263-265 Courage under Fire 188 Court Martial 256 257 Death 269 Death of Daughter 48 Decides to become a Farmer 61 Decides to Formally Join Union Army 20 Decides to Rejoin Command 168 Description 139 Did Not Get Along with Stanford Ing 30 Dislike for Mormons 253 Drinking and Arguments 253 Early Description 25 Elected Captain by Fellow Soldiers 21 Enjoyed Hunting in Colorado 120 Exhausted and Ill 244 Family at New Fort Hays 116 Family Troubles 232 Faulted Crook for Defeat at Rosebud River 202 First Cavalry Battle 25 Friendly toward Kiowa at Fort Sill 241 Feud with Custer Grows 107 Gathered Gossip about Custer 131 Given Honorary Title but Not Promoted 51 52 Gloats over Custer's Court Martial 85 Held in High Esteem by H Company 231 Helped Drill the Union Home Guard 17 His Son F W Born 74 His Wing to Unite with Reno's 156

Benteen, Frederick William (cont.)
Hunted and Fished during Nez Perce Campaign 214 Hunted and Fished during Yellowstone Expedition 133 Hunted in Dakota Territory 144 in Bowen's Cavalry Company 21 in Command at Fort Dodge 111 in Command When Winslow Becomes Ill 43 in St Louis Directory 12 Invites Kiowa Chief to Dinner 103 Items Taken on Little Bighorn Campaign 159 Leads Detachment to Nashville for Demobilization 60 Learns of Daughter's Birth 39 Left Father's Trade for Sign Painting 9 Left in Command of 10th Missouri Upon Bowen's Arrest 39 Lost Seven Horses while Serving with the 7th Cavalry 81 Love for Horses 62 Loved the Sport of Baseball 10 Married to Catherine Louisa Norman 26 Meets with Sheridan 92 on Black Hills Expedition 141 on Leave in St Louis 35 on Washita Campaign 97 98 Opinion of Buffalo Hunting, 112 Ordered to Attack Warriors at Washita 101 Ponders Post-War Career 59 Post Commander at Fort Rice 146 Post Commander at Fort Riley 240

Benteen, Frederick William (cont.)
  Praised by Curtis 51 Praised by Gen Wilson 58 Praised by McPherson 44 Praised by Reno in Official Battle Report 199 Praised for Participation in Iuka Battle 40 Promoted to Lt Col 44 Promoted to Major 235 Promoted to Second Major 10th Missouri Cavalry 35 Property Description outside South Atlanta 61 Provides Cavalry Escort for Sheridan 28 Question of His Father's Imprisonment 34 Questions Custer's Orders 168 Reburied at Arlington National Cemetery 269 Received Civil War Brevets 75 Recruits Replacements for 10th Missouri Cavalry 46 Refused Ing's Order 31 Relieved of Command 255 Reported No Evidence of Skirmish Line 178 Retires from Army Life on Disability 261 Retrieved Regimental Papers Which Were Then Lost 46 Rheumatism 104 Sent to Retrieve Regimental Records in Vicksburg 44 Sent to St Louis to Inspect Horses 120 Served at Lt Norman's Court Martial 57 Shoots Indian Boy 99 100 Shortcomings xi

Benteen, Frederick William (cont.)
  Supposedly Asked for Imprisonment of Charley during War 33 Takes Command of 138th USCT as Colonel 60 Takes up Weir's Offer of a Duel 201 Temporary Duty in St Louis and Rolla 37 Testifies on Reno's Behalf 209 227 Took in Gossip about Custer 121 Took Urgent Leave to Visit Wife and Gravely Ill Daughter, 42 Tried to Learn Kiowa Language 103 241 Views Custer's Remains 195 with Lyon during Attack on Price 18 19 Writes Scathing Letter about Custer Which Is Published 105

Benteen, Frederick Wilson "Freddie" (Son of Frederick William Benteen) 87 116 117 212 226 241-244 247 259 266 270 Birth 74 Contracted Osteomyelitis 232 Health Problems 267 Retired from Army as Lt Col 270

Benteen, Henrietta Elizabeth "En" 3 Marries James L Doyle 8

Benteen, Kate (See Benteen, Catherine)

Benteen, Name Used in Novel *Gone with the Wind* 270 Place Names 271

Index 327

Benteen, Theodore Charles (Theodore Karl) (See Benteen, Charley) 1 2
Benteen, Theodore Charles Jr (Theo) 10 Birth 3 at Sacramento 226 Death 232 in St Louis Directory 12 198 Paper Hanging 7 9
Benteen, Theodore Norman; Birth 144 Death 146
Benteen, William Henry 232
Benton, Riverboat, 205
Benzine Boards (Review Panels), 121 233
Bess, Benteen's Thoroughbred Mare 50
Bibb Naval Furnace, Destroyed by Benteen and His Men 54
Biersfield, Alabama 54
Big Hole, Montana 212
Bighorn River, 133 194 197
Bighorn Sheep, Hunted by Benteen 134
Bismarck, Dakota Territory 130 134 135 138 154 220 222
Black Cavalry Regiments, 65 Not Rotated as the Rest of the Army 122 (See 9th Cavalry and 10th Cavalry)
Black Hills Expedition, 138-140
Black Hills, 127 144 145 221 222 Gold 147 148
Black Kettle, (Cheyenne Chief) 90 98-100 Benteen Claimed to Have Shot Him 101 Tepees and Goods from Village Were Burned 101 Women and Children of Village Taken Hostage 101
Black Powder Smoke, Not Observed from Weir Point 178
Blacks, Murdered in Colfax, Louisiana 142
Blair, Gen Frances (Frank) P Jr 66
Blandsford Churchyard, Burial Place of Caroline Benteen 4
Bolivar, Tennessee 44 Woods' Flotilla Disembarks 34
Bolton, Mississippi; 10th Missouri Cavalry Skirmish 43
Booty, Found in Soldiers' Packs 59 Taken from Black Kettle's Village 100
Bowen, Capt William D 21 Argues with Second in Command 36 Arrested 39 Discharged from the Army 44 Kills Cornyn 41 Lt Col Becomes Acting Commander of 10th Missouri Cavalry 36 Lt Col Second in Command of 10th Missouri Cavalry 35 Maj Goes on Leave 30 Promoted 32 Wounded at Sugar Creek Battle 28
Bowen's Battalion, Attached to Curtis's Headquarters 27 Attacked near Salem, Missouri 25 26 Deployed to Dutch Hollow 24 Deployed to Dutch Hollow 25 First Battalion Missouri Cavalry 21 Joins 3rd Iowa Cavalry 31 Masters the Use of the Howitzer 28

Bowen's Battalion (cont.)
  on Woods' Flotilla towards
  Vicksburg 32 Reformation
  with 9th Missouri Cavalry 35
  Sent to Benton's Barracks in
  St Louis 35
Bows and Arrows, 191
Box, Mrs. 114
Bozeman Trail, Wyoming 148-
  159 204
Bozeman, Disaster 76
Brandy Station, Virginia;
  Pleasonton Victorious at 48
Breaux Bridge, Louisiana 143
Breckinridge, John C;
  Presidential Candidate 13
Brevets, Importance to Officers
  75
Brice's Crossroads, Mississippi
  227 Sturgis Routed by
  Forrest 45
Bronx Zoo, Received Animals
  Sent by Custer 131
Brooklyn Bridge, 231
Brown, B Gratz; Missouri
  Senator 75
Brown, Eliza; Custer's Black
  Cook 112 Unfair Gossip 132
Buchanan, President 14
Buffalo Hunting, 115
Buffalo Soldiers, 237 242 250
  251 266
Buffalo, Massacre 86
Bull Run, Battle; Casualty
  Percentage Compared to
  Wilson's Creek 20
Bulluno, Italy; Home of De
  Rudio 116
Cabildo, Louisiana 142

Cahaba Prison, Prisoners
  Liberated but Many Killed
  on the *Sultana* 56
Cairo, Illinois, 52 129
Calhoun Hill, 176 177
Calvary, Union; Uniform, Arms
  and Horses 22
Camas Meadows, Idaho 212
Camp Forsyth, 94 95
Camp Robinson, Nebraska 204
  222
Camp Sturgis, New Name for
  Fort Hays 120
Camp Supply, 96 97 103 109-
  111
Canadian River, 92 North 96
  South 98
Canyon Creek, Montana
  Territory 215 Battle 218 263
  Benteen Breveted Brigadier
  General for Gallantry 262
Carbines, Could Be Fired by
  Warriors from Galloping
  Ponies 181
Carr, Maj Eugene A 109
Carter Station 249
Cartridges, Linen or Paper
  Could Malfunction in the
  Rain 41
Cattle Drives, 85
Cavalry, Both Armies
  Recognized the Need for 21
  Clothing 159 Difference
  Between Eastern and
  Western Union Horsemen 21
  Intensive Training 23
  Limited Use during an
  Ongoing Engagement 24
  Rivalry with Infantry 68

Cavalry (cont.)
  Time and Cost Required for Training 21 Training 71 72
  Used for Scouting and Harassment 24
Cavalry Arms, Great Variety 22
Cavalry Horses, and Mules 22
  Poor Quality 22 Union and Confederate 23
Cedar Coulee, 174
Cedar Creek, Montana 209 211
Centennial Exposition, 206
Chandler, John S 266
Charlestown Harbor, Fort Sumter 14
Chattahoochee River, Bridges Destroyed or Captured 57
Chattanooga, Tennessee in Union Hands 44
Cherokee Outlet, Oklahoma Panhandle 239
Cherokee, Tribe 85
Cheyenne, 67 105 239 at Fort Larned 88 Attacking Along the Saline River 92 Women Saw Custer's Approach while Viewing Reno Battle 175 Chiefs Meet with Gen Hancock 77 Continue to Be Pursued by Custer and 7th Cavalry 108 Effects of Washita Battle 102 Finally Move Onto Reservation 109 in Washita Valley 100 Intercepted by Crook 201 Marauders 90 Offered Reservation Area in Western Indian Territory 86 Prisoners Rounded up 219 Prisoners 220 Raids 80

Cheyenne (cont.)
  Village on Powder River Attacked by Crook 204
Cheyenne, Northern 127 148 Astonishing Exodus 222 Ordered to Indian Territory in Oklahoma 205 Prisoners 221
Cheyenne, Southern 205
Chicago, Illinois 206
Chickasaw Bluffs, Mississippi; Sherman Turned Back from Vicksburg 36
Chickasaw, Tribe 85
Chief Gall, 177 182 190 196 247
Chief Joseph, Nez Perce, 212 216 217 a National Hero 219 Surrenders at Bear Paw, Montana 219
Chilloco, Indian Territory 242
China Set, Bought by Benteen in Chicago 225 230
Chisholm Trail, 85 86
Cholera, at Fort Wallace 84
Cimarron River, 86
Civil War, Control of Mississippi River the Key to Success 15 End of 58
Clark's Fork Canyon, 213 214
Clark's Fork River, 215
"Clay Eaters" (Poor White Immigrants from the South), 9
Clearwater River, Idaho 212
Clemens, Samuel (Mark Twain) 12
Cleveland, Grover 258
Clymer, Hiester 151

Cody, Buffalo Bill 201 202
Colfax, Louisiana 142
Colorado, 248
Colored Troops, Services Valued by the Army 60
Colt Peacemaker Revolver, 22 90 140 Reloading Requires Two Hands, 180 181 Sympathetic Firing 41 Rapid Fire Revolving Rifles 38
Columbus, Georgia 75 Manufacturing Center Attacked 57
Comanche 67 Offered Reservation Area in Western Indian Territory 86 Reservation 240
Constitutional Union Party 1860 Presidential Race 13
Cooke, First Lt William 87 88 97 108 110 123 161 172 173 263
Corinth, Mississippi; 10th Missouri to Join New Division under Gen Dodge 35 Important Railroad Junction 35 36
Cornyn, Col Florence; Commander of 10th Missouri Cavalry 35 in Raid near Iuka Mississippi 40 Killed by Bowen 41 Ordered to Disengage 38 Proceeds to Tupelo Mississippi to Join Grierson's Remnants 38 Promoted to Cavalry Brigade Commander 36
Cornyn's Brigade, Ordered to Raid Florence, Alabama 39

Cornyn's Brigade (cont.) Part of Dodge's Raid to Distract Forrest 37 Problems Arise 39
Couch, W L 239 240 242 Elected Mayor of Oklahoma City 243
Crane Creek, Missouri; Cavalry Charge 28
Crazy Horse, 176 177 196 203 204 Retaliates against Crook's Destruction of Roamers' Village 149
Creek, Tribe 85
Crook, Gen George 145 148 149 156 157 201 202 204 242 249 250 254-257 268 Attacked by Crazy Horse and 1000 Warriors 150 Desperately Needed a Victory 203 Defeat Unknown to Custer's Command 158
Crow Scouts, 164 165 170 181 184 185 193 195 212 216 217 247 Appearance Described 158 Report Reno's Retreat 175 Tell Custer of Ford B 172 with Custer 158
Crow, 213 Camping Grounds 173 Enjoyed Prosperity as Sioux Fortunes Declined 212 Refused Aid to the Nez Perce 214 Relatives of Nez Perce 211 Reservation 212
Crow's Nest, 167 Disputed Location 164
Curley, Crow Scout 195 247

Index

Curtis, Gen Samuel R 29 30 32 49 66 92 Commander of Union Forces in Missouri 27 Succeeds Pleasonton in Command 51 Pursues Price 50

Custer Battlefield, 176 177 190 191 247 Not Visible from Base of Hillock at Weir Point 185

Custer City, Dakota Territory 145

Custer, Boston; Civilian Brother of Tom and George with the Wagon Train 174 175

Custer, Elizabeth (Libby) Bacon 70 (See Custer, Libby)

Custer, George Armstrong 69 71 72 76 78 81 83 84 87 88 91 93-98 100 102 103 105 106 110 111 119 122 123 129 131 133 134 137 139 141 142 148 153-158 160 161 163 166 168-173 176 177 180 184-187 190 195 202 205 224 233 237 242 247 249 263 264 268 279 and Men Annihilated 177 178 Argues with Benteen 158 at Lee's Retreat at Williamsport 70 Begins Civil War Memoirs during Court Martial Sentence 85 Begins Literary Career 120 Biography by Whittaker 207 208 Blamed by Benteen for Defeat at Little Bighorn 200 Changes Day of Little Bighorn Attack 165

Custer, George Armstrong (cont.) Claimed by Benteen to Be Bribed by the Fort Hays Post Trader 79 Commander of 7th Cavalry 69 Continues to Pursue Cheyenne 108 109 Court Martialed 84 85 Estranged from Citizens of Bismarck 138 Feud with Benteen Grows 107 Freemason 124 Friends and Foes 118 Gambling Problems 73 126 Gossip about 121 Had Information Needed to Make Decision 175 Ignores Scout's Warnings 165 Ill-Fated Nebraska Expedition 82 in New York Complains about Post Traders and Indian Agents 150 in Washington Testified about Post Traders 151 Irked by Hancock 80 Issues Orders to Prepare to Attack 166 Learns That Reno Has Encountered Warriors 173 Life Insurance Policy and Unpaid Debts 198 Makes Enemy of President Grant 152 Marries Elizabeth Bacon 70 Movements during Little Bighorn Battle 176 177 Ordered to Expel Hostiles Between Platte and Republican Rivers 82 Orders Benteen to March a Battalion to the Left 167 Orders Dogs Killed 99

Custer, George Armstrong (cont.) Praised by Pleasonton and Sheridan 70 Questionable Motives Behind Orders to Benteen 167 Sees Part of Huge Village 174 Suspended from Command 85 Swift Promotion 69 70 Takes Lead of March from Benteen 167

Custer, Libby 71 73 84 95 106 112 118 122 125 132 138 139 153 154 207 228 230 246 264 265 270 Arrives at Fort Hayes 80 Entertained Visitors at New Fort Hays 115 Said to Have Written Husband's Articles 120

Custer, Lt Tom 106 115 122 123 137 Captain of C Company 153

Custer's Trail, Probable Location 180

Dakota Boom, 129

Dakota Territory, 128

Dandy, Custer's Horse 166

Davis, Caroline 2

Davis, Jefferson; Captured 59 Elected President of Confederate States 14

De Rudio, Lt Charles xi 129 146 153 160 163 195-197 203 212 268 Second Lt Charles 116 Capt Charles 235 Freemason 124 Included in Buffalo Bill's Autobiography 202 Left Behind 183 Transferred to 7th Cavalry 117

De Rudio, Lisa 135 212

De Rudio, Roma 117

Deadwood, Dakota Territory 221 222

Deep Coulee, 176

Deep Ravine, 176 191

Delaware Scouts, 120

Delmonico's, New York 122

Denison, Eliza Brown; Custer's Black Cook, Unfair Gossip 132 (See Brown, Eliza)

Denver, Colorado 74

Depredations, against White Settlers in Kansas 68

Depression of 1873, 138 147

Desertion, during Custer's Nebraska Expedition 82 from Fort Hayes 79 Penalties 81 83

Detroit Audubon Club, Received Specimens from Custer 131

Detroit, Michigan 120

Diaz/Dice, Anita Norman, 230 241 246 252 Troublesome to Benteen 232

Dick, Benteen's U S Horse, 169 220

Discipline, among Soldiers; a Problem at the End of the War 59

Doane, Lt Gustavus C 197 212

Dodge, Brig Gen Grenville 35 38 Promoted Cornyn to Cavalry Brigade Commander 36

Dodge, Col R I 230

Dodge's Raid, to Distract Forrest 37

Dog Soldiers, 86 90 99 100 119

Dogs, Custer's 158

Index

Dorman, Isaiah; Black Plainsman at Little Bighorn 136 238
Douglas, Stephen; Presidential Candidate 13
Doyle, Henrietta Benteen 8 26
Doyle, James L 8
Draft Evaders, in North Alabama Hill Country 57
Drill Companies, Popular in St Louis in the 1850s 12
Drinking, a Problem among Many Officers 212 the Ruin of French and Benteen, 201
Du Chesne River, 250
Dull Knife, Chief 204
Dysentery, among Custer's Men 82
Early, Jubal; Held Off by Custer at Gettysburg 70
Ebenezer Church, Alabama; Battle with Forrest 54
Edison, Thomas 232
Elizabethtown, Kentucky 123 126
Elk Horn Creek, Cheyenne Raid 90 First Victory for 7th Cavalry 91
Elliott, Maj Joel H 85 86 88 98 99 104 105 158 Body Found with Bodies of His Men 103 Conducted Training at Fort Riley 71 Killed outside of Black Kettle's Village 100 Search for His and His Men's Bodies 101
Elmira, New York; Union Prison 34
Elsworth City, Kansas 86

Emmet Guards, Drill Company 12
Enforcement Act of 1870, 123
Escape, from Reno Hill Possibly Discussed 191
Fair Play, Confederate Steamboat 32 33
Far West, River Steamer 155 156 197 202
Fifth Avenue Hotel, New York 132
"Fighting Tenth," at Tupelo 38
Firearms, Many Kinds Used by Warriors at Little Bighorn 191
First Battalion Missouri Cavalry, Bowen's Battalion 21
Five Civilized Tribes; Creeks, Seminoles, Chickasaw, Choctaw, and Cherokee 85
Five Forks, Virginia; Sheridan Pierced Confederate Line 54
Following the Guidon, Libby Custer's Book 106
Ford B, 172-176 180
Forrest, Gen Nathan Bedford xii 45 37 128 227 Attacks Winslow's Brigade at Canton, Mississippi 43 Defended Huge Arsenal at Selma, Alabama 55 Continued Marauding 46 Cuts Grant's Supply Lines 36 Escapes at Selma 56 Outnumbers Cornyn's Brigade 37 Wounded and Outflanked by Winslow Brigade 54

Forsyth, Maj G A, 92 93
Fort Laramie Treaty of 1878, 127
Fort Abercrombie, 209
Fort Abraham Lincoln, Dakota Territory 130 134 135 137 138 148 151 152 154 198 203 205 206 208 209 219 219-221 226 Baseball Team 141
Fort Bascom, New Mexico 94
Fort Bridger, Wyoming Territory 249 251 252
Fort Buford, Dakota Territory 209 220
Fort Cobb, 103 104 106
Fort Custer, 247
Fort "Damn Shame," 252
Fort Dodge, 74 83 94 110
Fort Douglas, 257
Fort Du Chesne, 250 255 256 258 259 Difficulties 251 252
Fort Ellis, Montana Territory 148 149 203
Fort Fetterman, Wyoming 148 201 204
Fort Fisher, North Carolina 124
Fort Harker, xii 74 77 82 87 86 90 91 95 Description 87
Fort Hays, 74 78 83 84 94 118 120 212 Flooded 82 New 85 109 111 New, Description 112
Fort Jefferson, Prison in Dry Tortugas 34
Fort Keogh, Montana Territory 209 217
Fort Laramie, 141
Fort Larned, 74 77 85 88 89
Fort Leavenworth, 74 76 85 104 119 122 261
Fort Lyon, Colorado 94
Fort McKinney, Wyoming 244-246 248 249
Fort McPherson, 83
Fort Meade, 221 222 226 228 229
Fort Niobrara, Nebraska 248 260
Fort Randall, 144 145
Fort Reno, 239
Fort Rice, 130 134 145 152 192 196 200 205 206 208 229 Abandoned with Benteen's Two Infants in the Cemetery 221 Description 135-137 Activities and Entertainment 137 Winter Activities 136
Fort Riley, xii 66 68 70 71 74 76 77 80 82 84 236 239 240 244
Fort Robinson, Nebraska 248
Fort Scott, Kansas 51
Fort Sill, Indian Territory; in Disrepair 240106 108 151 241 243 Malaria 240
Fort Snelling, 128
Fort Sumter, Fired Upon Beginning the Civil War 14
Fort Supply, 239
Fort Thornburg, 251
Fort Union, 74
Fort Vancouver, Washington Territory 225
Fort Wallace, 74 83-85
Fort Yates, 221 246
Fort Zarah, 74
Fossils, Sent by Custer to University of Michigan 131

Index

Foster, Stephen; Composer 2
Franklin, Battle of 239
Free Blacks, House Painting Competition for Charley Benteen 4
Freemasons, 124
French Guyana, 116
French, Capt Thomas H 121 171 1146 83 185 186 201 229 Drinking and Court Martial 222 224 Drinking Problem 212
Fuller, Lt Ezra, 1005
Garibaldi, Giuseppe, 116
Gatling Guns, 153 148 Benteen Had a Poor Opinion 84 Impeded Reno's March 156
Georgetown, Colorado, 122
Georgia, Governor, 266 269
Germany, Possible Benteen Origin 1
Geronimo, 249
"Gettysburg of the Transmississippi", Second Largest Cavalry Engagement in Civil War 49
Gettysburg, Custer Held Off Jubal Early 70 Victory Celebrated 39
Gibbon, Col John, 148-150 155-158 200 202 212 Relief Column 195 197
Gibbs Breech-Loading Carbine, 40
Gibson, First Lt Francis (Frank) v 125 146 162 163 168 188 190 192 194 229 267
Girard, Fred; Guide and Interpreter 153 223 224 with Reno 173

Glendive River, 132
Glenn, Private 188
Gobright, Lawrence A; Benteen's Cousin and Co-Founder of Associated Press 153
Godfrey Lt Edward S 100 121 137 186 190 200 203 Capt Edward 223 230 246 247 264-266 268 269 at Reno Court of Inquiry 224 Awarded Medal of Honor 219 Cited in Bear Paw Battle Report 220 221 Instructor at West Point 232 Never Found Fault with Custer 233
Gold Rush, Effect on Eastern Businessmen 6
Gold, Found in Black Hills 141 142 Prospectors in the Black Hills 144
Goldin, Theodore W; Correspondence with Benteen 263-265
Goodnight-Loving Trail, 85
Goose Creek, Wyoming 150
Grand Ball, 232
Grand River Agency, 206
Grant Park, Atlanta 262
Grant, Capt Fred (President's Son); Court Martialed by Custer 152
Grant, Ulysses S 17 32 48 65 66 148 151 Accepts Lee's Surrender 58 and Winslow at Vicksburg 41 Begins Canal Construction across Millikin's Loop 37 Brother Named by Custer in Belknap Investigation 151 152

Grant, Ulysses S (cont.)
  Lays Siege to Vicksburg 39
  Defeats Confederates at Jackson Mississippi 39
  Devises Final Plan to Take Vicksburg 38 Prepares to Capture Vicksburg 36
  President U S 264 Removes Custer from Command 152
Gratiot Street, Union Prison 34
Great Platte (Oregon) Trail, 67
Great Sioux Reservation, 127 204 206 229 260
Grierson, Brig Gen Benjamin 44 Commanded Cavalry Division Which Included Winslow's Brigade 42
Grierson's Cavalry Corps, Included Winslow's Brigade and the 10th Missouri Cavalry 45
Grierson's Raid, 239 Remnants Joined by Cornyn's Brigade 38 to Distract Forrest 37
Hale, Lt Owen 87
Halleck, Gen 92
Hancock, Gen Winfield, 76-78 80 92 109 Visits Fort Hayes 79
Hardtack, 161 165 242
Harris, Joel Chandler 266
Hart River, 154
Hatch, Col Edward, 239 242 244 245 255 256 260
Hayes, Lucy "Lemonade Lucy"; President's Wife 227
Hayes, Rutherford B; President 227 228
Hays City, 85 112 115 120 Crime and Violence 114

Hazen, Gen W B 102 104 105
Henrietta, Texas 240 243 244
Herendeen, George; Scout v
Hermitage Heights, Name of Benteen's Farm 62
Hickok, James Butler "Wild Bill" 29 115
Hinricks, Capt Charles F 53 59
Homesteaders (Boomers), 239
Horner, Pvt Jacob 1005
Horses, Appaloosa 211 Army Vs Warrior Pony 93 Belonging to Nez Perce, Captured Affecting Outcome of War 217 Benteen Purchases for Regiment and Self 125 Benteen's Continued Interest 268 Benteen's Love for 62 Carefully Inspected Before Little Bighorn Campaign 159 "Coloring" the 96 Exhausted 215 Grooming, Feeding, Inspecting, and Picketing 160 Need for Protection from Warriors 200 Nez Perce Had Large Supply 215 Officers to Purchase Their Own 129 Officers' 113 Theft by Deserters 81 Watered Before Little Bighorn Battle 169 Watered by Reno at Little Bighorn River 179 White; Carried Regimental Band 153
Hotchkiss Gun, 218 249 250 269
House Committee on Military Affairs, 222

Household Furnishings, at Army Forts 230
Howard, Gen Oliver O "the Praying General" 211-214 217
Howitzer, Twelve-Pound 218 Advantages of Smooth Bore Vs Rifled 27 28 Gave Cavalry a More Meaningful Role in Battle 24 Smoothbore 216
Huetter, 253
Illinois Central Railroad, 129
Independence, Missouri 49
Indian Territory, 92 103 105 119 221 222 239 240 Eastern and Western 85 Western Areas Offered to Kiowa Comanche Cheyenne and Arapaho 86
Ing, Capt Stanford, 30 31
Inspector General, Visits Fort Harker 111
International Order of Odd Fellows (IOOF), Benteen Inducted into 124 (See Also Odd Fellows)
Iuka, Mississippi; Benteen Led Battle Charge 40
Jackson, Andrew 62
Jackson, Mississippi; Grant Defeats Confederates 39
James Brothers, Desperadoes 26
Janesville, Wisconsin 263
"Jaywalker" (a Union Irregular), 110
Jefferson Barracks, Cavalry Center Ten Miles from St Louis 35

Jefferson City, Missouri; Not Attacked by Price 49
Johnson Island, Union Prison 34
Johnson, President Andrew 65 71 91
Johnston, Gen; Commander of Last Confederate Army in the Field 58
Journalists, at Tenth Anniversary of Battle of Little Bighorn 247 on Black Hills Expedition 139 on Yellowstone Expedition 131 133 with Custer at Little Bighorn 176
Judith Gap, Blocked by Sturgis 213
Jumbo, the Elephant 232
Junction City, Kansas 68
Kane, Beulah; Married to Charley Benteen 7
Kansas City, Missouri 49 66
Kansas Pacific Railroad, 68 85 86 93 114
Keogh, Capt Myles 75 163 164 173 263
Kickapoo, 239
Kiowa, 67 239 at Fort Larned 88 in Washita Valley 100 102 Offered Reservation Area in Western Indian Territory 86 Reservation 240 Said to Be Peaceful 104 Tracks Followed from Washita 104
Kiowa-Apache, 67
Knabe, William 2
Know Nothing Party, 3
Koch, Robert 257

Krag-Jorgensen Turnbolt Carbine, 231
Ku Klux Klan, 123 124 262
Ladd, Lt Eugene F 257 258
Lakota Sioux, 200 Fort Laramie Treaty of 1878 127 Govt Wanted Conveyance of Title of Black Hills 14 Burial Place in Rosebud Valley 201 Camping Grounds 173 Miniconjou; Defeated at Muddy Creek 204 Warriors Pursued by Custer 172
Lapwai Reservation, Washington Territory 211
Laramie Treaty, 139 148
Laramie, Wyoming 249
Leavenworth, Kansas 120 255
Lee Bolt-Action, 231
Lee, Gen Robert E 54 and Army Engineers in St Louis 7 Surrenders 58
Lee-Enfield, Adopted by British Army 231
Leonard, Steven M; Author/Historian xi
Lexington, Missouri 49
Liberated Slaves, Comprised 138th USCT 60
Life on the Plains, Custer's Book 142 143 268
Lincoln Conspirators, Held at Fort Jefferson Prison in Dry Tortugas 34
Lincoln, Abraham; Elected as President 14 Initially Saw No Need for Cavalry 21 Presidential Candidate 13 Rejected Anaconda Plan 1
Lincoln, Robert; Secretary of War 228
Liquor, Availability to Soldiers 79
Little Bighorn Battle, 124 190 198 208 230 235 246 263 Benteen Awarded Brevet of Brigadier General for Gallantry 262 Benteen Invited to a Talk 268 Custer Held Responsible for Disaster 224 Difficult Transportation of Wounded 197 Godfrey's Account Angered Benteen 186 Medals of Honor 265 Plan of Action 157 Press Clippings Used in Whittaker's Custer Biography 207 Soldier and Indian Casualties 196 Tenth Anniversary 247
Little Bighorn National Monument, 265
Little Bighorn River, 156 171 173 179 196 263
Little Bighorn Valley, 163
"Little Dixie," North of St Louis 9
Little Missouri River, 155 229
Little Wolf, 204
Lolo Trail, 212
"Lone Tepee," Found by Custer's Men 172
Louisiana, Civil Unrest 142
Louisville, Kentucky 123-125
Lowrey, Elizabeth 11
Lyon, Brig Gen Nathaniel 18 19 Capt Nathaniel; Commander of Union Home Guard 17

Index

Macon, Georgia 58
Madison Square Garden, New York 232
Madison, President James 67
Malaria, 269 at Fort Sill 240
Mardi Gras, 143
Maria, River Steamer; Explosion Killed Some of Benteen's Men 52
Marmaton River, Kansas 51
Martin, John (Giovanni Martini) 176 185 Duty Trumpeter 166 263 Trumpeter/Messenger from Custer 170 171 Horse Wounded 174 Only White Survivor 173
Mathey, First Lt Edwin G 137 146 163 187
Mazzini, Giuseppe 116
McClellan Saddle, Issued to Union Cavalry 23
McClellan, George B 15 23
McCurry, Joseph 125
McDougall, Capt 163
McIntosh, Lt Donald 87 88 121 125 171
McKinley, President 270
McPherson, Gen James B 42 Praises Benteen 44
Medical Care, Officers' Families 114
Medicine Bluff Creek, 106 108
Medicine Lodge Creek, Kansas; Important Treaty Talks, 85 86 Treaty 88 127
Medicine Tail Coulee, 174-176
Memphis, Tennessee 44 128 Benteen Returns 46
Merchant's Hotel, St Paul Minnesota 205

Meridian, Mississippi 42 Captured 43 Winslow's Brigade Prepared to Raid 42
Merrill, Maj Lewis 216 219 245 246 Lt 262
Merrill's Light Horse (2nd Missouri Cavalry), Absorbs 10th Missouri 60
Merritt, Gen Wesley 261
Mess Bills, 110
Metropolitan Opera, New York 232
Metropolitan Police, New Orleans 142
Michigan, University of; Received Fossils Sent by Custer 131
Midnight, Benteen's Horse 80
Miles, Gen Nelson 201 203 204 209 217 218 249 268 a Custer Partisan 157
Military Education, Expected of Well-Bred Virginians 5 6
Milk Creek Battle, Colorado, 251
Millikin's Bend, Louisiana 32 33
Mills, Charles K; Author/Historian xi
Mine Creek, Kansas; "the Battle of the Osage" 50 75
Minieball, Used against Cavalry 24
Minute Men, Democratic Paramilitary Units 13
Mississippi River, 143 Firmly in Union Control 44
Missouri Compromise, Extension Rejected by Lincoln 14

Missouri, Governor of, 51
Missouri River, 128 134 135 198 200 209 218 220
Bouyer, Mitch; Guide 165
Mitchell, Margaret, 270
Mona, "Mo-Nah-Se-Tah"; Indian Woman Hostage 106
Monroe, Michigan; Custer Inspects Property 120 Custer Travels to 122
Montana Territory, 128 149 219 222
Montgomery, Alabama 57
Mosby, John Singleton 24
Mosquitoes, 160
Mountain Meadows Massacre, 253
Moylan, Myles, 19 71 80 110 125 153 171 178 184 190 264 Awarded Medal of Honor 219 "Hardtack Mick" 189 Promoted by Custer 69
Muddy Creek, 163 204
Mules, Problems with 161 Qualities 149
Music, Appreciation by German Immigrants in Baltimore 2
Musselshell River, 213 217
Myers, Capt Edward, 101 104
Napoleon III, 116
Napoleon Cannon, 153
Napoleon, Employment of Horsemen 23
Nash, Joseph 266
Nashville, Battle of 239
National Road (Cumberland Road), 1 Maryland to Illinois 8
Native Americans (Anti-Immigrant Whites), 13

Netherlands, Benteen Family Lineage Tradition 1
New Orleans, Louisiana 142
New York Ontario and Western Railway, 232
New York, Benteen Assigned to 229
Nez Perce War, 189
Nez Perce, 211 213 217 at Bear Paw, Montana 218 Campaign 225 Captives Sent to Barren Lands in Kansas and Oklahoma Territory 219 Epic Exodus 212 Flee to Canada 214 Pursuit 215 Sent to Colville Reservation in Washington 219 Surrender after Bear Paw Battle 219
Noell, Hon Tom, 76
Norman, Anita 11 (See Diaz, Anita)
Norman, Catherine Louisa (Kate) 10 11 21 26 Courted by Fred Benteen 12 (See Benteen, Catherine)
Norman, Elizabeth Lowrey 11 Death 241
Norman, First Lt Leslie R; Younger Brother of Kate 11 46 252 Court Martialed and Allowed to Resign 57
Norman, Henry R 11
Norman, Violet 241-244 252 256 258 261
Norman, William H 11
North Carolina, Supplanted by Kentucky for Horse Breeding 125
Northern Militia, Peacetime; Lack of Discipline 15

Index 341

Northern Pacific Railroad, Surveyors Protected by 7th Cavalry 128 130 133
Occidental Hotel, San Francisco; a Favorite with Army Officers 225
Odd Fellows (IOOF), 129
 Benteen Inducted into 124
Oglala Sioux, Battle at Slim Buttes 203
"Oh Susanna," Song 2
Ohio Canal, 2
Oklahoma District, 239 243
Oklahoma Territory, 220
"Ole-Tankel" (Greyhair), Benteen's Indian Name 241
Oregon, 211
Osage Indian Guides, with 7th Cavalry 97 98
Palmer House, Chicago; Reno Court of Inquiry 223
Pawnee Killer, Notorious Sioux War Chief 83
Payne, David L 239
Pea Ridge Mountain, Arkansas; Battle 29
Pennsylvania Cavalry, 117
Pershing, Gen John "Black Jack" 238
Pershing, Gen 270
Peters, Willie 164
Petersburg Classical Institute, Attended by Fred Benteen 4 5
Petersburg, Virginia 66
 Business Opportunities 3
Philadelphia, Pennsylvania 206
Philippines, 270
Piano Makers, Established Early in Baltimore 2
Pierre, Dakota Territory 222
Platte River Trail (Oregon Trail), 81 82
Platte, Department of the 258 259
Pleasonton, Gen Alfred 47 48 66 75 Engages Price near Kansas City Missouri 49 Praise for Custer 70 Pursues Price 50 Succeeded by Curtis in Command 51
Point Pleasant, New Jersey 233
Polygamy, among Mormons 253
Pompey's Pillar, 213
Ponies, Killed by Custer 100 Warriors' vs Army Horses 93
Post Traders (Sutlers), 110
Potowmack and Chesapeake Canal, 2
Powder River, 155 156 202 203 229 244
Price, Brig Gen Sterling (Old Pap), 18 19 70 Advances into Missouri 47 Advances into St Louis 48 Decides Not to Attack Jefferson City 49 Moves toward Jefferson City, Missouri 48 Pursued by Curtis 51 Retreats to Kansas 49 Wanted to Capture St Louis 27
Quantrill, Capt William 26
Quarters, Officers'; and Furnishings 113 114
Rabid Wolf, at Fort Larned 89
Railroad Passes, for Custer 150 151

Railroads, Petitioned Congress for Land Grants Within Indian Territory 239 Right-of-Way Lands in the Dakotas 151
Rations, Shortages at End of War 59
Rattlesnakes, at Fort Rice 136
Red Cloud Agency, 201
Red River, 86 243
Redfield, Bill 164
Reno Creek, 171 173
Reno Hill, 173 180 185-187 190 192 195 197 202 233 265 Escape Possibly Discussed 191 Renamed Reno-Benteen Hill 229
Reno, Maj Gen Jesse L; Altercation with Rutherford Hayes 228
Reno, Maj Marcus 117 123 134 152 155 157 165 171 173 176 178 179 181 182 185 187 191 192 194 195 198 200 203 207 233 243 246 258 262-264 268 269 Brawls with Benteen 118 Charges Dismissed in 1967 228 Courage under Fire 189 Court of Inquiry 222-224 Court-Martialed 209 Criticized by Several Officers 200 Disgrace and Death 228 Drinking and Court Martial 226 227 Drinking and Other Problems after Little Bighorn 208 209 Freemason 124 in Full Retreat 175
Reno, Maj Marcus (cont.) Ordered to Pursue Warriors to Village 172 Orders Withdrawal 183 Praises Benteen in Official Battle Report 199 Reburied at Little Bighorn Battlefield 228 Said to Have Suggested Abandoning the Wounded 189 190 Takes up Defensive Position 184
Revolution of 1848, Italy 116
Rex Balls, New Orleans 143
Richmond, Virginia; the Fall of 57
Roamers, Lakota and Northern Cheyenne on Unceded Lands 127 128 149 162 204 205 to Be Dislodged 148
Rock Creek, Wyoming 249
Rock Island, Illinois; Union Prison 34
Rodman Gun, 133 153 158
Rolla, Missouri; Railroad Terminus 20 26 52
Roosevelt, President Theodore 269
Rosebud Agency, 260
Rosebud River, 156-159 201
Rosebud Valley, 150 163 201
Rosencrans, Gen 66
Roy, Sgt Stanislas v
Ryan, First Sgt John v
Sabers, Supplanted by Firearms 24
Saint Luca Military Academy, Milan, Italy 116
Salaries, Officers' 114
Saline River, 89-92 Battle 76 Raids 99

Index

Salt Lake City, Utah 248 253 257
San Francisco, Benteen Did Not Enjoy 225
Sand Creek, Colorado; Massacre 77 98
"Sand Diggers," Poor White Immigrants from the South 9
Sandy Hill River, 68
Santa Fe Trail, 67 68 74 77 88 95
Savannah, Georgia; Captured by End of 1864 53
Schultz, Carl; Secretary of the Interior 248
Scott, Gen Hugh v 73 Praise for Benteen 74
Scott, Gen Winfield 15
Scouts, Deserted the Relief Column 195 Reliability 166
Scurvy, among Custer's Men 82 at Fort Hays 79
Selma, Alabama 54 Captured by Upton's Division 56 Huge Arsenal Defended by Forrest 55 Victory Anticlimactic 56 57
Seminole Tribe, 85
Seventh Regiment Armory, 232
Sharps Carbine, 22 118 188
Sharpshooter Ridge, 180 188
Sheridan, Gen Philip H 28 85 88 91-93 98 103 105 107 109 117 120 126 141 143 145 148 149 199 236 256 258 a Favorite of Grant Replaced Pleasonton 48 Appeals to Grant to Reinstate Custer 152 at Five Forks, Virginia 54

Sheridan, Gen Philip H (cont.) Devises Three-Pronged Attack on Tribes 94 Orders Custer to Destroy Indian Villages 97
Sherman, Gen William T 17 44 81 83 Approaches Vicksburg 36 Arranged Armistice in North Carolina with Gen Johnston 58 Begins Atlanta Campaign 44 Chose Meridian Mississippi in Preparation for Atlanta Campaign 42 Moving into South Carolina after Sweeping through Georgia 54
Shreveport, Texas 143
Sibley Tent, 112 250 Description 80
Sigel, Col Franz 19
Sigil's Dutch Brigade, at Battle of Wilson's Creek 20
Sioux City, Dakota Territory 129
Sioux Reservation, 203
Sioux War, 191 204 249
Sioux, 67 127 157 179 244 Black Hills Gold Needed by Fed Govt 148 Camped at Rosebud River 157 Encountered during Yellowstone Expedition 133 Fortunes in Decline as Crow Enjoy Prosperity 212 Use of Decoy or Ambush 133
Sioux, Lakota 204-206
Sioux, Miniconjou 269
Sioux, Oglala 203

Sitting Bull, 196 204 209 211 218 229 Lakota Shaman 162
Slave Craftsmen, Could Be Hired out for House Painting 4
Slave Interests, Unyielding Grasp on the South 14
Slave Patrols, Policed Black Section of Town 6
Slave Uprising, Feared by Virginians 6
Slavery, in Missouri 8 9 in St Louis; Competition from Immigrant Labor 11
Slaves, Owned by Charley Benteen 3
Slemo, Hon Campbell 270
Slim Buttes, Battle with Oglala Sioux 203
Smith and Wesson Revolvers, 181
Smith, Col A J 47 48 Commander of 7th Cavalry 70 111 119
Smith, Maj Gen Andrew J 45
Smoky Hill River, 78 86
Smoky Hill Trail, 67 68 74 78 80
Solomon River, 89
South Carolina 142 Votes Ordinance of Secession 14
South Dakota, 127
Southern Industry, Question of Necessity of Its Destruction 58
Southern Soldier, Honed by Night Patrols and Trained Militia 15
Spanish-American War, 270
Spartanburg, South Carolina 123
Specie Resumption Act of 1875, 147
Spencer Repeating Carbine, 118
Spencer Repeating Rifles, 90 91 Issued to Wilson's Army 53 Issued to Cavalry Soldiers 47 Benteen's Dry Comment 55 Instrumental in Union Victory at Battle of the Osage 50
Spencer Repeating Shotgun, 241
Spotted Horn Bull, Mrs; Heard Trumpet Calls 179 Lakota Witness 175
Springfield Carbine, 231 1873 Model Issued to Soldiers 139 Breech Block Criticized by Reno 224
Springfield, Massachusetts; National Arsenal 231
Springfield Rifle Not Used by Cavalry while Mounted 181
Springfield Trapdoor Carbine 192 Praised by Benteen 191
St Charles Hotel, New Orleans 143
St Louis Armory, Large Stock of Cavalry Gear 22 Largest in the Country 17
St Louis Greys, Drill Company 12
St Louis Museum of Art, in Early Stages of Formation 9
St Louis, Missouri 46-48 51 52 65 206 230 Academy of Art 12 Agricultural and Mechanical Fair 12

St Louis, Missouri (cont.)
Benteen Kept His Home
There 241 252 Black
Population; Free and Slave
11 Commerce and
Manufacture 6 7 Importance
during Civil War 27 Kate
Benteen and Son Return
from Fort Harker for
Recuperation 111
Philharmonic Concerts 12
Union Vs Confederate
Hostilities 18 Violent Civil
Disorder Following
Secession 17 Visited by the
Prince of Wales 12
St Paul, Minnesota 128 130 143 205 209
Stagecoaches, 222
Standing Rock Reservation, 221
Standing Rock Lakota Agency, 135 206
Stanley, Gen David 131 133
Stanley's Stockade, 132-134
Statue of Liberty, Head and Torch on Display at Centennial Exposition 206
Steiff, Charles 2
Steves, Maria Louisa Benteen 270
Stinkwater (Shoshone) River, 214
Streight's Raid, to Distract Forrest 37
"Strikers," Soldiers Who Did Chores for Officers 113
Stumbling Bear, Kiowa Chief and Friend of Benteen 241
Sturgis, Col Samuel D 19 119 121 123 205 208 213-217

Sturgis, Col Samuel D (cont.)
219 221 226 235 246
Furious with Benteen for
Testifying in Reno's Behalf,
227 (Brig Gen) 45
Sturgis, James (Jack); Col's Son Killed at Little Bighorn 227
Sturgis, Mrs 227
Sugar Creek, Arkansas; Battle 28 29
Suicide, Committed by One of Custer's Officers 82
Sully, Lt Col Alfred 92 94
Sultana, Riverboat Full of Liberated Union Prisoners Explodes 56
Summit Springs, Colorado; Western Cheyenne Defeated 109
Sun Dance, 162
Sutlers (Post Traders), 110
Sweetwater Creek, 108
Talbot's Ferry, Arkansas; Raid 31
Taliaferro County, Georgia 260 262
Yankton, Dakota Territory 144
Tennessee River, 52
Terry, Brig Gen Alfred H, 123 124 128 145 152 153 156-160 176 185 191 197 199 200-202 205 220 228
Appeals to Grant to Reinstate Custer 152
Problems with Custer 155
Texas Panhandle, 108
"The Very Last Polka," Sheet Music Cover Scene Painted by Fred Benteen 5

Tongue River Cantonment (Fort Keogh), 209
Tongue River, 150 156 202 218
Tupelo, Mississippi; Smith's Standoff with Forrest 45
Turner, Nat; Leader of Slave Uprising 6
Tuscombia, Alabama; Stormed by 10th Missouri Cavalry 37
Tuskegee, Alabama 57
Uintah Mountains, 250
Uintah Reservation, 248 249
Uintah River, 250
Unceded Lands, 127 Surrendered to the Government 229
Union Home Guard, Mobilized in St Louis Following Secession 17
Union Pacific Railroad, 225
Union Prisons, High Mortality Rates 34
Upton, Brig Gen Emory 53 65
Upton's Division, Deployed on the Selma Road 54 Destroys Iron Works at Birmingham, Alabama 53 Ordered to Make Frontal Attack at Selma 55
USCT, 116 238 Got the Worst of Everything 236
Utah Territory, 248
Utes, in Colorado 102 Warriors 248 250 251
Van Dorn, Gen Earl, 29
Vancouver Barracks, Washington 225
Varnum, Lt Charles A v 159 164 165 167 179 188 230
Vic, Custer's Mare 166

Vicksburg, Mississippi 32 Grant Prepares to Capture 37 Victory Celebrated 39
Virginia, Supplanted by Kentucky for Horse Breeding 125
Waddell's Farm, Wagon Train Attack 32
Wales, Prince of; Visited St Louis 12
Wallowa Valley, Oregon 219 Gold Discovery and Attempt to Drive out Nez Perce 211
War Bonnet Creek, 201
Warriors, Identification 90 Tactics 177
Washington Artillery Ball, 143
Washington Guards, Drill Company, 12
Washington Territory, 211
Washita Battle, a Costly Victory 102 "Army Massacre" 102 Custer's After-Action Report Resented by Officers 102 103 Hostages 106 Hostages at New Fort Hays 114 Hostages Released to Abate Raids 119 Mentioned 158 168 174 255 266 Victory Criticized 102 Women and Children 109
Washita Battlefield, 108 Revisited 103
Washita Letter, Written by Benteen 110
Washita River, 86 97 98 104
Weaver, Cpl 31
Weir, Capt Thomas 121 169 185 200 201 205 2026 223 224

Index

Weir, Capt Thomas (cont.)
  Death by Indirect Effects of Alcoholism 207 Interviewed by Whittaker in New York 207
Weir Point, 173 180 185 269
West Point, 235 Class Ring Recovered from Body 184 Custer's Remained Reburied There 247 Favoritism Believed by Benteen 61 Godfrey an Instructor 230 Officers Were Appointed by President of United States 21
West Point Graduates, Black 252 Samuel Curtis 27 Edward S Godfrey 121 137 George Armstrong Custer 69 James Sturgis 227 Marcus Reno 117
Western Trail, 85
Westport, Missouri 49
Whiskey Point, near Bismarck 138
White Brotherhood 123
White Camellia 123 142
"White Man's Crow's Nest," 164
Whittaker, Frederick 223 228 Accusations against Reno 222 Author of Custer's Biography 207 208 Continued to Attack Reno 224 withdraws Charge of Cowardice against Benteen 224
Wickiup, Described 174
"Wide Awakes" (Republican Immigrants), 13

Wilmington, North Carolina 124
Wilson, Gen James H 52 54 58-60 75 229 74 Rests His Men at Selma 57 Sends a Division on Diversionary Attack Northwest of Selma 55
Wilson's Campaign, Overshadowed by Other Events 54
Wilson's Cavalry Corps, Central Alabama Raid 53
Wilson's Creek, Missouri; Battle 19 45 Casualties 20 Cornyn Given Field Command 35
Winchester Rifles, 153 Repeating Carbine 231
Windolph, Sgt Charles, v 125
Winslow, Gen Edward F 43 229 232 265 with Grant at Vicksburg 41 Becomes Ill and Leaves Benteen in Command 43 Wounded and Relinquishes Command to Benteen 49 Resumes Command 52
Winslow's Brigade, at Battle of the Osage 50 Benteen Joins 41 Benteen Recruited Officers for 138th USCT 60 Fired Upon near Brownsville Mississippi 42 Forced to Abandon 1300 Horses 47 Hurried to Benton's Barracks 48 Incorporated into Grierson's Cavalry Corps 45 Outflanks Forrest at Ebenezer Church Alabama 54

Winslow's Brigade (cont.)
  Reinforces Pleasonton in St Louis 47 Sent to Fort Scott, Kansas 51
Winter Campaigns, 97 98 149 204
Wisconsin National Guard, 263
Wolf Mountain, Montana 167
  Sioux-Cheyenne Defeated by Miles 204
Women, at Fort Abraham Lincoln 138 Indian, Killed at Black Kettle's Village 99 Lack of Decent Quarters in Dakota Territory 130 Pastimes at Forts 113 144
Woods' Flotilla, 33 34
  Delivered Prisoners and Spoils Back to Headquarters 35
Woods, Col Charles 32

Wounded Knee, 269
Wyncoop, Edward W 102
  Indian Agent 76 89
Wyoming Territory, 222 243 249
Yankton, Dakota Territory 129 130
Yellowstone District, 209
Yellowstone Expedition, 130 133 134
Yellowstone National Park, 212 213 217
Yellowstone River, 132 133 148 150 155-157 197 198 201 203 209 212 215 218 220
Yellowstone Valley, 128
Young, Brigham 253 257
Young, Lt Richard W 257
Younger, Cole 26
Zoaves, Drill Company 12

About the Author

Dr. J. C. Ladenheim is a retired neurosurgeon and a dedicated student of nineteenth-century American history. In addition to his books on neurosurgery, he has writeen on firearms and ballistics and on the life of Charles De Rudio, a participant in the Little Bighorn battle.

www.ingramcontent.com/pod-product-compliance
Lightning Source LLC
Chambersburg PA
CBHW050428240426
43661CB00055B/2312